CRAYON Shinchan

By Yoshito Usui

Volume 1

CRAYON Shinchan

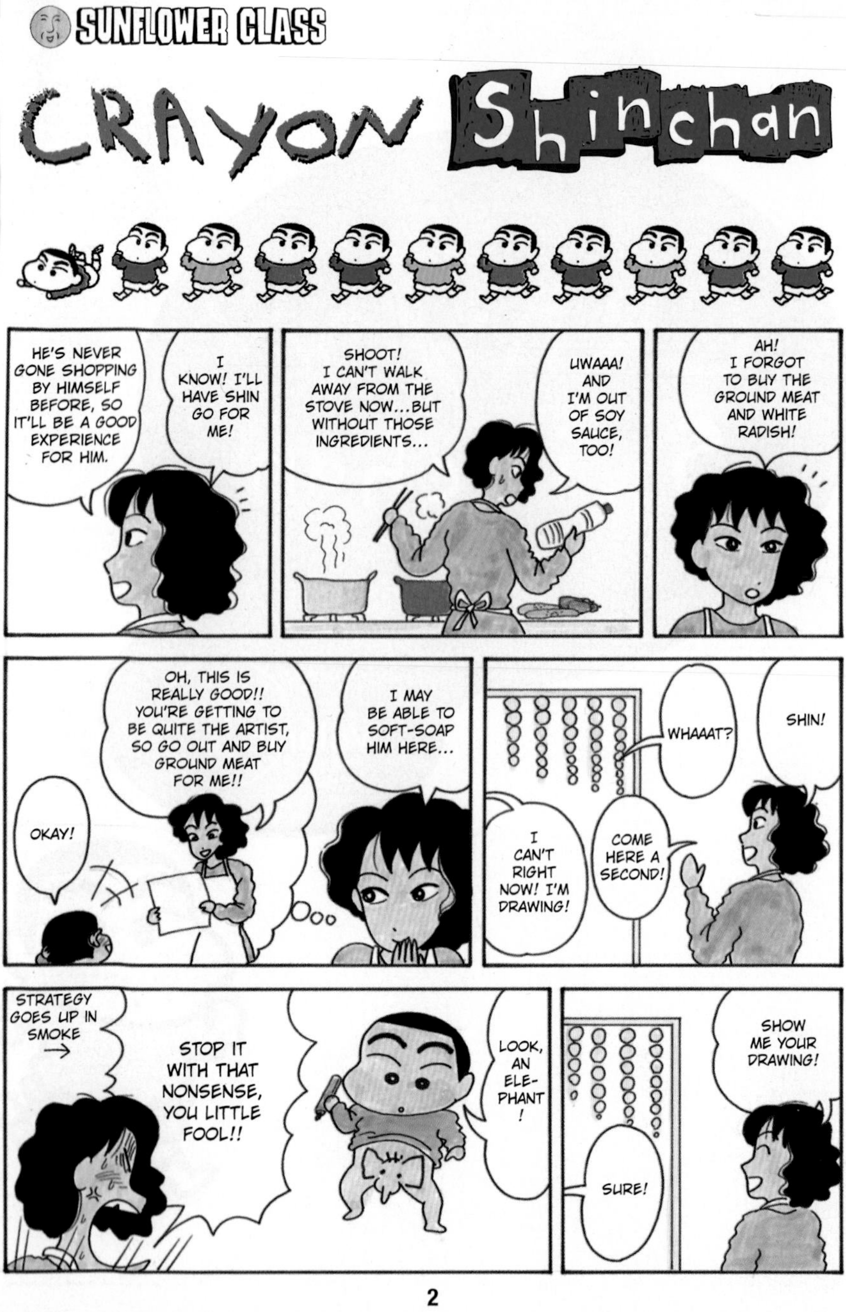
AH! I FORGOT TO BUY THE GROUND MEAT AND WHITE RADISH!
UWAAA! AND I'M OUT OF SOY SAUCE, TOO!
SHOOT! I CAN'T WALK AWAY FROM THE STOVE NOW...BUT WITHOUT THOSE INGREDIENTS...
I KNOW! I'LL HAVE SHIN GO FOR ME!
HE'S NEVER GONE SHOPPING BY HIMSELF BEFORE, SO IT'LL BE A GOOD EXPERIENCE FOR HIM.
SHIN!
WHAAAT?
COME HERE A SECOND!
I CAN'T RIGHT NOW! I'M DRAWING!
I MAY BE ABLE TO SOFT-SOAP HIM HERE...
OH, THIS IS REALLY GOOD!! YOU'RE GETTING TO BE QUITE THE ARTIST, SO GO OUT AND BUY GROUND MEAT FOR ME!!
OKAY!
SHOW ME YOUR DRAWING!
SURE!
LOOK, AN ELE-PHANT!
STOP IT WITH THAT NONSENSE, YOU LITTLE FOOL!!
STRATEGY GOES UP IN SMOKE →

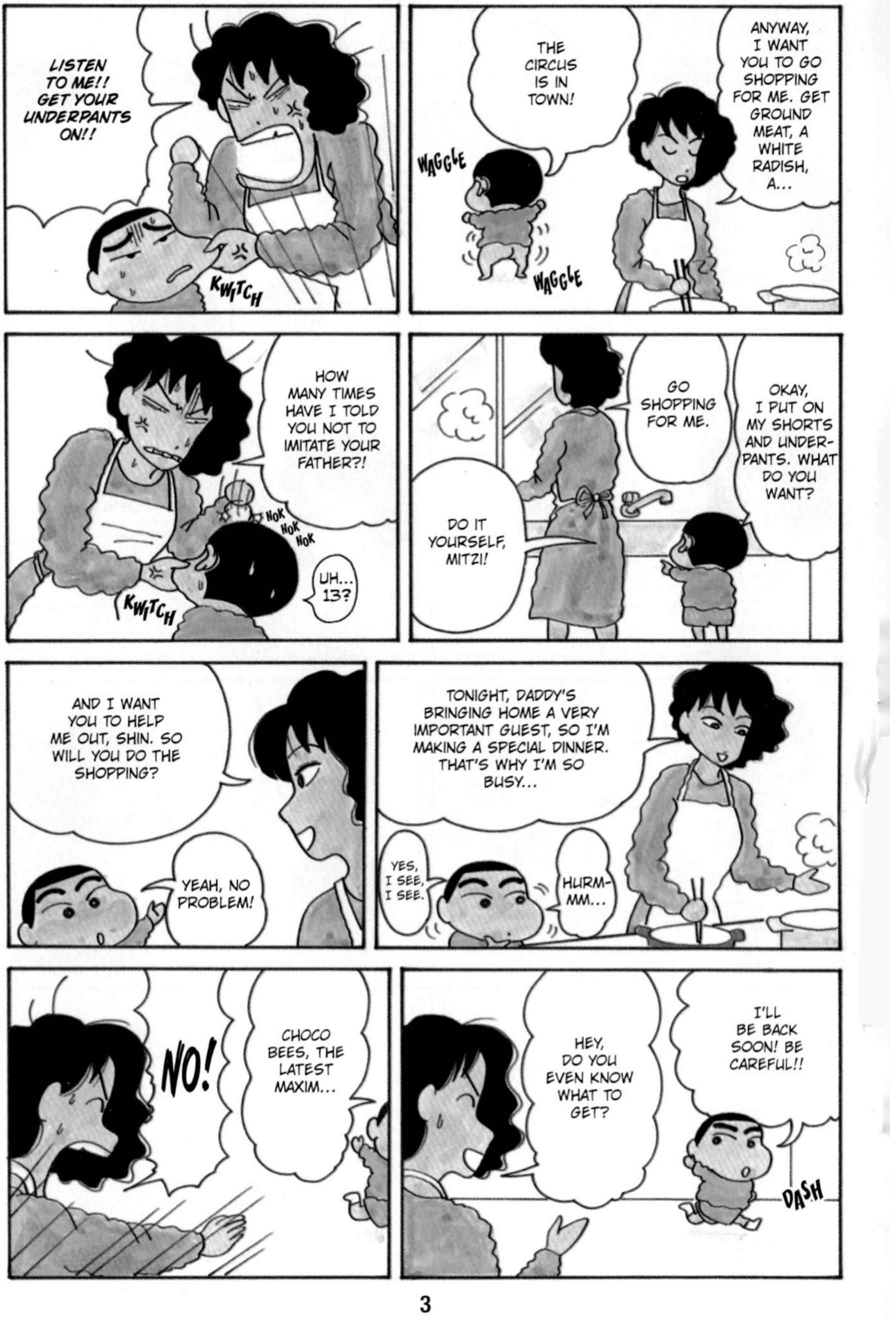

LISTEN TO ME!! GET YOUR UNDERPANTS ON!!
KWITCH
THE CIRCUS IS IN TOWN!
WAGGLE
WAGGLE
ANYWAY, I WANT YOU TO GO SHOPPING FOR ME. GET GROUND MEAT, A WHITE RADISH, A...
HOW MANY TIMES HAVE I TOLD YOU NOT TO IMITATE YOUR FATHER?!
NOK NOK NOK
KWITCH
UH... 13?
OKAY, I PUT ON MY SHORTS AND UNDER-PANTS. WHAT DO YOU WANT?
GO SHOPPING FOR ME.
DO IT YOURSELF, MITZI!
AND I WANT YOU TO HELP ME OUT, SHIN. SO WILL YOU DO THE SHOPPING?
YEAH, NO PROBLEM!
TONIGHT, DADDY'S BRINGING HOME A VERY IMPORTANT GUEST, SO I'M MAKING A SPECIAL DINNER. THAT'S WHY I'M SO BUSY...
HURMM-MM...
YES, I SEE, I SEE.
CHOCO BEES, THE LATEST MAXIM...
NO!
HEY, DO YOU EVEN KNOW WHAT TO GET?
I'LL BE BACK SOON! BE CAREFUL!!
DASH

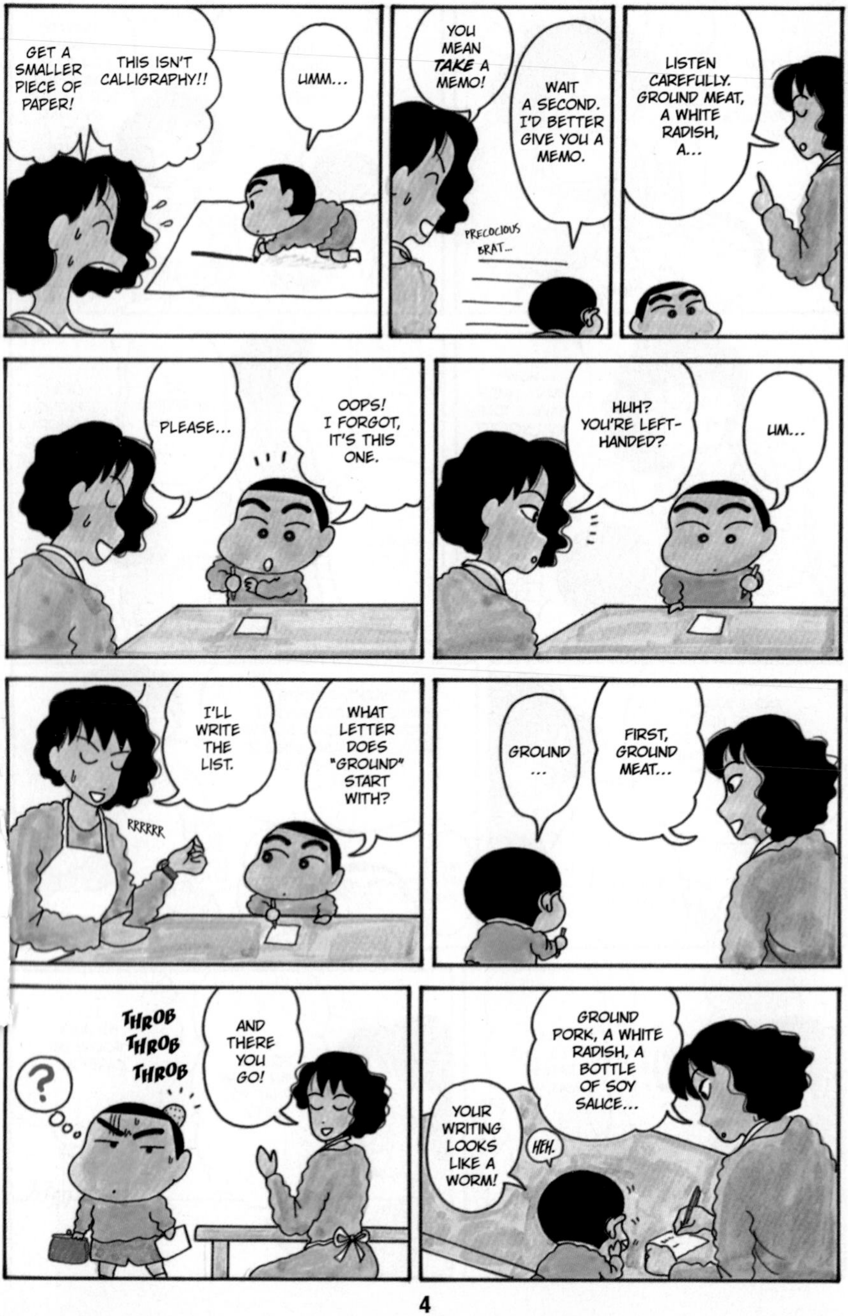
LISTEN CAREFULLY. GROUND MEAT, A WHITE RADISH, A...
WAIT A SECOND. I'D BETTER GIVE YOU A MEMO.
YOU MEAN *TAKE* A MEMO!
PRECOCIOUS BRAT...
UMM...
THIS ISN'T CALLIGRAPHY!!
GET A SMALLER PIECE OF PAPER!
UM...
HUH? YOU'RE LEFT-HANDED?
OOPS! I FORGOT, IT'S THIS ONE.
PLEASE...
FIRST, GROUND MEAT...
GROUND...
WHAT LETTER DOES "GROUND" START WITH?
I'LL WRITE THE LIST.
RRRRRR
GROUND PORK, A WHITE RADISH, A BOTTLE OF SOY SAUCE...
HEH.
YOUR WRITING LOOKS LIKE A WORM!
AND THERE YOU GO!
THROB THROB THROB
?

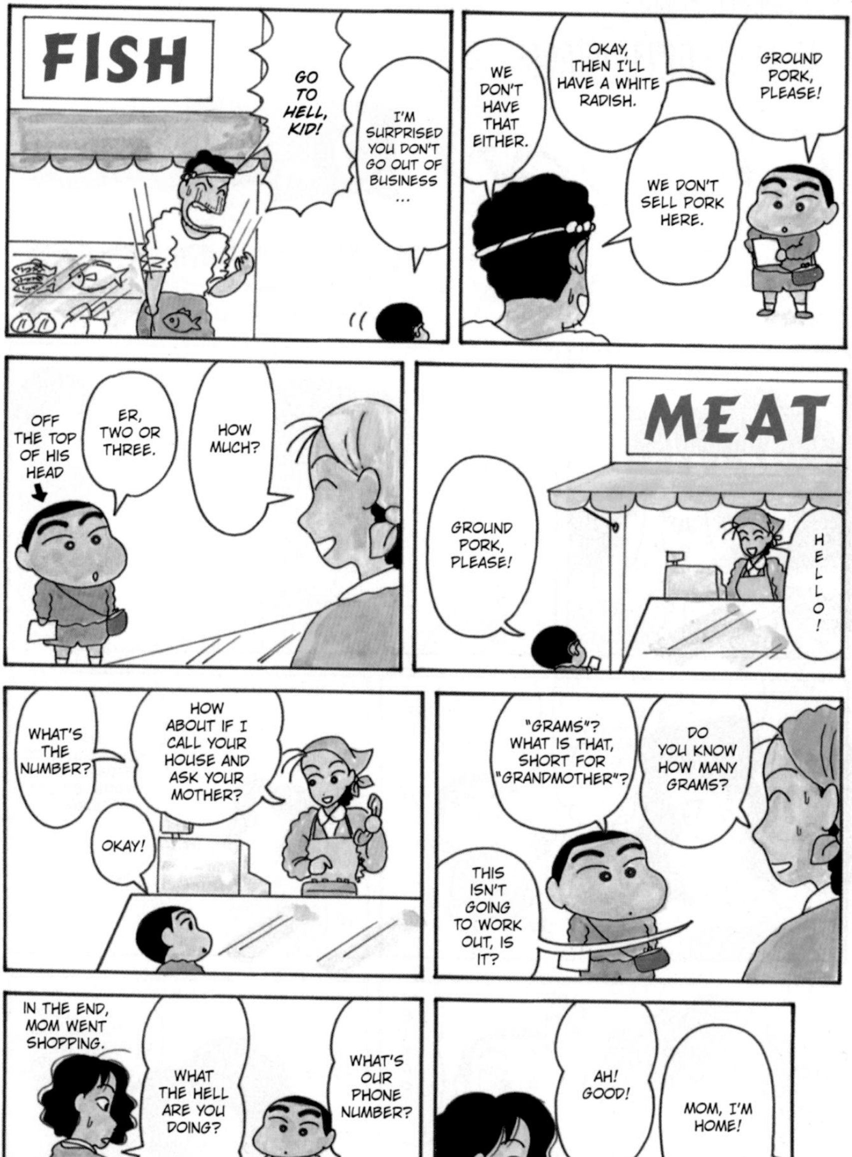
GROUND PORK, PLEASE!
WE DON'T SELL PORK HERE.
OKAY, THEN I'LL HAVE A WHITE RADISH.
WE DON'T HAVE THAT EITHER.
I'M SURPRISED YOU DON'T GO OUT OF BUSINESS ...
GO TO HELL, KID!
FISH
MEAT
HELLO!
GROUND PORK, PLEASE!
HOW MUCH?
ER, TWO OR THREE.
OFF THE TOP OF HIS HEAD
DO YOU KNOW HOW MANY GRAMS?
"GRAMS"? WHAT IS THAT, SHORT FOR "GRANDMOTHER"?
THIS ISN'T GOING TO WORK OUT, IS IT?
HOW ABOUT IF I CALL YOUR HOUSE AND ASK YOUR MOTHER?
WHAT'S THE NUMBER?
OKAY!
MOM, I'M HOME!
AH! GOOD!
WHAT'S OUR PHONE NUMBER?
WHAT THE HELL ARE YOU DOING?
IN THE END, MOM WENT SHOPPING.

SUNFLOWER CLASS

CRAYON Shinchan

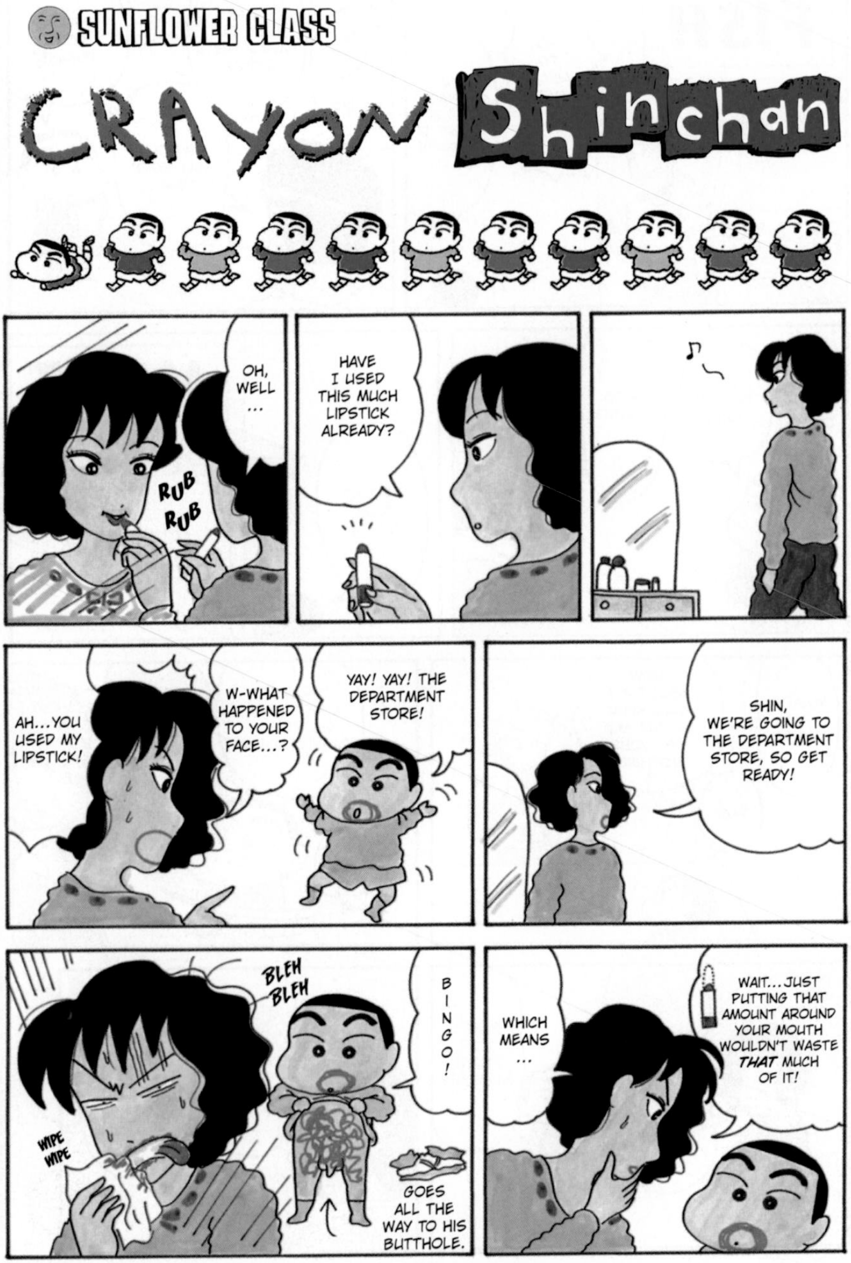
♪
HAVE I USED THIS MUCH LIPSTICK ALREADY?
OH, WELL...
RUB RUB
SHIN, WE'RE GOING TO THE DEPARTMENT STORE, SO GET READY!
YAY! YAY! THE DEPARTMENT STORE!
W-WHAT HAPPENED TO YOUR FACE...?
AH...YOU USED MY LIPSTICK!
WAIT...JUST PUTTING THAT AMOUNT AROUND YOUR MOUTH WOULDN'T WASTE *THAT* MUCH OF IT!
WHICH MEANS...
BINGO!
BLEH BLEH
WIPE WIPE
GOES ALL THE WAY TO HIS BUTTHOLE.

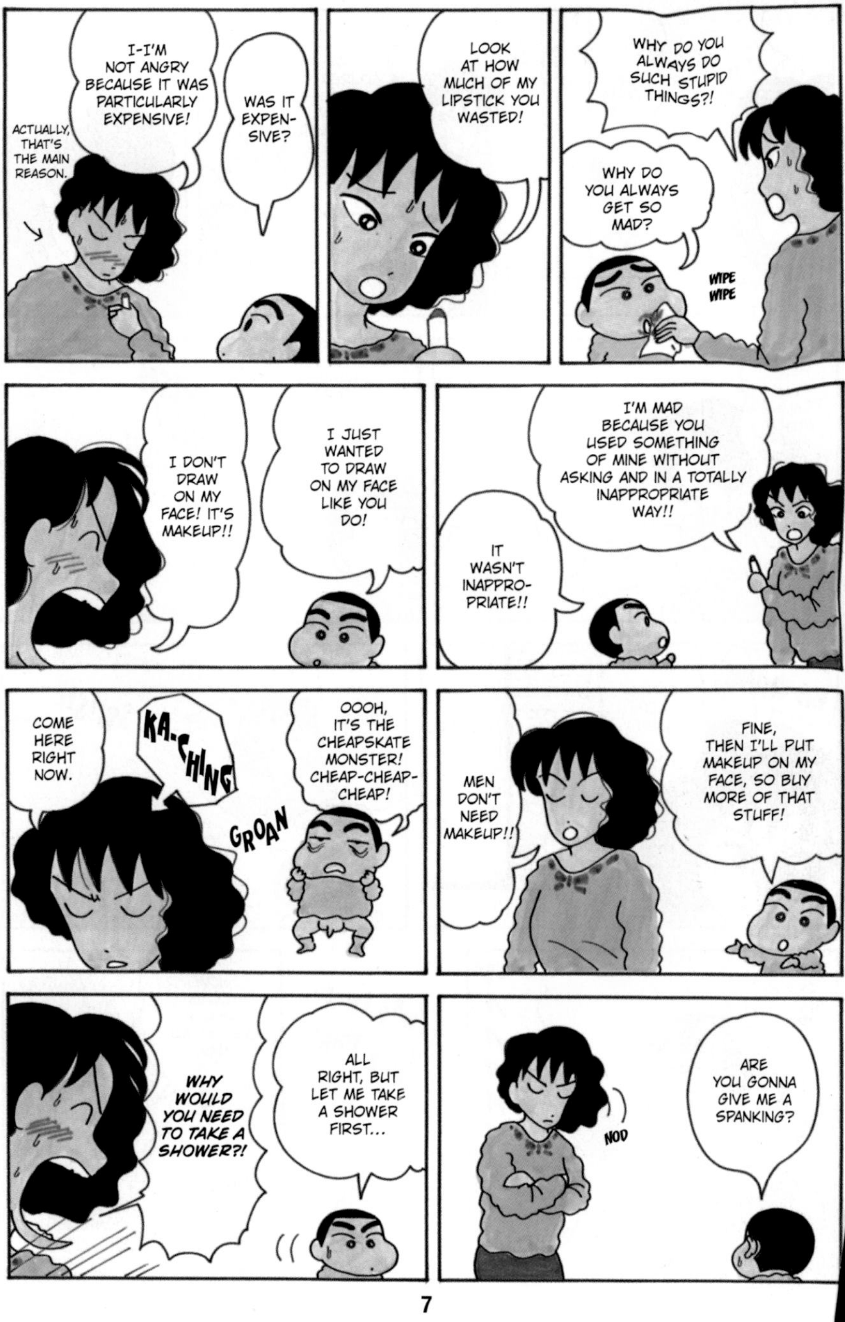
WHY DO YOU ALWAYS DO SUCH STUPID THINGS?!
WHY DO YOU ALWAYS GET SO MAD?
WIPE WIPE
LOOK AT HOW MUCH OF MY LIPSTICK YOU WASTED!
WAS IT EXPEN-SIVE?
I-I'M NOT ANGRY BECAUSE IT WAS PARTICULARLY EXPENSIVE!
ACTUALLY, THAT'S THE MAIN REASON.
I'M MAD BECAUSE YOU USED SOMETHING OF MINE WITHOUT ASKING AND IN A TOTALLY INAPPROPRIATE WAY!!
IT WASN'T INAPPRO-PRIATE!!
I JUST WANTED TO DRAW ON MY FACE LIKE YOU DO!
I DON'T DRAW ON MY FACE! IT'S MAKEUP!!
FINE, THEN I'LL PUT MAKEUP ON MY FACE, SO BUY MORE OF THAT STUFF!
MEN DON'T NEED MAKEUP!!
OOOH, IT'S THE CHEAPSKATE MONSTER! CHEAP-CHEAP-CHEAP!
KA-CHING
GROAN
COME HERE RIGHT NOW.
ARE YOU GONNA GIVE ME A SPANKING?
NOD
ALL RIGHT, BUT LET ME TAKE A SHOWER FIRST...
WHY WOULD YOU NEED TO TAKE A SHOWER?!

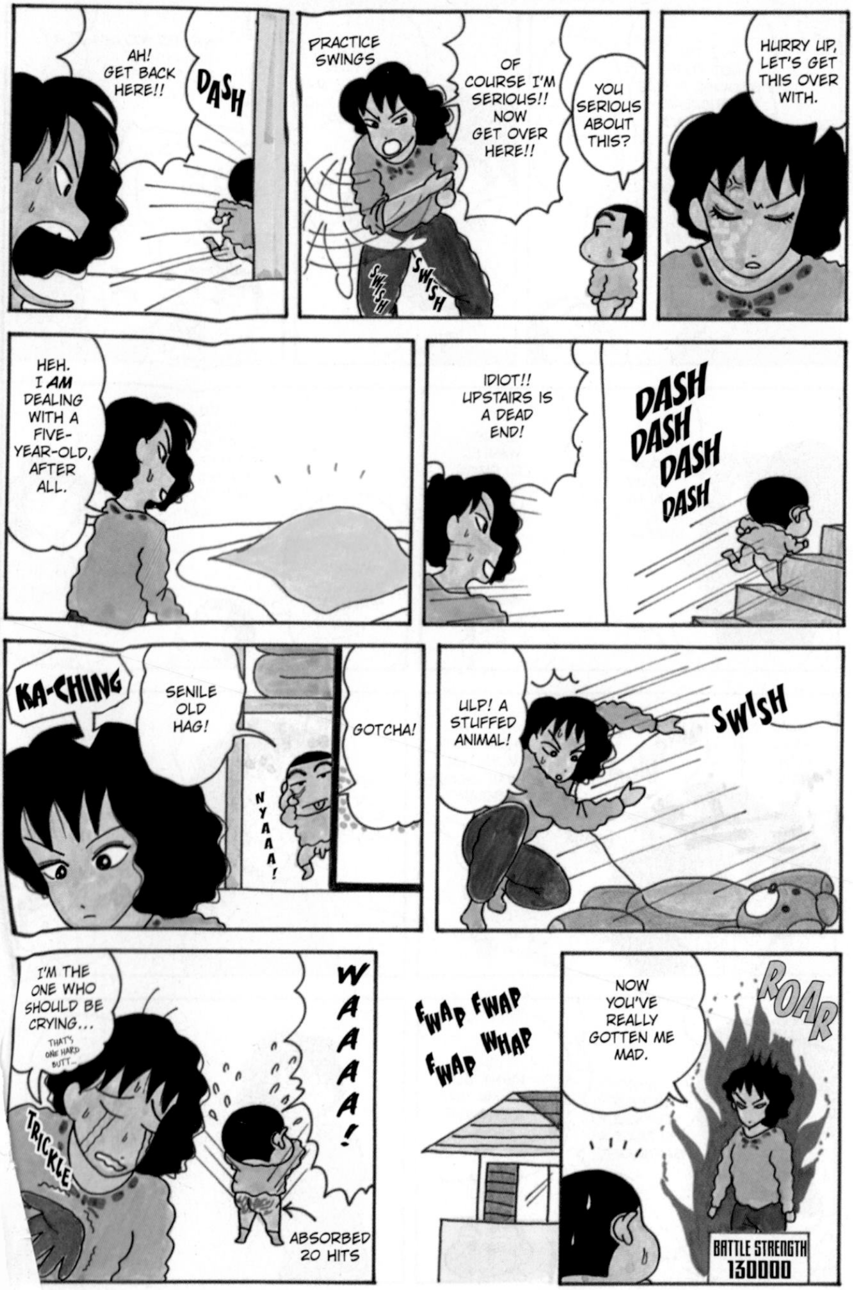
HURRY UP, LET'S GET THIS OVER WITH.
YOU SERIOUS ABOUT THIS?
OF COURSE I'M SERIOUS!! NOW GET OVER HERE!!
PRACTICE SWINGS
SWISH
SWISH
DASH
AH! GET BACK HERE!!
DASH DASH DASH DASH
IDIOT!! UPSTAIRS IS A DEAD END!
HEH. I AM DEALING WITH A FIVE-YEAR-OLD, AFTER ALL.
SWISH
ULP! A STUFFED ANIMAL!
GOTCHA!
NYAAAA!
SENILE OLD HAG!
KA-CHING
ROAR
NOW YOU'VE REALLY GOTTEN ME MAD.
BATTLE STRENGTH 130000
FWAP FWAP FWAP WHAP
WAAAAA!
I'M THE ONE WHO SHOULD BE CRYING...
THAT'S ONE HARD BUTT...
TRICKLE
ABSORBED 20 HITS

MOM AND I ARE BEST FRIENDS

PART 1

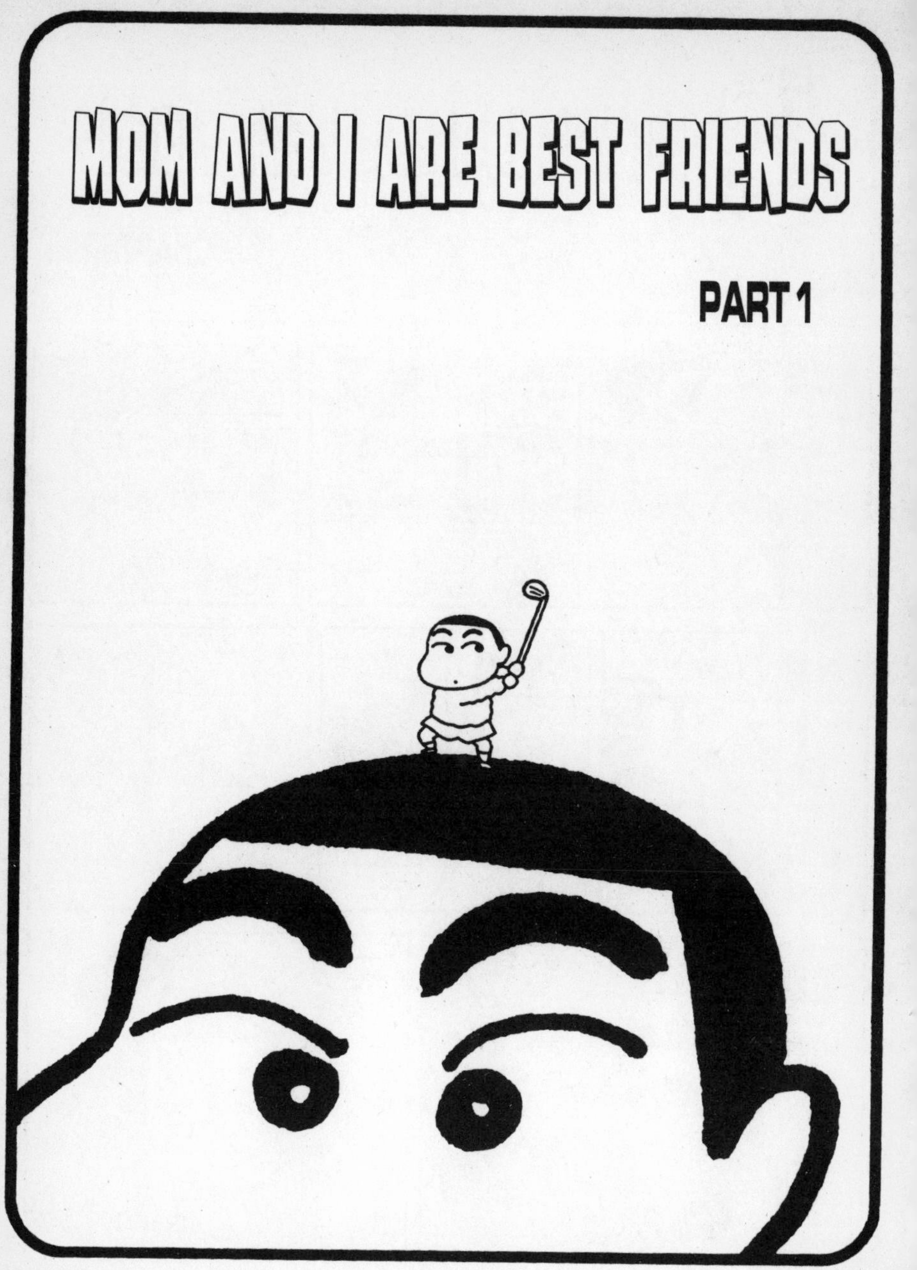

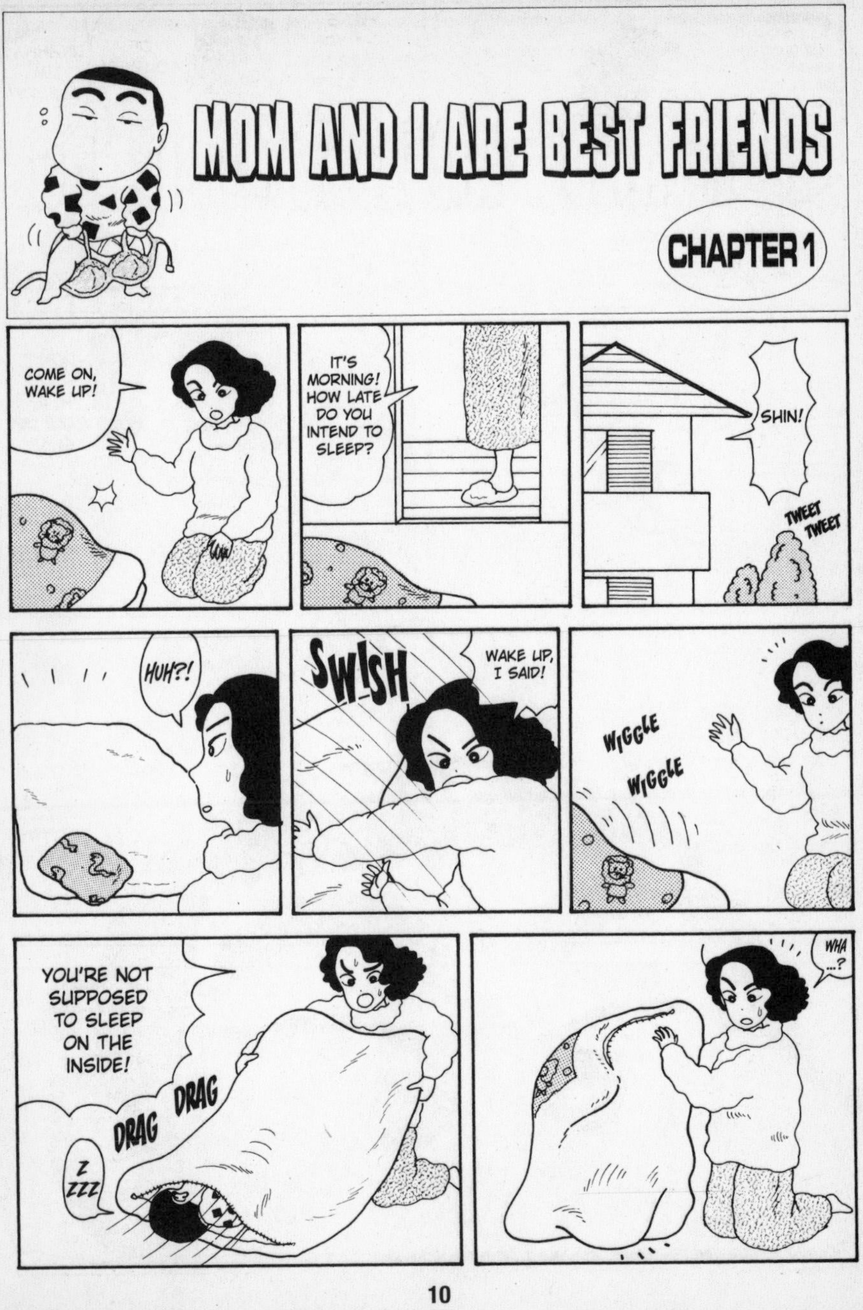
MOM AND I ARE BEST FRIENDS
CHAPTER 1
SHIN!
TWEET TWEET
IT'S MORNING! HOW LATE DO YOU INTEND TO SLEEP?
COME ON, WAKE UP!
WIGGLE WIGGLE
SWISH
WAKE UP, I SAID!
HUH?!
WHA ...?
YOU'RE NOT SUPPOSED TO SLEEP ON THE INSIDE!
DRAG DRAG
Z ZZZ

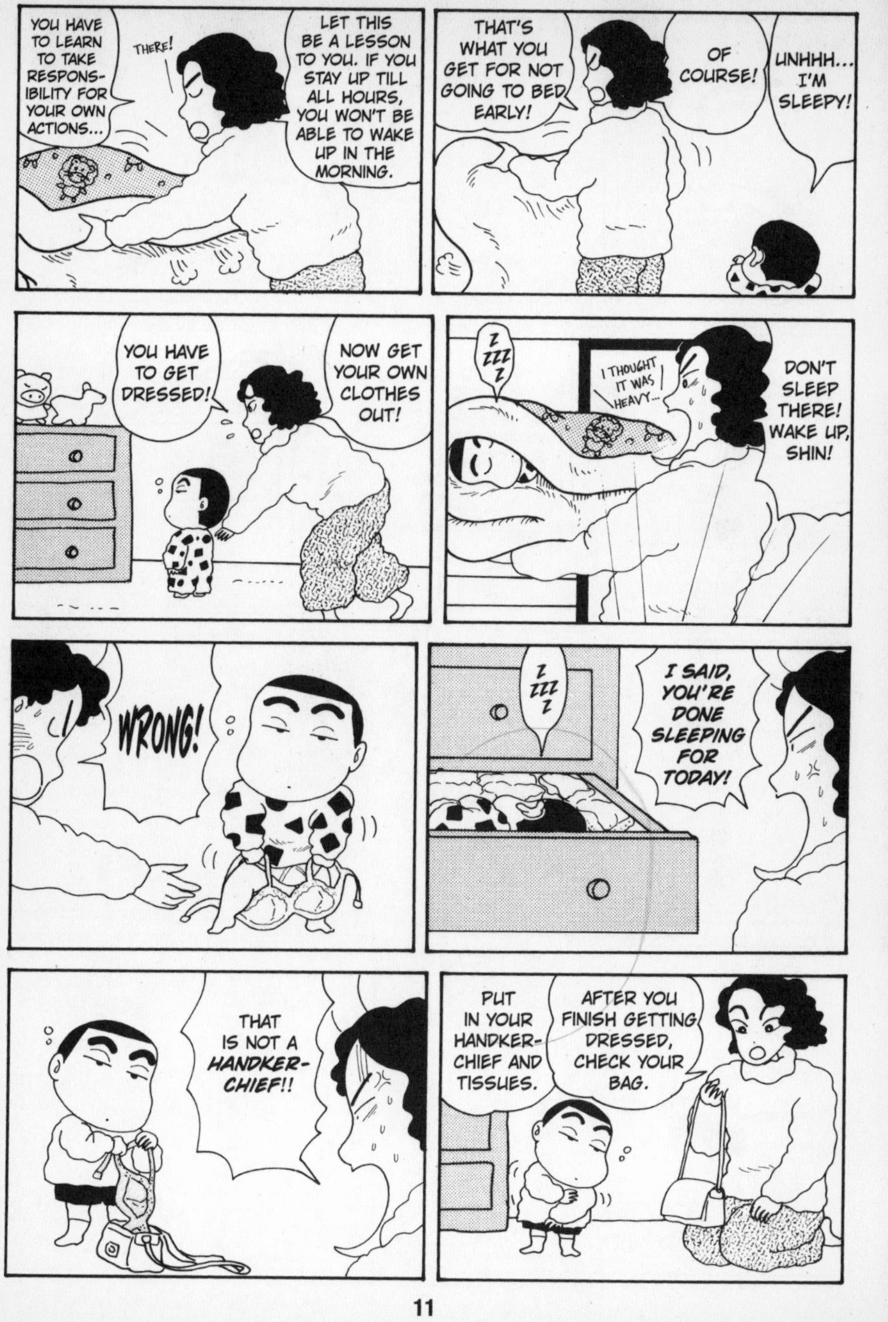

UNHHH... I'M SLEEPY!
OF COURSE!
THAT'S WHAT YOU GET FOR NOT GOING TO BED EARLY!
LET THIS BE A LESSON TO YOU. IF YOU STAY UP TILL ALL HOURS, YOU WON'T BE ABLE TO WAKE UP IN THE MORNING.
THERE!
YOU HAVE TO LEARN TO TAKE RESPONSIBILITY FOR YOUR OWN ACTIONS...
DON'T SLEEP THERE! WAKE UP, SHIN!
I THOUGHT IT WAS HEAVY...
Z ZZZ Z
NOW GET YOUR OWN CLOTHES OUT!
YOU HAVE TO GET DRESSED!
I SAID, YOU'RE DONE SLEEPING FOR TODAY!
Z ZZZ Z
WRONG!
AFTER YOU FINISH GETTING DRESSED, CHECK YOUR BAG.
PUT IN YOUR HANDKERCHIEF AND TISSUES.
THAT IS NOT A HANDKERCHIEF!!

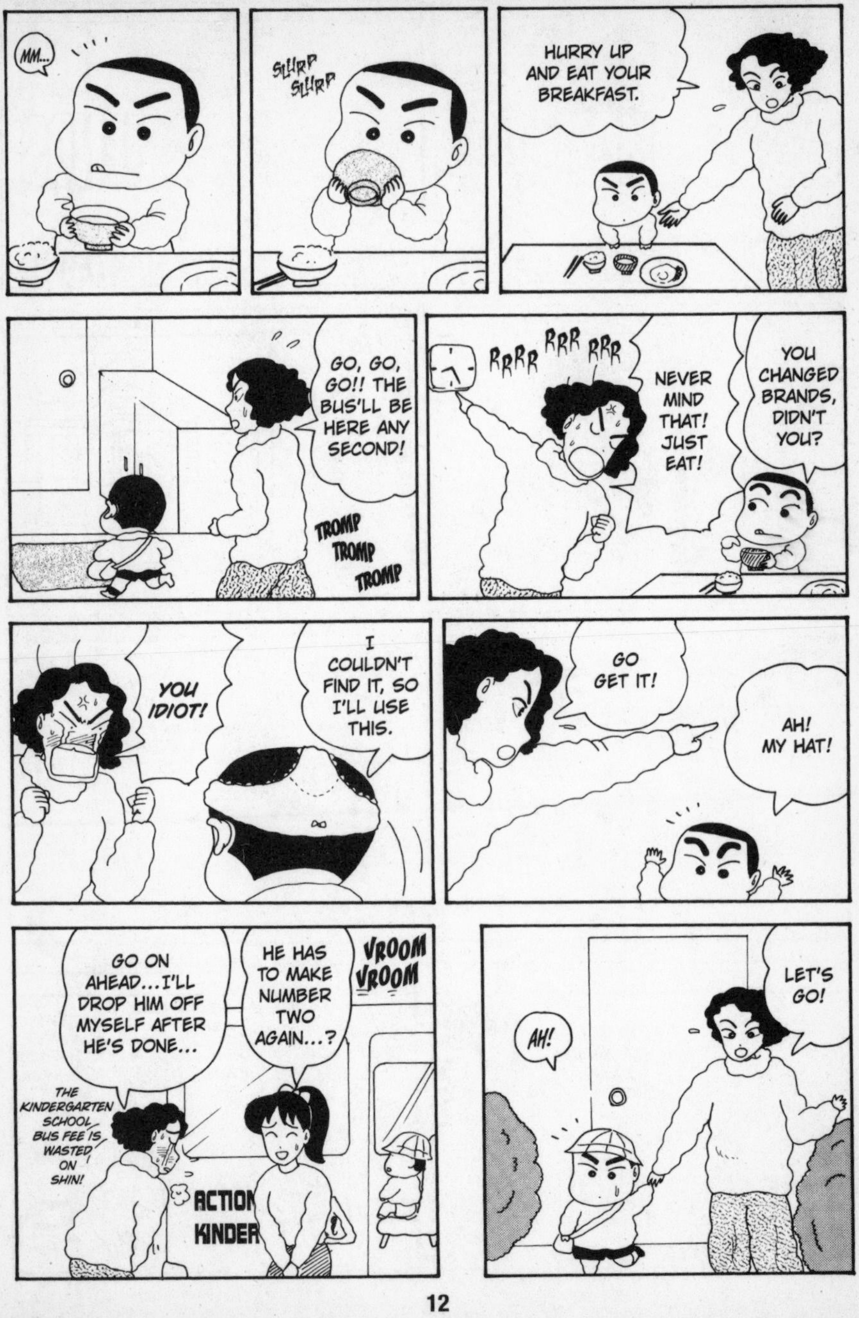
HURRY UP AND EAT YOUR BREAKFAST.
SLURP SLURP
MM...
YOU CHANGED BRANDS, DIDN'T YOU?
NEVER MIND THAT! JUST EAT!
RRRR RRR RRR
GO, GO, GO!! THE BUS'LL BE HERE ANY SECOND!
TROMP TROMP TROMP
AH! MY HAT!
GO GET IT!
I COULDN'T FIND IT, SO I'LL USE THIS.
YOU IDIOT!
LET'S GO!
AH!
VROOM VROOM
HE HAS TO MAKE NUMBER TWO AGAIN...?
GO ON AHEAD...I'LL DROP HIM OFF MYSELF AFTER HE'S DONE...
THE KINDERGARTEN SCHOOL BUS FEE IS WASTED ON SHIN!
ACTION KINDER

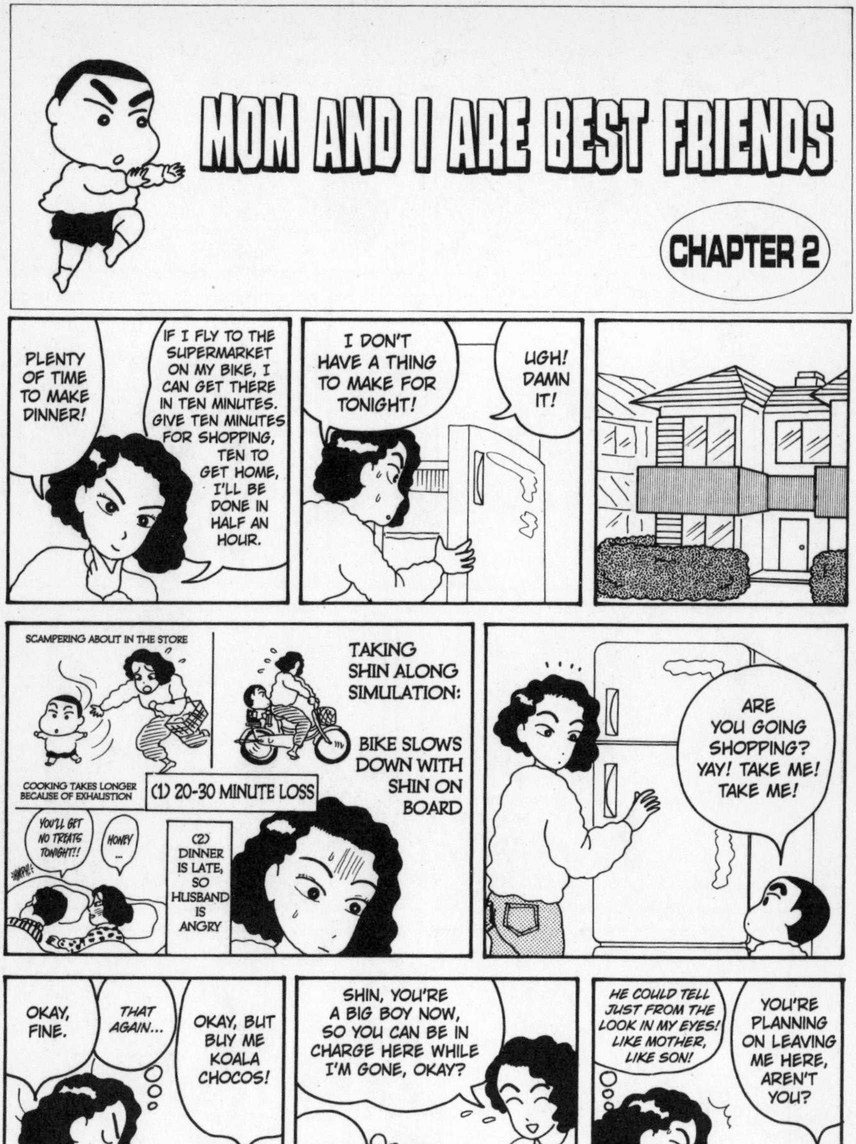
MOM AND I ARE BEST FRIENDS
CHAPTER 2
UGH! DAMN IT!
I DON'T HAVE A THING TO MAKE FOR TONIGHT!
IF I FLY TO THE SUPERMARKET ON MY BIKE, I CAN GET THERE IN TEN MINUTES. GIVE TEN MINUTES FOR SHOPPING, TEN TO GET HOME, I'LL BE DONE IN HALF AN HOUR.
PLENTY OF TIME TO MAKE DINNER!
...
ARE YOU GOING SHOPPING? YAY! TAKE ME! TAKE ME!
TAKING SHIN ALONG SIMULATION:
BIKE SLOWS DOWN WITH SHIN ON BOARD
SCAMPERING ABOUT IN THE STORE
COOKING TAKES LONGER BECAUSE OF EXHAUSTION
(1) 20-30 MINUTE LOSS
(2) DINNER IS LATE, SO HUSBAND IS ANGRY
HONEY ...
YOU'LL GET NO TREATS TONIGHT!!
HMPH!
YOU'RE PLANNING ON LEAVING ME HERE, AREN'T YOU?
HE COULD TELL JUST FROM THE LOOK IN MY EYES! LIKE MOTHER, LIKE SON!
THUMP
SHIN, YOU'RE A BIG BOY NOW, SO YOU CAN BE IN CHARGE HERE WHILE I'M GONE, OKAY?
THAT LINE AGAIN...
OKAY, BUT BUY ME KOALA CHOCOS!
THAT AGAIN...
OKAY, FINE.

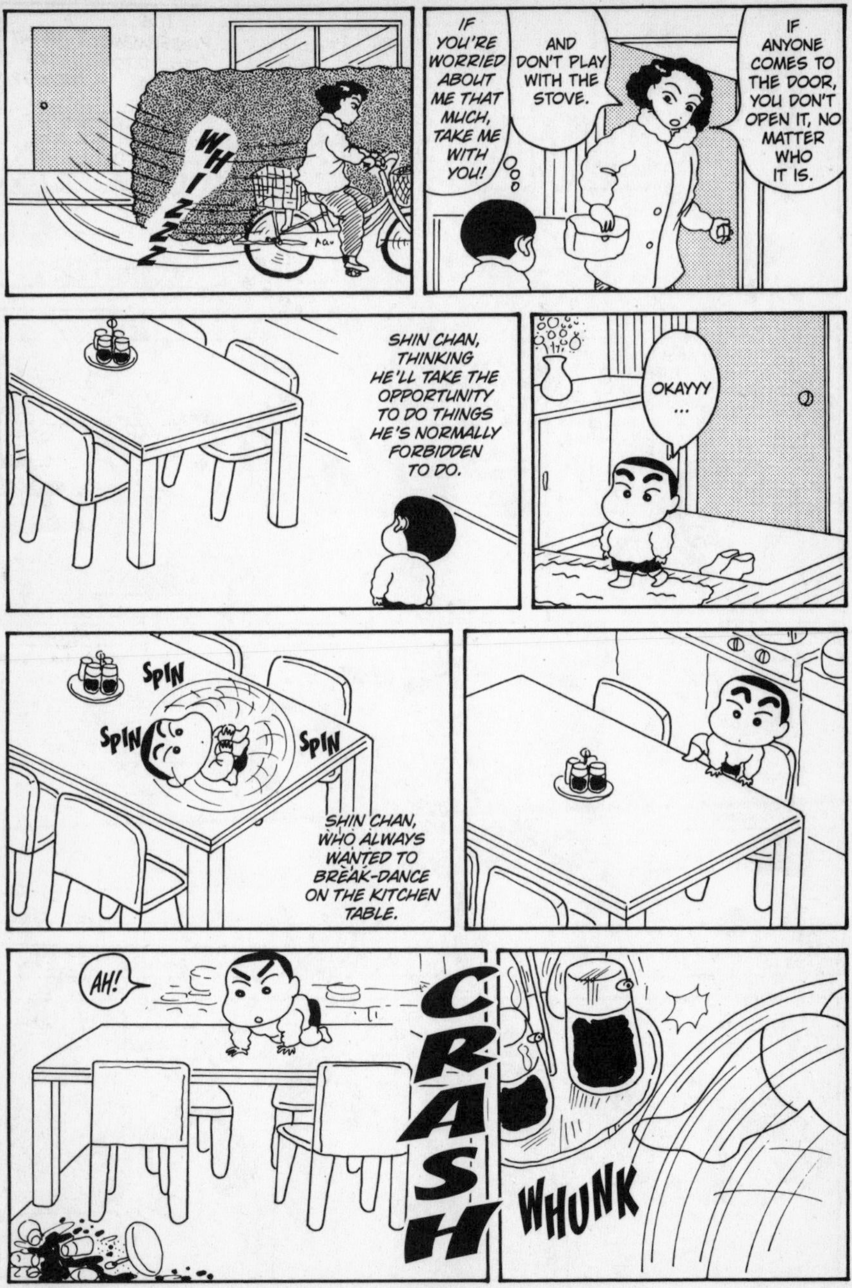
IF ANYONE COMES TO THE DOOR, YOU DON'T OPEN IT, NO MATTER WHO IT IS.
AND DON'T PLAY WITH THE STOVE.
IF YOU'RE WORRIED ABOUT ME THAT MUCH, TAKE ME WITH YOU!
WHIZZZZ
OKAYYY ...
SHIN CHAN, THINKING HE'LL TAKE THE OPPORTUNITY TO DO THINGS HE'S NORMALLY FORBIDDEN TO DO.
SPIN
SPIN
SPIN
SHIN CHAN, WHO ALWAYS WANTED TO BREAK-DANCE ON THE KITCHEN TABLE.
CRASH
WHUNK
AH!

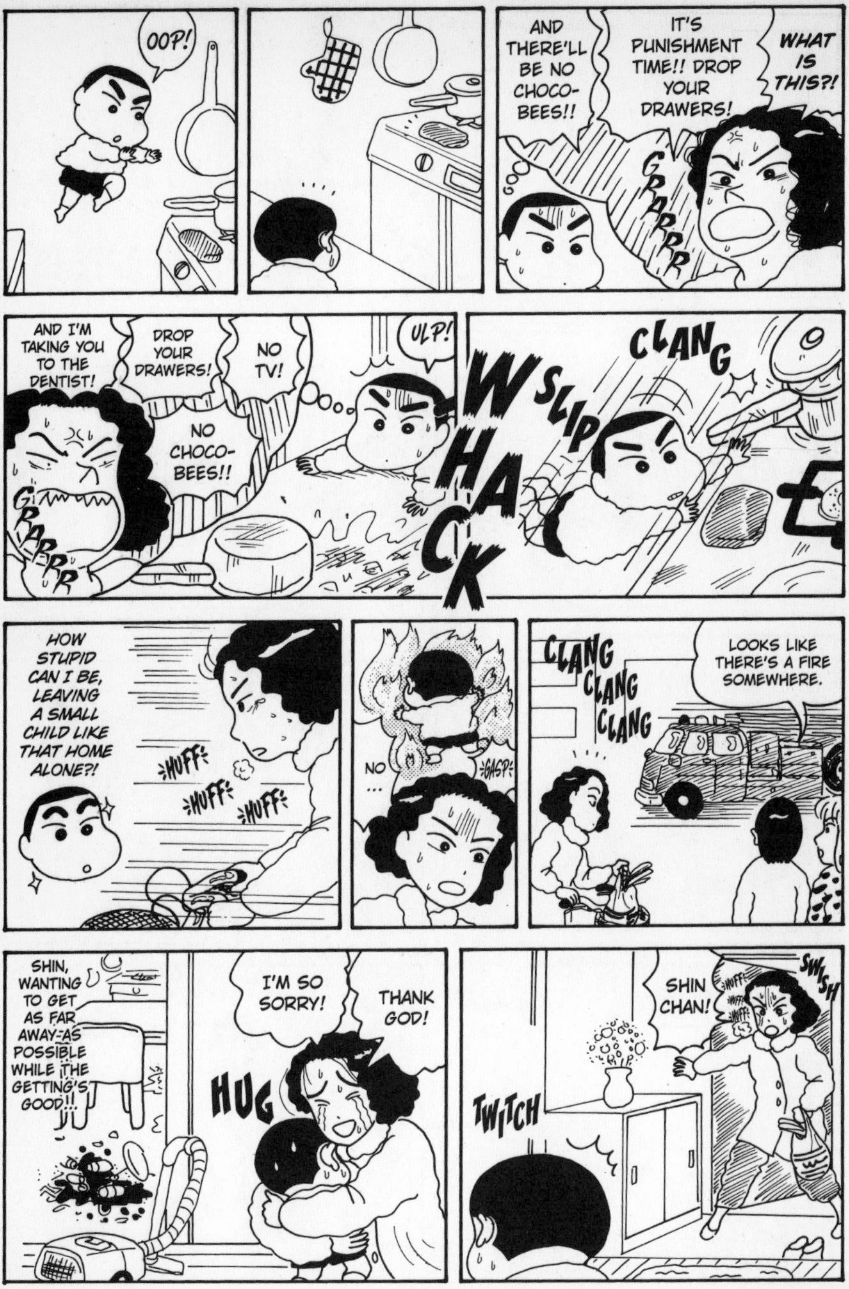
WHAT IS THIS?!
IT'S PUNISHMENT TIME!! DROP YOUR DRAWERS!
AND THERE'LL BE NO CHOCO-BEES!!
GRARRR
OOP!
CLANG
SLIP
WHACK
ULP!
NO TV!
DROP YOUR DRAWERS!
AND I'M TAKING YOU TO THE DENTIST!
NO CHOCO-BEES!!
GRARRR
CLANG CLANG CLANG
LOOKS LIKE THERE'S A FIRE SOMEWHERE.
GASP
NO ...
HOW STUPID CAN I BE, LEAVING A SMALL CHILD LIKE THAT HOME ALONE?!
HUFF
HUFF
HUFF
SWISH
SHIN CHAN!
HUFF
HUFF
HUFF
TWITCH
THANK GOD!
I'M SO SORRY!
HUG
SHIN, WANTING TO GET AS FAR AWAY AS POSSIBLE WHILE THE GETTING'S GOOD!!

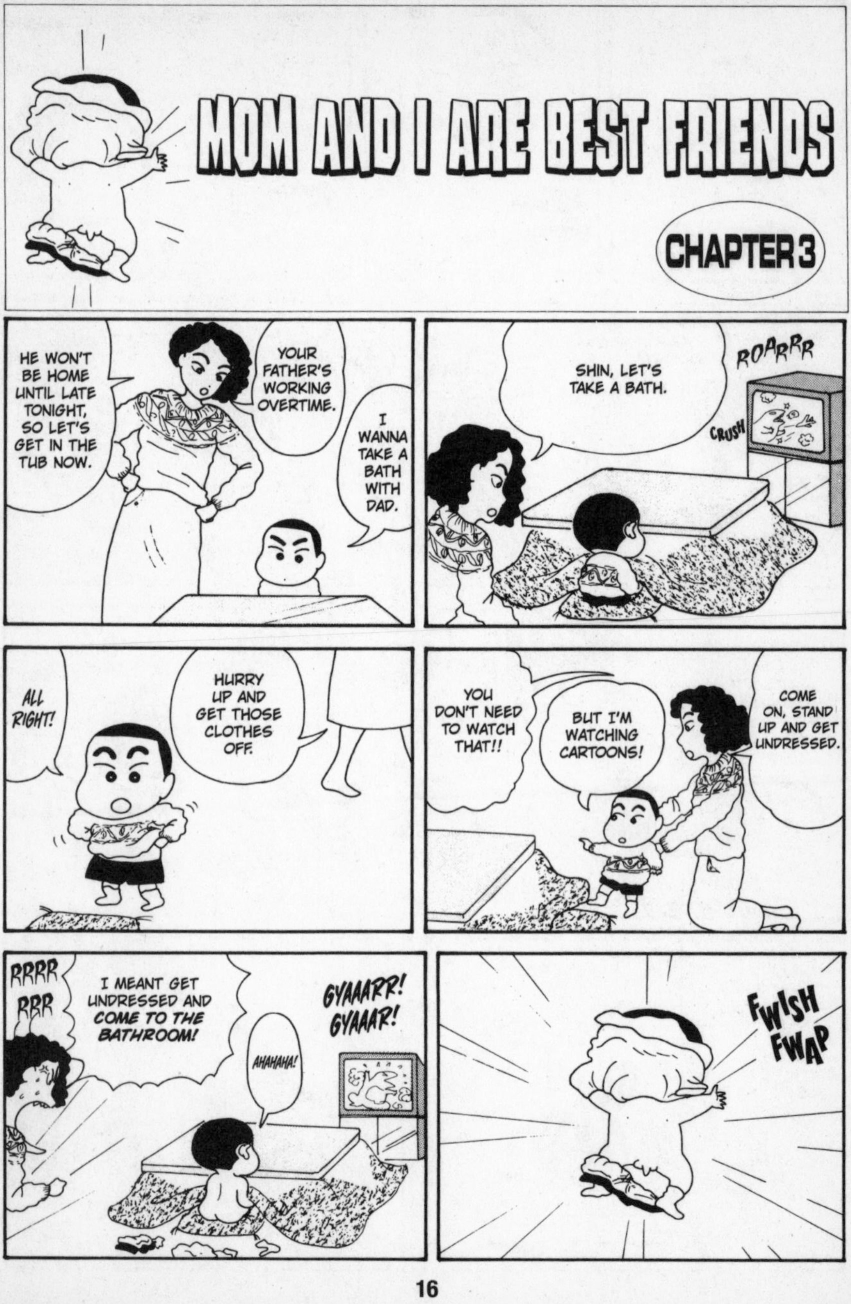
MOM AND I ARE BEST FRIENDS
CHAPTER 3
SHIN, LET'S TAKE A BATH.
ROARRR
CRUSH
YOUR FATHER'S WORKING OVERTIME.
I WANNA TAKE A BATH WITH DAD.
HE WON'T BE HOME UNTIL LATE TONIGHT, SO LET'S GET IN THE TUB NOW.
COME ON, STAND UP AND GET UNDRESSED.
BUT I'M WATCHING CARTOONS!
YOU DON'T NEED TO WATCH THAT!!
HURRY UP AND GET THOSE CLOTHES OFF.
ALL RIGHT!
FWISH FWAP
GYAAARR! GYAAAR!
AHAHAHA!
I MEANT GET UNDRESSED AND *COME TO THE BATHROOM!*
RRRR RRR

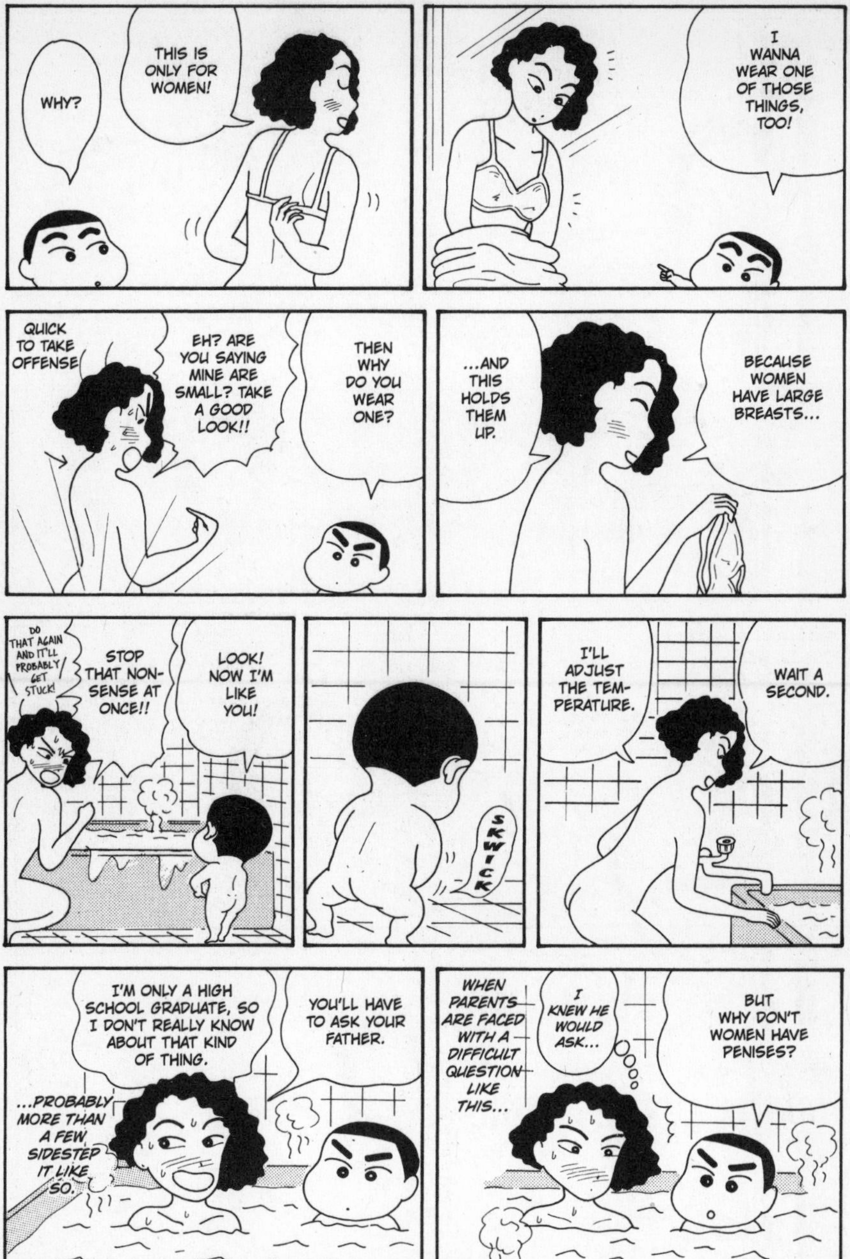
I WANNA WEAR ONE OF THOSE THINGS, TOO!
THIS IS ONLY FOR WOMEN!
WHY?
BECAUSE WOMEN HAVE LARGE BREASTS...
...AND THIS HOLDS THEM UP.
THEN WHY DO YOU WEAR ONE?
EH? ARE YOU SAYING MINE ARE SMALL? TAKE A GOOD LOOK!!
QUICK TO TAKE OFFENSE
WAIT A SECOND.
I'LL ADJUST THE TEMPERATURE.
SKWICK
LOOK! NOW I'M LIKE YOU!
STOP THAT NONSENSE AT ONCE!!
DO THAT AGAIN AND IT'LL PROBABLY GET STUCK!
BUT WHY DON'T WOMEN HAVE PENISES?
I KNEW HE WOULD ASK...
WHEN PARENTS ARE FACED WITH A DIFFICULT QUESTION LIKE THIS...
YOU'LL HAVE TO ASK YOUR FATHER.
I'M ONLY A HIGH SCHOOL GRADUATE, SO I DON'T REALLY KNOW ABOUT THAT KIND OF THING.
...PROBABLY MORE THAN A FEW SIDESTEP IT LIKE SO.

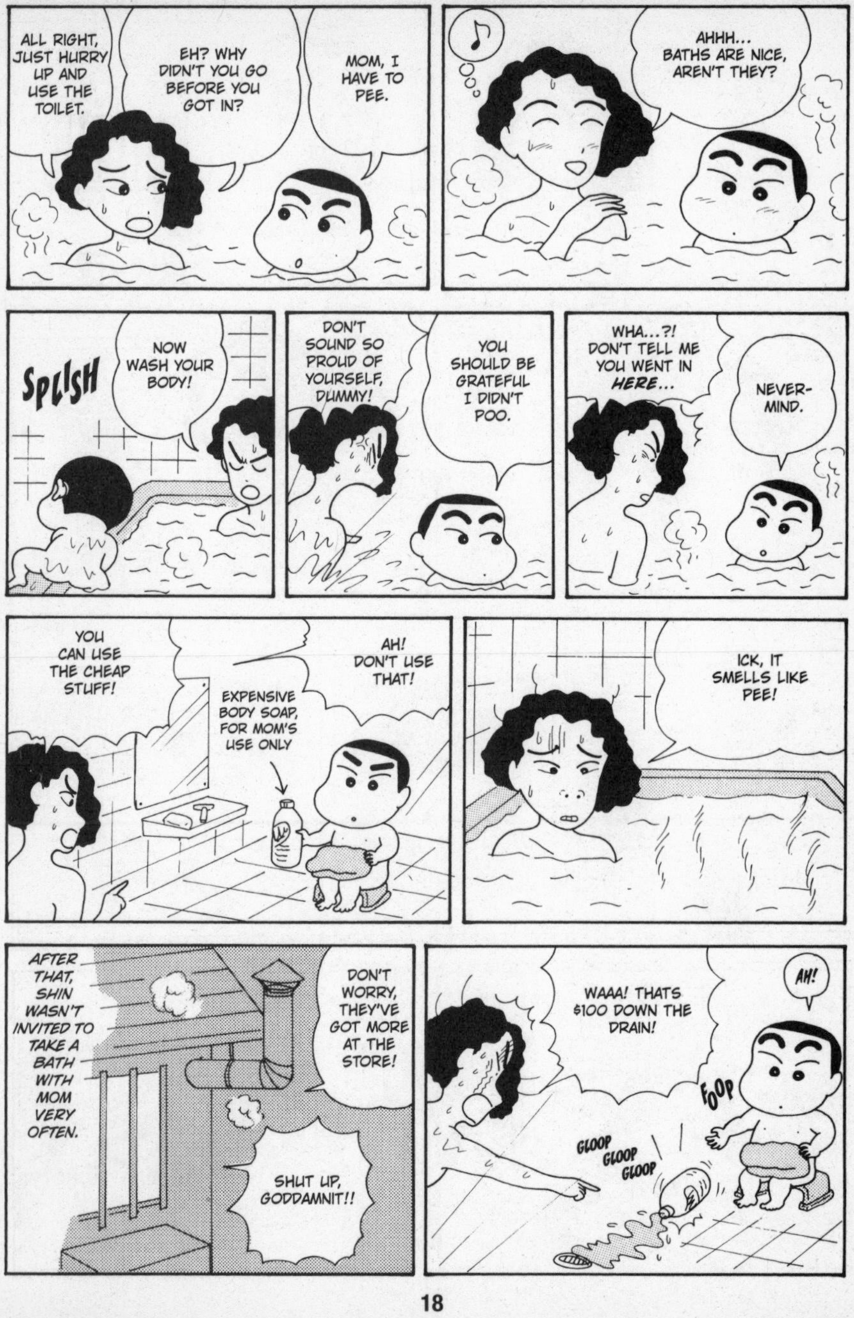
AHHH... BATHS ARE NICE, AREN'T THEY?
MOM, I HAVE TO PEE.
EH? WHY DIDN'T YOU GO BEFORE YOU GOT IN?
ALL RIGHT, JUST HURRY UP AND USE THE TOILET.
NEVER-MIND.
WHA...?! DON'T TELL ME YOU WENT IN *HERE*...
YOU SHOULD BE GRATEFUL I DIDN'T POO.
DON'T SOUND SO PROUD OF YOURSELF, DUMMY!
NOW WASH YOUR BODY!
SPLISH
ICK, IT SMELLS LIKE PEE!
AH! DON'T USE THAT!
EXPENSIVE BODY SOAP, FOR MOM'S USE ONLY
YOU CAN USE THE CHEAP STUFF!
AH!
WAAA! THATS $100 DOWN THE DRAIN!
FOOP
GLOOP GLOOP GLOOP
DON'T WORRY, THEY'VE GOT MORE AT THE STORE!
SHUT UP, GODDAMNIT!!
AFTER THAT, SHIN WASN'T INVITED TO TAKE A BATH WITH MOM VERY OFTEN.

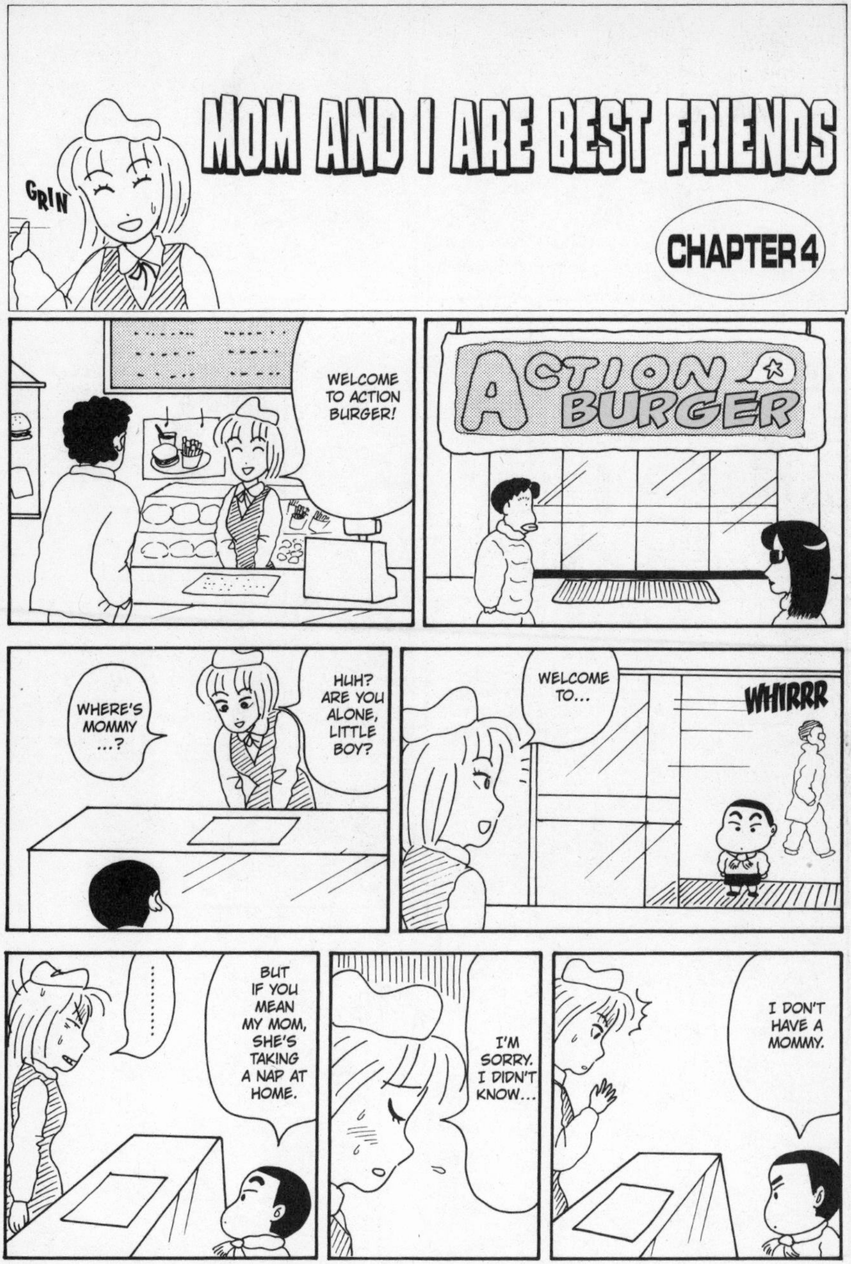
MOM AND I ARE BEST FRIENDS
CHAPTER 4
GRIN
ACTION BURGER
WELCOME TO ACTION BURGER!
WHIRRR
WELCOME TO...
HUH? ARE YOU ALONE, LITTLE BOY?
WHERE'S MOMMY ...?
I DON'T HAVE A MOMMY.
I'M SORRY. I DIDN'T KNOW...
BUT IF YOU MEAN MY MOM, SHE'S TAKING A NAP AT HOME.
....

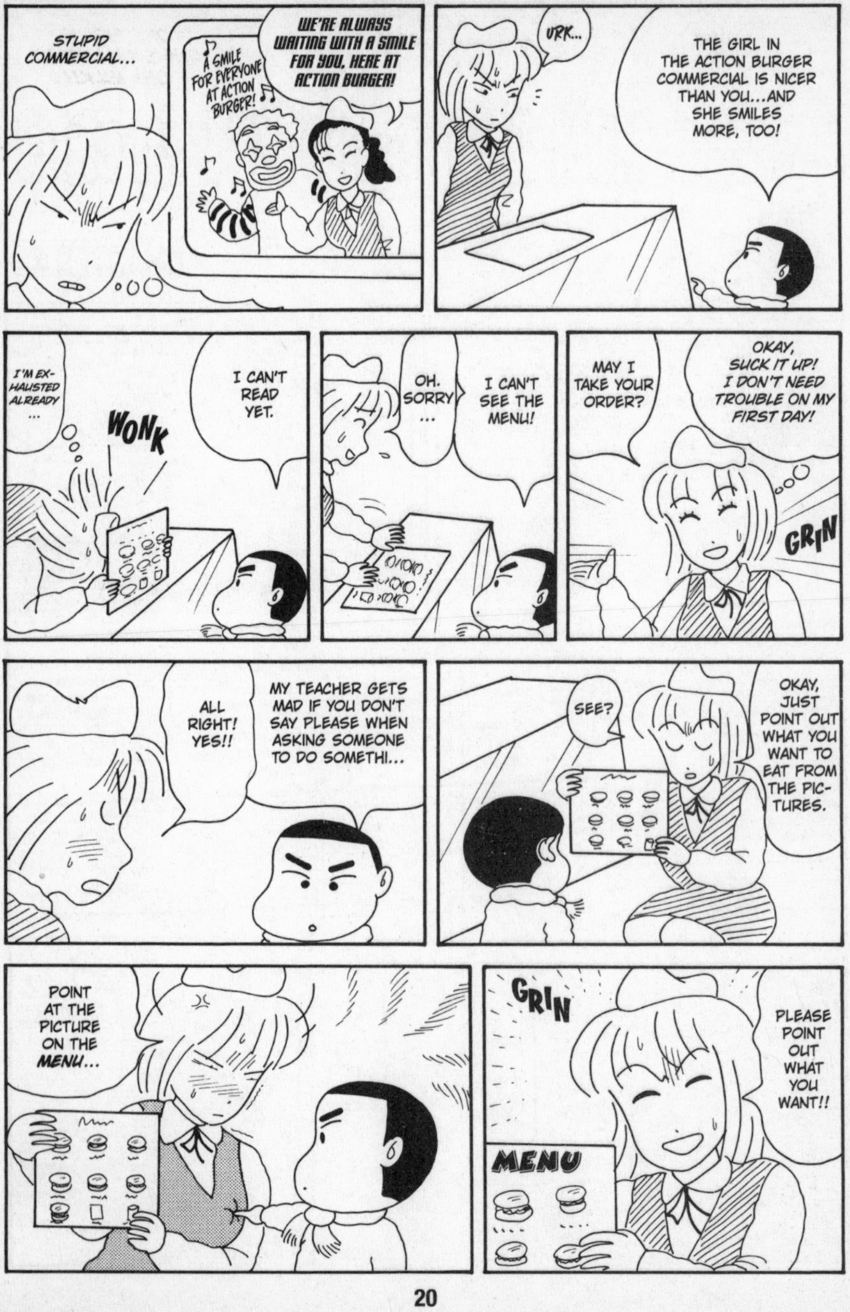
THE GIRL IN THE ACTION BURGER COMMERCIAL IS NICER THAN YOU...AND SHE SMILES MORE, TOO!
URK...
WE'RE ALWAYS WAITING WITH A SMILE FOR YOU, HERE AT ACTION BURGER!
A SMILE FOR EVERYONE AT ACTION BURGER!
STUPID COMMERCIAL...
OKAY, SUCK IT UP! I DON'T NEED TROUBLE ON MY FIRST DAY!
MAY I TAKE YOUR ORDER?
GRIN
I CAN'T SEE THE MENU!
OH. SORRY ...
I CAN'T READ YET.
WONK
I'M EX-HAUSTED ALREADY ...
OKAY, JUST POINT OUT WHAT YOU WANT TO EAT FROM THE PIC-TURES.
SEE?
MY TEACHER GETS MAD IF YOU DON'T SAY PLEASE WHEN ASKING SOMEONE TO DO SOMETHI...
ALL RIGHT! YES!!
PLEASE POINT OUT WHAT YOU WANT!!
GRIN
MENU
POINT AT THE PICTURE ON THE MENU...

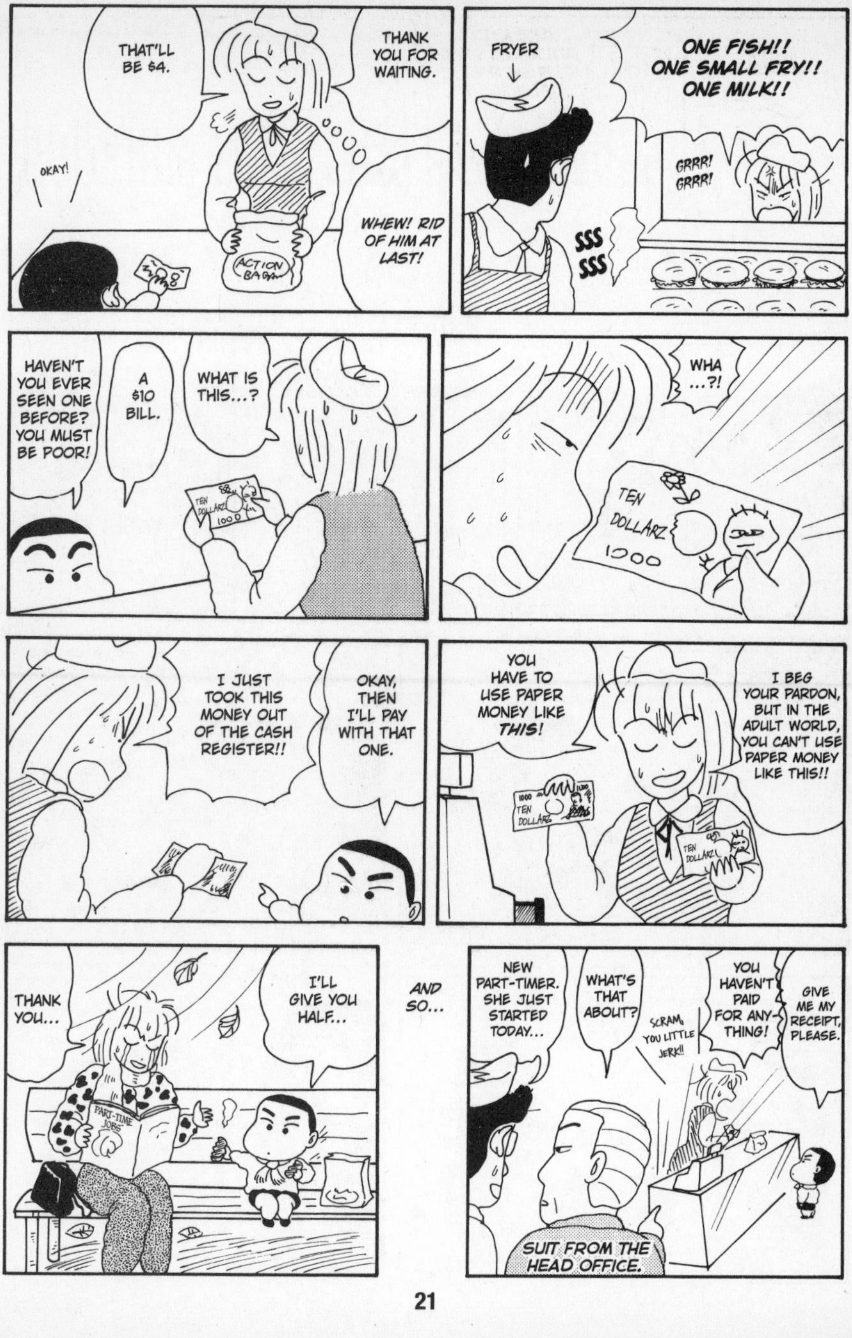
FRYER
ONE FISH!! ONE SMALL FRY!! ONE MILK!!
GRRR! GRRR!
SSS SSS
THANK YOU FOR WAITING.
THAT'LL BE $4.
OKAY!
WHEW! RID OF HIM AT LAST!
ACTION BAG
WHA ...?!
TEN DOLLARZ 1000
WHAT IS THIS...?
A $10 BILL.
HAVEN'T YOU EVER SEEN ONE BEFORE? YOU MUST BE POOR!
TEN DOLLARZ 1000
I BEG YOUR PARDON, BUT IN THE ADULT WORLD, YOU CAN'T USE PAPER MONEY LIKE THIS!!
YOU HAVE TO USE PAPER MONEY LIKE *THIS!*
1000 TEN DOLLARZ
TEN DOLLARZ
OKAY, THEN I'LL PAY WITH THAT ONE.
I JUST TOOK THIS MONEY OUT OF THE CASH REGISTER!!
GIVE ME MY RECEIPT, PLEASE.
YOU HAVEN'T PAID FOR ANY-THING!
SCRAM, YOU LITTLE JERK!!
WHAT'S THAT ABOUT?
NEW PART-TIMER. SHE JUST STARTED TODAY...
SUIT FROM THE HEAD OFFICE.
AND SO...
I'LL GIVE YOU HALF...
THANK YOU...
PART-TIME JOBS

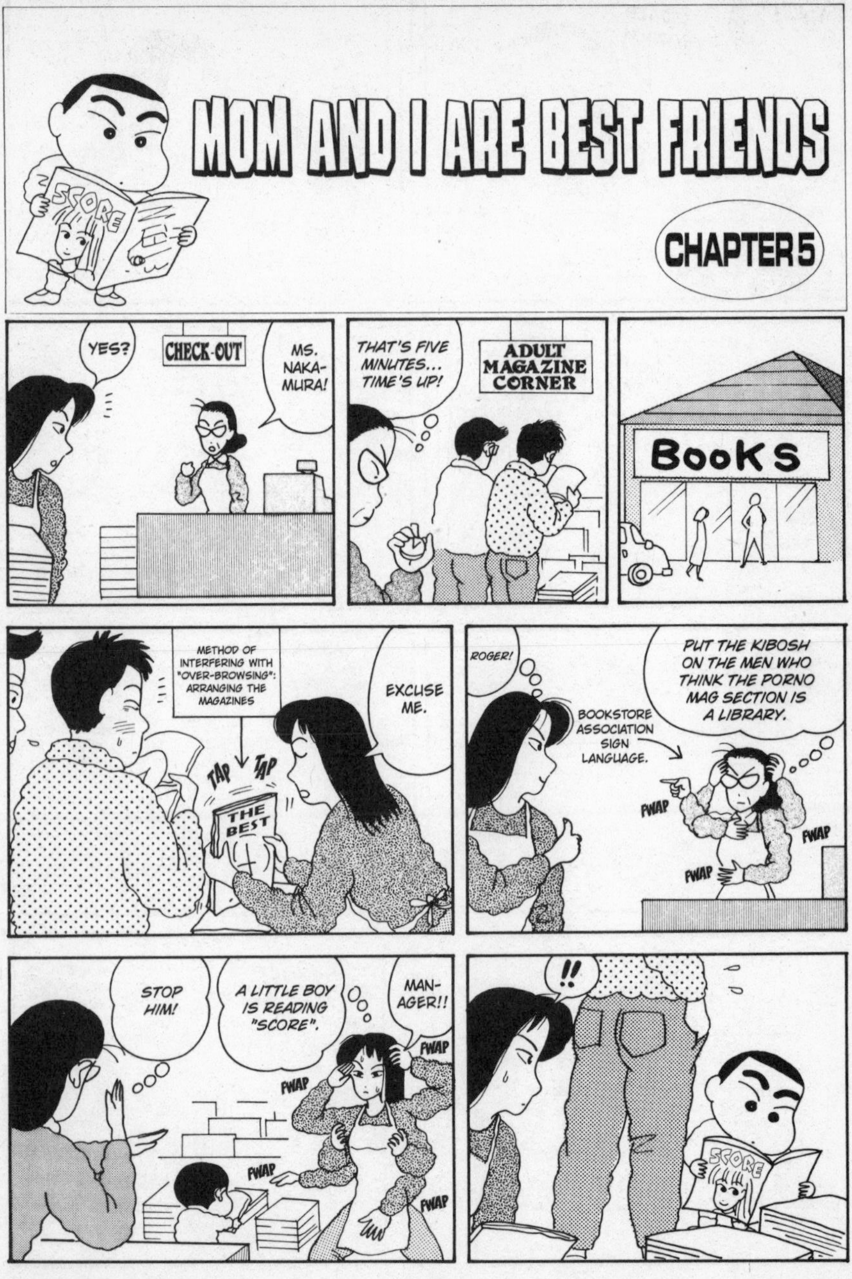
MOM AND I ARE BEST FRIENDS
CHAPTER 5
SCORE
ADULT MAGAZINE CORNER
THAT'S FIVE MINUTES... TIME'S UP!
MS. NAKA-MURA!
CHECK-OUT
YES?
BOOKS
PUT THE KIBOSH ON THE MEN WHO THINK THE PORNO MAG SECTION IS A LIBRARY.
ROGER!
BOOKSTORE ASSOCIATION SIGN LANGUAGE.
FWAP
FWAP
FWAP
EXCUSE ME.
METHOD OF INTERFERING WITH "OVER-BROWSING": ARRANGING THE MAGAZINES
TAP TAP
THE BEST
!!
SCORE
MAN-AGER!!
FWAP
A LITTLE BOY IS READING "SCORE".
STOP HIM!
FWAP
FWAP
FWAP

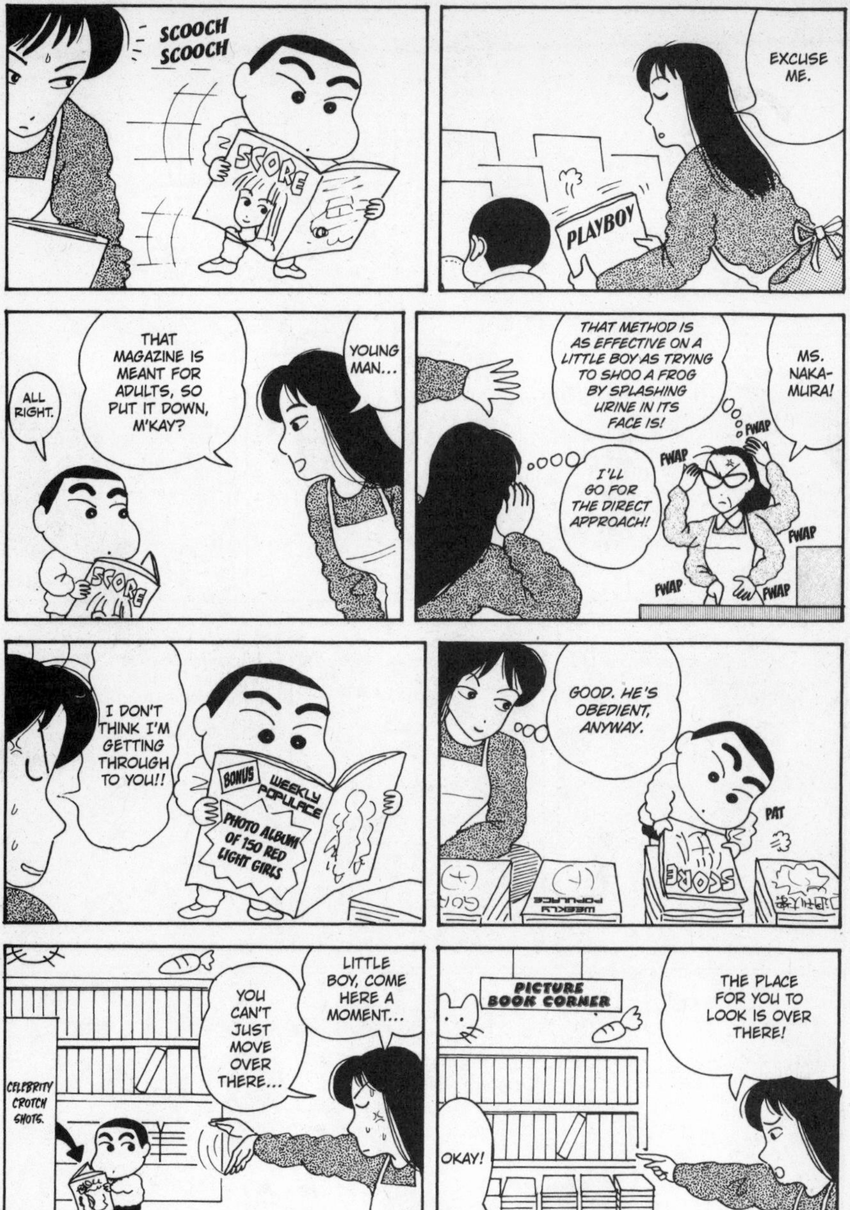
EXCUSE ME.
PLAYBOY
SCOOCH SCOOCH
SCORE
MS. NAKAMURA!
THAT METHOD IS AS EFFECTIVE ON A LITTLE BOY AS TRYING TO SHOO A FROG BY SPLASHING URINE IN ITS FACE IS!
FWAP
I'LL GO FOR THE DIRECT APPROACH!
FWAP
FWAP
FWAP
FWAP
YOUNG MAN...
THAT MAGAZINE IS MEANT FOR ADULTS, SO PUT IT DOWN, M'KAY?
ALL RIGHT.
SCORE
GOOD. HE'S OBEDIENT, ANYWAY.
PAT
I DON'T THINK I'M GETTING THROUGH TO YOU!!
BONUS
WEEKLY POPULACE
PHOTO ALBUM OF 150 RED LIGHT GIRLS
PICTURE BOOK CORNER
THE PLACE FOR YOU TO LOOK IS OVER THERE!
OKAY!
LITTLE BOY, COME HERE A MOMENT...
YOU CAN'T JUST MOVE OVER THERE...
CELEBRITY CROTCH SHOTS.

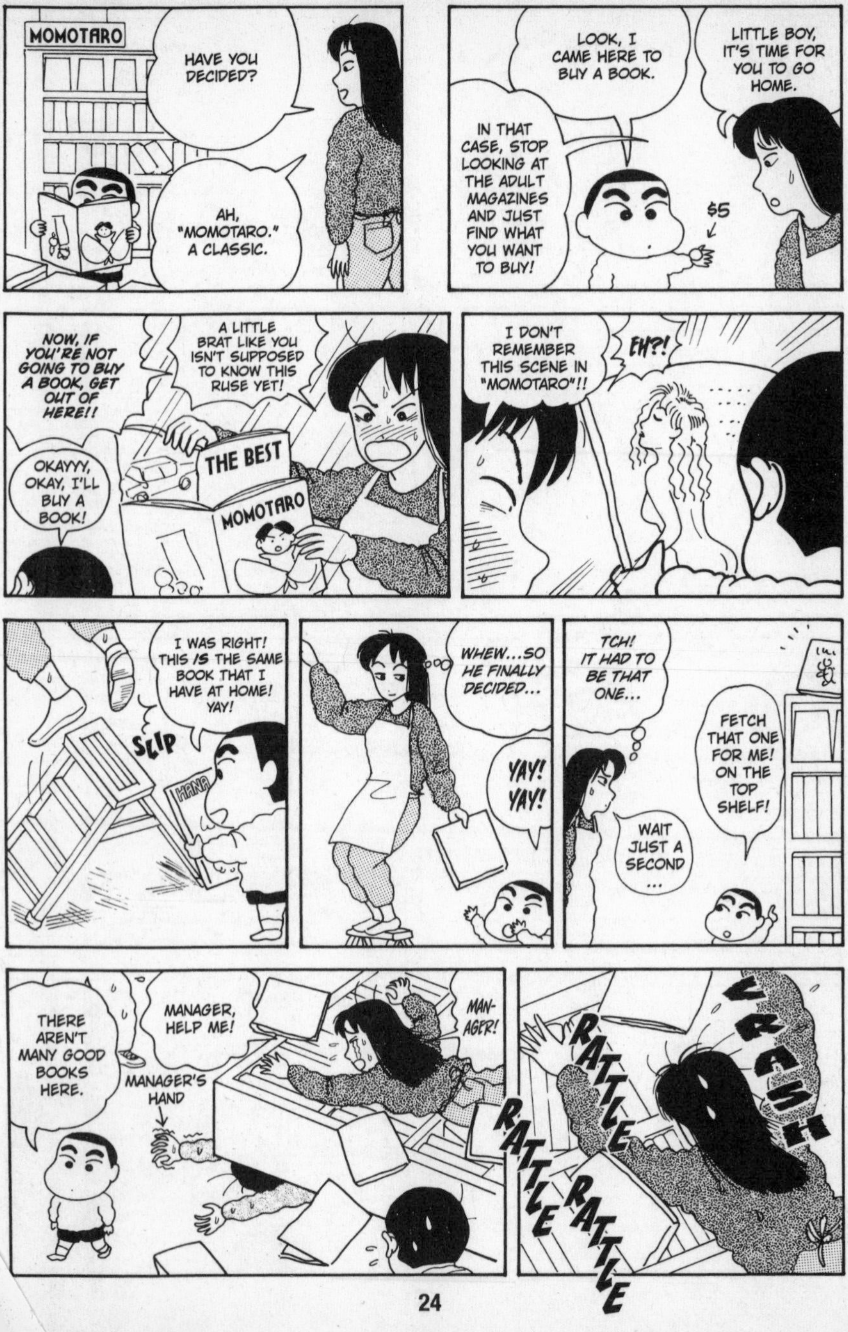
LITTLE BOY, IT'S TIME FOR YOU TO GO HOME.
LOOK, I CAME HERE TO BUY A BOOK.
IN THAT CASE, STOP LOOKING AT THE ADULT MAGAZINES AND JUST FIND WHAT YOU WANT TO BUY!
$5
MOMOTARO
HAVE YOU DECIDED?
AH, "MOMOTARO." A CLASSIC.
EH?!
I DON'T REMEMBER THIS SCENE IN "MOMOTARO"!!
A LITTLE BRAT LIKE YOU ISN'T SUPPOSED TO KNOW THIS RUSE YET!
NOW, IF YOU'RE NOT GOING TO BUY A BOOK, GET OUT OF HERE!!
THE BEST
MOMOTARO
OKAYYY, OKAY, I'LL BUY A BOOK!
FETCH THAT ONE FOR ME! ON THE TOP SHELF!
TCH! IT HAD TO BE THAT ONE...
WAIT JUST A SECOND ...
WHEW...SO HE FINALLY DECIDED...
YAY! YAY!
I WAS RIGHT! THIS IS THE SAME BOOK THAT I HAVE AT HOME! YAY!
SLIP
HANA
VRASH
RATTLE
RATTLE
RATTLE
RATTLE
MAN-AGER!
MANAGER, HELP ME!
MANAGER'S HAND
THERE AREN'T MANY GOOD BOOKS HERE.

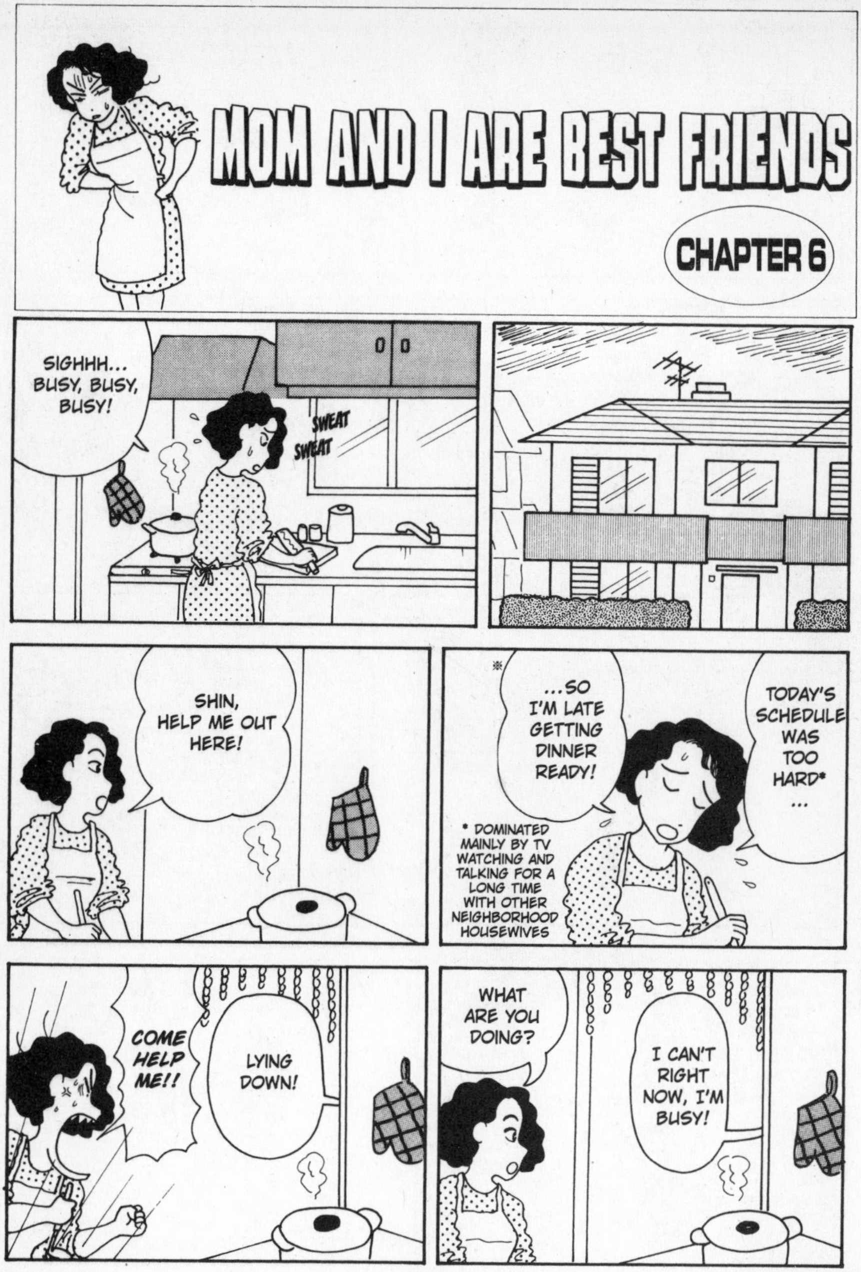
MOM AND I ARE BEST FRIENDS
CHAPTER 6
SIGHHH... BUSY, BUSY, BUSY!
SWEAT SWEAT
TODAY'S SCHEDULE WAS TOO HARD* ...
...SO I'M LATE GETTING DINNER READY!
* DOMINATED MAINLY BY TV WATCHING AND TALKING FOR A LONG TIME WITH OTHER NEIGHBORHOOD HOUSEWIVES
SHIN, HELP ME OUT HERE!
I CAN'T RIGHT NOW, I'M BUSY!
WHAT ARE YOU DOING?
LYING DOWN!
COME HELP ME!!

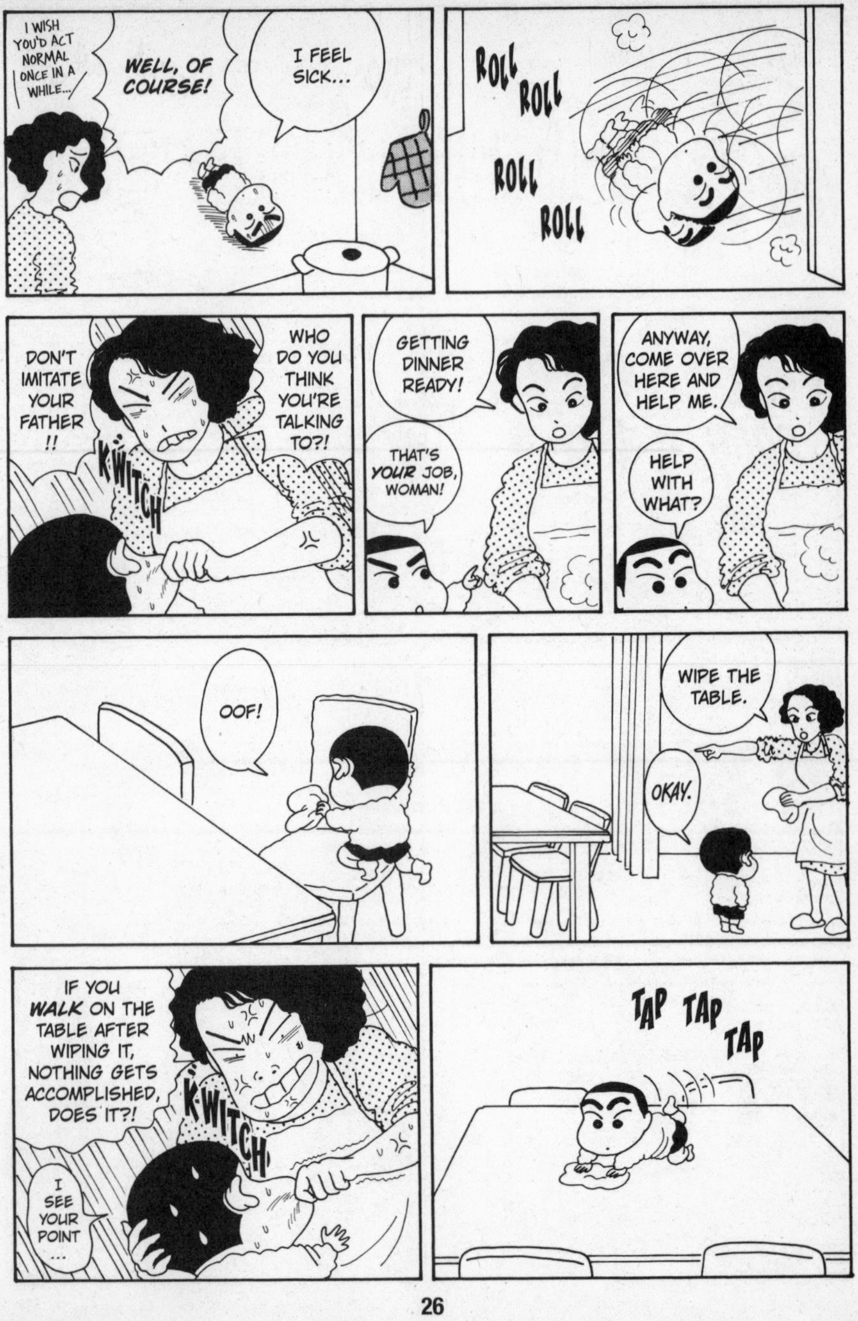
ROLL ROLL ROLL ROLL
I FEEL SICK...
WELL, OF COURSE!
I WISH YOU'D ACT NORMAL ONCE IN A WHILE...
ANYWAY, COME OVER HERE AND HELP ME.
HELP WITH WHAT?
GETTING DINNER READY!
THAT'S YOUR JOB, WOMAN!
WHO DO YOU THINK YOU'RE TALKING TO?!
DON'T IMITATE YOUR FATHER!!
KWITCH
WIPE THE TABLE.
OKAY.
OOF!
TAP TAP TAP
IF YOU WALK ON THE TABLE AFTER WIPING IT, NOTHING GETS ACCOMPLISHED, DOES IT?!
KWITCH
I SEE YOUR POINT...

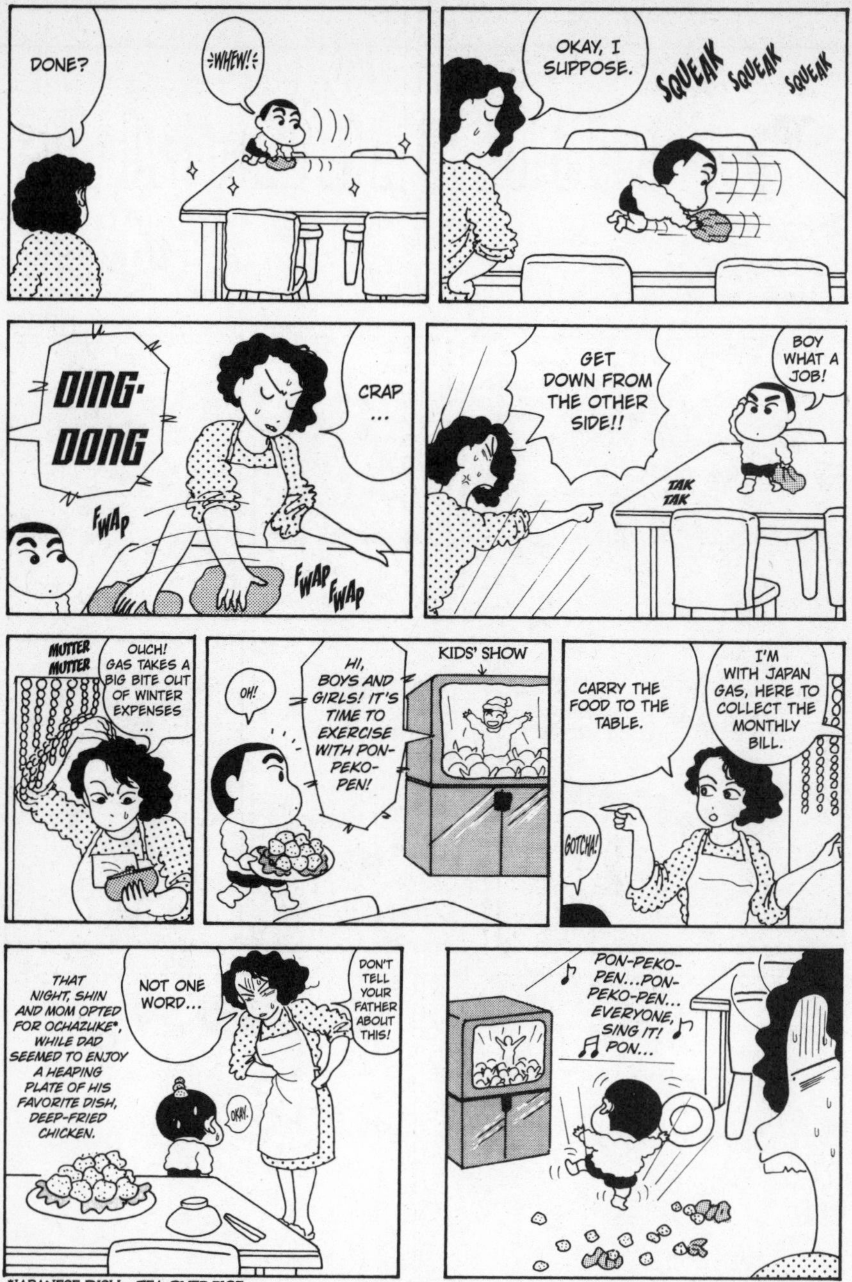

OKAY, I SUPPOSE.
SQUEAK SQUEAK SQUEAK
DONE?
WHEW!
BOY WHAT A JOB!
GET DOWN FROM THE OTHER SIDE!!
TAK TAK
CRAP ...
DING-DONG
FWAP
FWAP FWAP
I'M WITH JAPAN GAS, HERE TO COLLECT THE MONTHLY BILL.
CARRY THE FOOD TO THE TABLE.
GOTCHA!
KIDS' SHOW
HI, BOYS AND GIRLS! IT'S TIME TO EXERCISE WITH PON-PEKO-PEN!
OH!
OUCH! GAS TAKES A BIG BITE OUT OF WINTER EXPENSES ...
MUTTER MUTTER
PON-PEKO-PEN...PON-PEKO-PEN... EVERYONE, SING IT! PON...
DON'T TELL YOUR FATHER ABOUT THIS!
NOT ONE WORD...
OKAY.
THAT NIGHT, SHIN AND MOM OPTED FOR OCHAZUKE*, WHILE DAD SEEMED TO ENJOY A HEAPING PLATE OF HIS FAVORITE DISH, DEEP-FRIED CHICKEN.

*JAPANESE DISH - TEA OVER RICE.

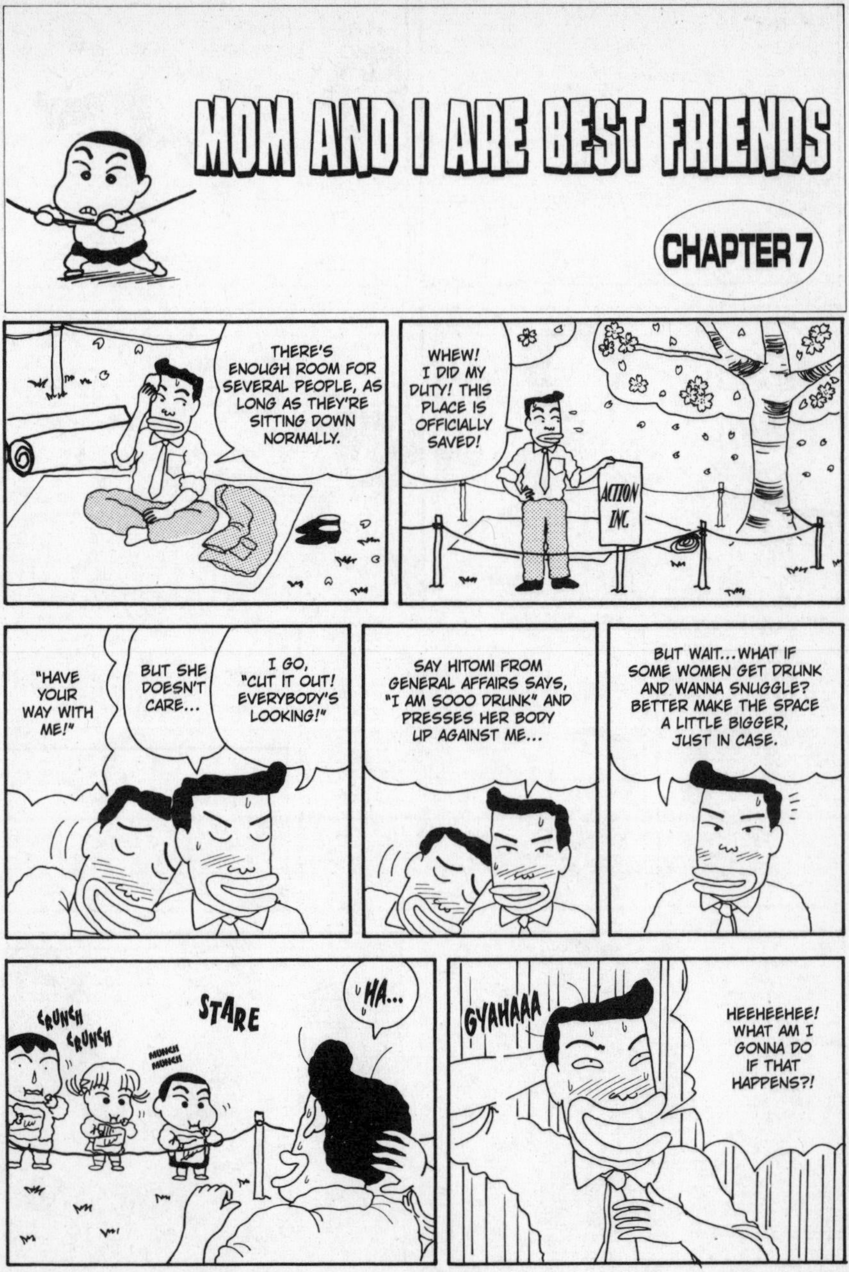
MOM AND I ARE BEST FRIENDS
CHAPTER 7
WHEW! I DID MY DUTY! THIS PLACE IS OFFICIALLY SAVED!
ACTION INC.
THERE'S ENOUGH ROOM FOR SEVERAL PEOPLE, AS LONG AS THEY'RE SITTING DOWN NORMALLY.
BUT WAIT...WHAT IF SOME WOMEN GET DRUNK AND WANNA SNUGGLE? BETTER MAKE THE SPACE A LITTLE BIGGER, JUST IN CASE.
SAY HITOMI FROM GENERAL AFFAIRS SAYS, "I AM SOOO DRUNK" AND PRESSES HER BODY UP AGAINST ME...
I GO, "CUT IT OUT! EVERYBODY'S LOOKING!"
BUT SHE DOESN'T CARE...
"HAVE YOUR WAY WITH ME!"
HEEHEEHEE! WHAT AM I GONNA DO IF THAT HAPPENS?!
GYAHAAA
HA...
STARE
MUNCH MUNCH
CRUNCH CRUNCH

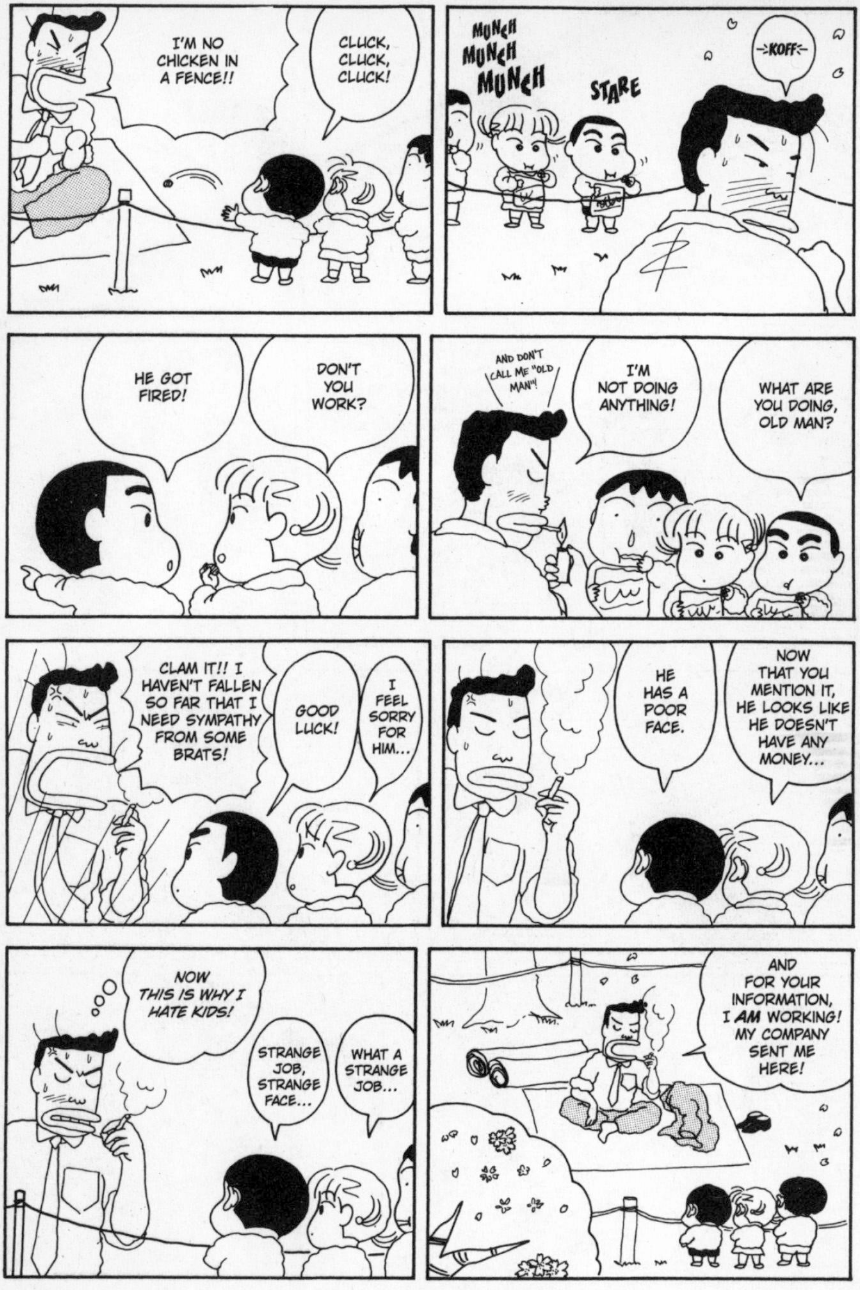

-KOFF-
STARE
MUNCH MUNCH MUNCH
CLUCK, CLUCK, CLUCK!
I'M NO CHICKEN IN A FENCE!!
WHAT ARE YOU DOING, OLD MAN?
I'M NOT DOING ANYTHING!
AND DON'T CALL ME "OLD MAN"!
DON'T YOU WORK?
HE GOT FIRED!
NOW THAT YOU MENTION IT, HE LOOKS LIKE HE DOESN'T HAVE ANY MONEY...
HE HAS A POOR FACE.
I FEEL SORRY FOR HIM...
GOOD LUCK!
CLAM IT!! I HAVEN'T FALLEN SO FAR THAT I NEED SYMPATHY FROM SOME BRATS!
AND FOR YOUR INFORMATION, I ***AM*** WORKING! MY COMPANY SENT ME HERE!
WHAT A STRANGE JOB...
STRANGE JOB, STRANGE FACE...
NOW THIS IS WHY I HATE KIDS!

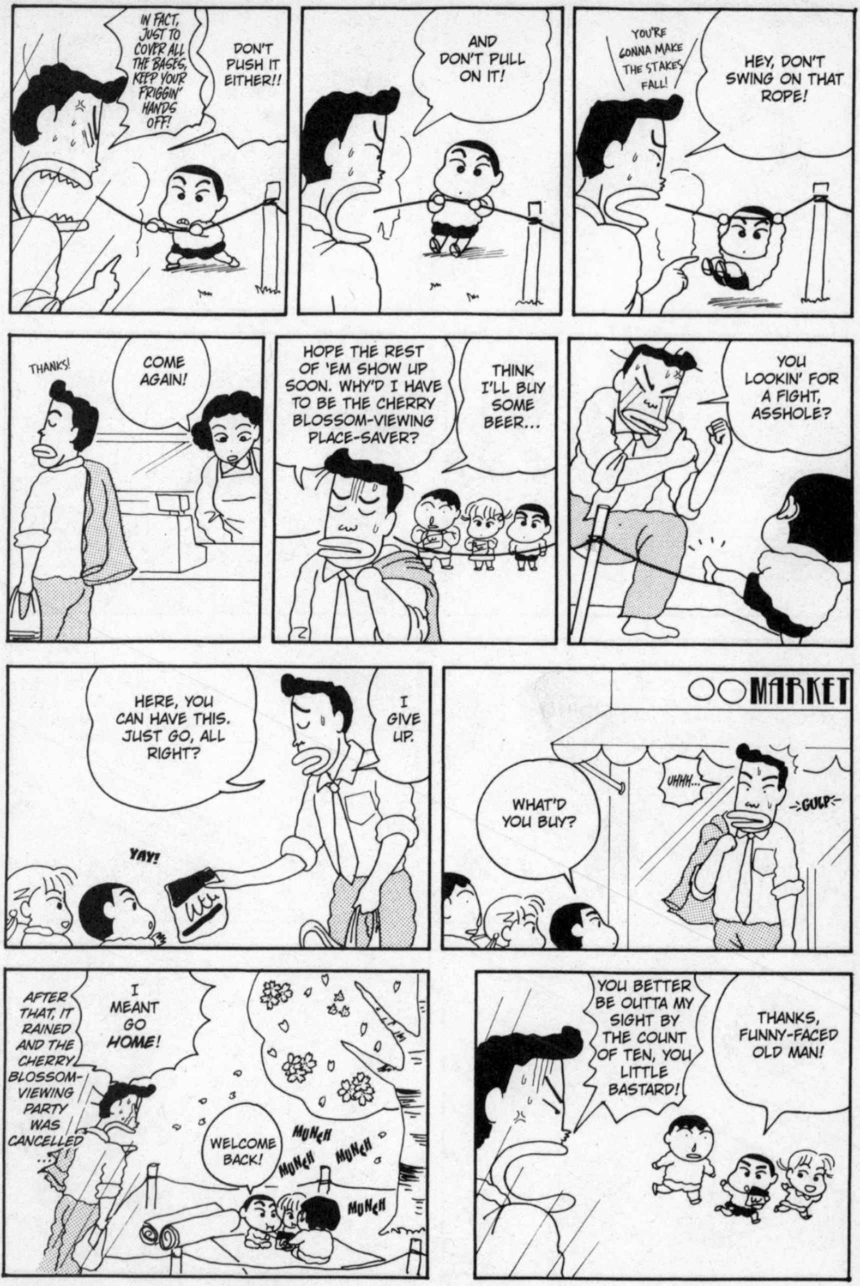
HEY, DON'T SWING ON THAT ROPE!
YOU'RE GONNA MAKE THE STAKES FALL!
AND DON'T PULL ON IT!
DON'T PUSH IT EITHER!!
IN FACT, JUST TO COVER ALL THE BASES, KEEP YOUR FRIGGIN' HANDS OFF!
YOU LOOKIN' FOR A FIGHT, ASSHOLE?
THINK I'LL BUY SOME BEER...
HOPE THE REST OF 'EM SHOW UP SOON. WHY'D I HAVE TO BE THE CHERRY BLOSSOM-VIEWING PLACE-SAVER?
COME AGAIN!
THANKS!
OO MARKET
GULP
UHHH...
WHAT'D YOU BUY?
I GIVE UP.
HERE, YOU CAN HAVE THIS. JUST GO, ALL RIGHT?
YAY!
THANKS, FUNNY-FACED OLD MAN!
YOU BETTER BE OUTTA MY SIGHT BY THE COUNT OF TEN, YOU LITTLE BASTARD!
I MEANT GO **HOME**!
AFTER THAT, IT RAINED AND THE CHERRY BLOSSOM-VIEWING PARTY WAS CANCELLED...
WELCOME BACK!
MUNCH
MUNCH
MUNCH
MUNCH

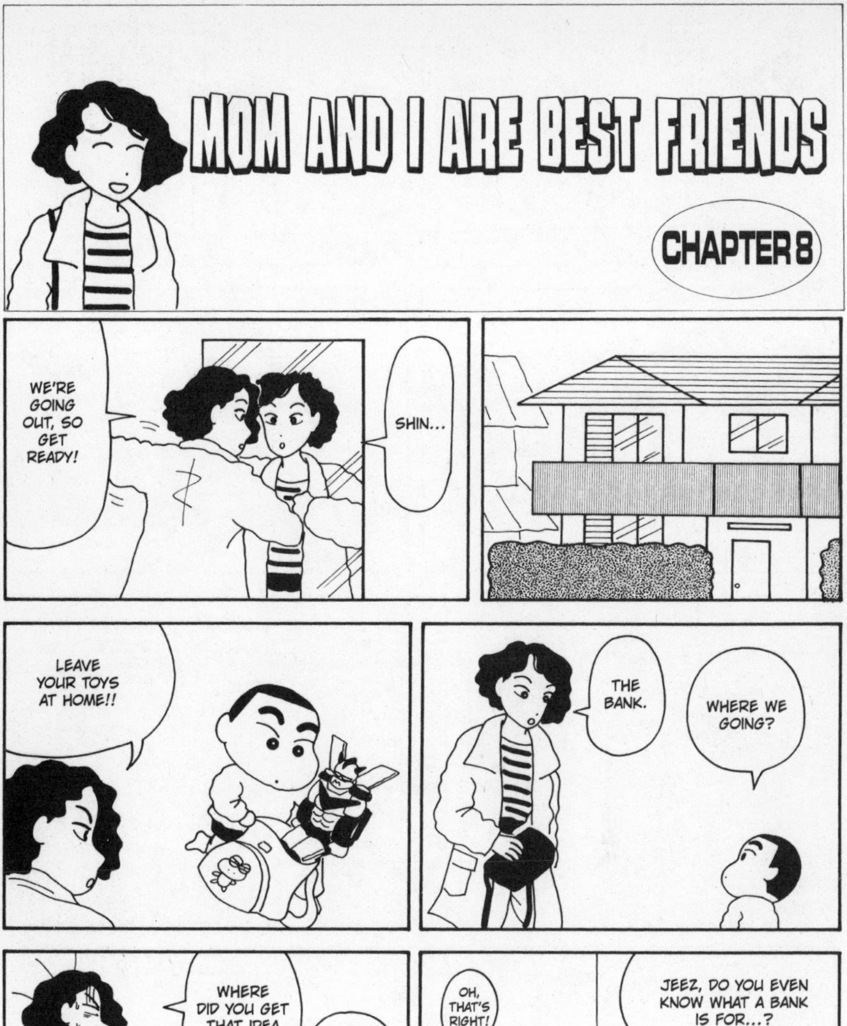
MOM AND I ARE BEST FRIENDS
CHAPTER 8
SHIN...
WE'RE GOING OUT, SO GET READY!
WHERE WE GOING?
THE BANK.
LEAVE YOUR TOYS AT HOME!!
JEEZ, DO YOU EVEN KNOW WHAT A BANK IS FOR...?
OH, THAT'S RIGHT!
HERE, MOM!
WHERE DID YOU GET THAT IDEA FROM...?

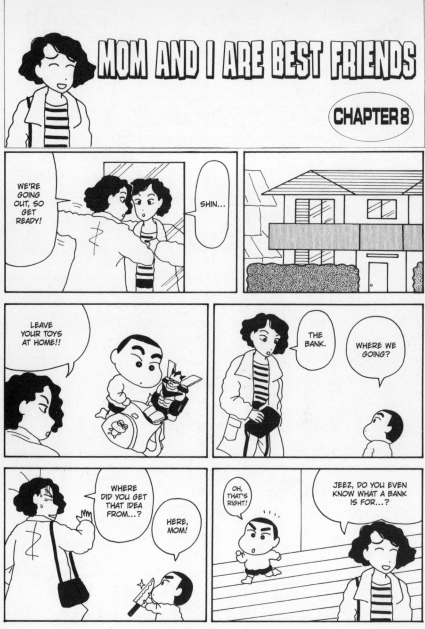

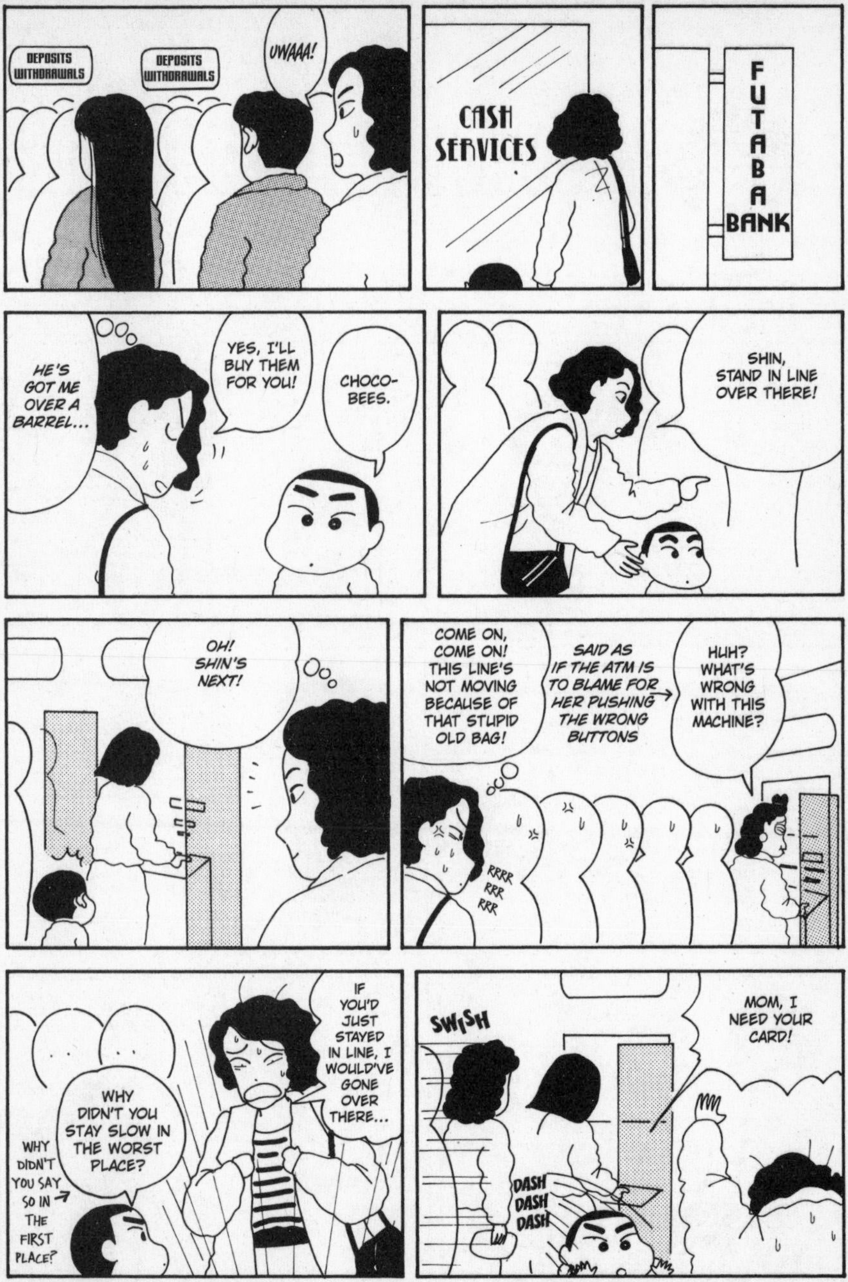
FUTABA BANK
CASH SERVICES
UWAAA!
DEPOSITS WITHDRAWALS
DEPOSITS WITHDRAWALS
SHIN, STAND IN LINE OVER THERE!
CHOCO-BEES.
YES, I'LL BUY THEM FOR YOU!
HE'S GOT ME OVER A BARREL...
HUH? WHAT'S WRONG WITH THIS MACHINE?
SAID AS IF THE ATM IS TO BLAME FOR HER PUSHING THE WRONG BUTTONS
COME ON, COME ON! THIS LINE'S NOT MOVING BECAUSE OF THAT STUPID OLD BAG!
RRRR RRR RRR
OH! SHIN'S NEXT!
MOM, I NEED YOUR CARD!
SWISH
DASH DASH DASH
IF YOU'D JUST STAYED IN LINE, I WOULD'VE GONE OVER THERE...
. . .
. . .
WHY DIDN'T YOU STAY SLOW IN THE WORST PLACE?
WHY DIDN'T YOU SAY SO IN THE FIRST PLACE?

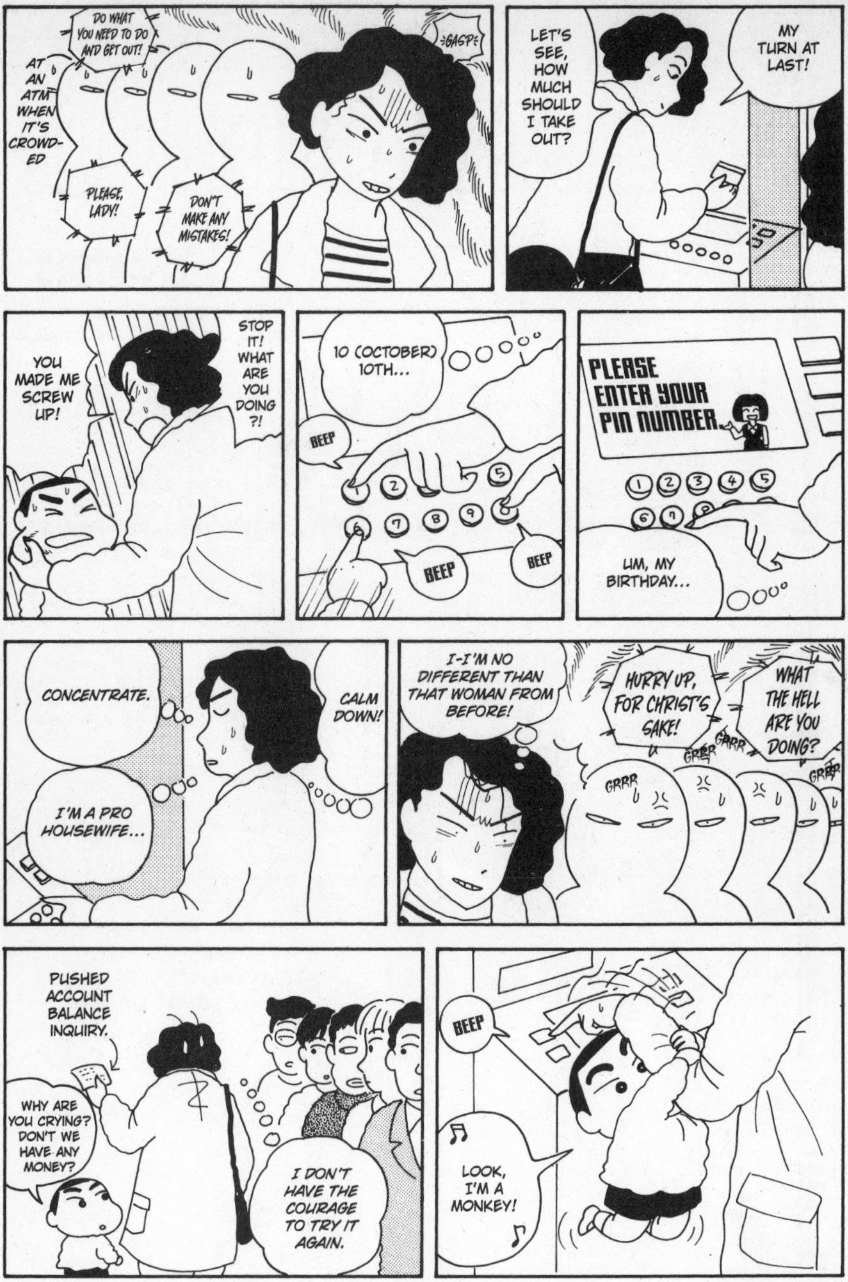
MY TURN AT LAST!
LET'S SEE, HOW MUCH SHOULD I TAKE OUT?
GASP
DO WHAT YOU NEED TO DO AND GET OUT!
AT AN ATM WHEN IT'S CROWDED
DON'T MAKE ANY MISTAKES!
PLEASE, LADY!
PLEASE ENTER YOUR PIN NUMBER.
UM, MY BIRTHDAY...
10 (OCTOBER) 10TH...
BEEP
BEEP
BEEP
STOP IT! WHAT ARE YOU DOING?!
YOU MADE ME SCREW UP!
WHAT THE HELL ARE YOU DOING?
HURRY UP, FOR CHRIST'S SAKE!
I-I'M NO DIFFERENT THAN THAT WOMAN FROM BEFORE!
GRRR
GRRR
GRRR
GRRR
CALM DOWN!
CONCENTRATE.
I'M A PRO HOUSEWIFE...
BEEP
LOOK, I'M A MONKEY!
PUSHED ACCOUNT BALANCE INQUIRY.
I DON'T HAVE THE COURAGE TO TRY IT AGAIN.
WHY ARE YOU CRYING? DON'T WE HAVE ANY MONEY?

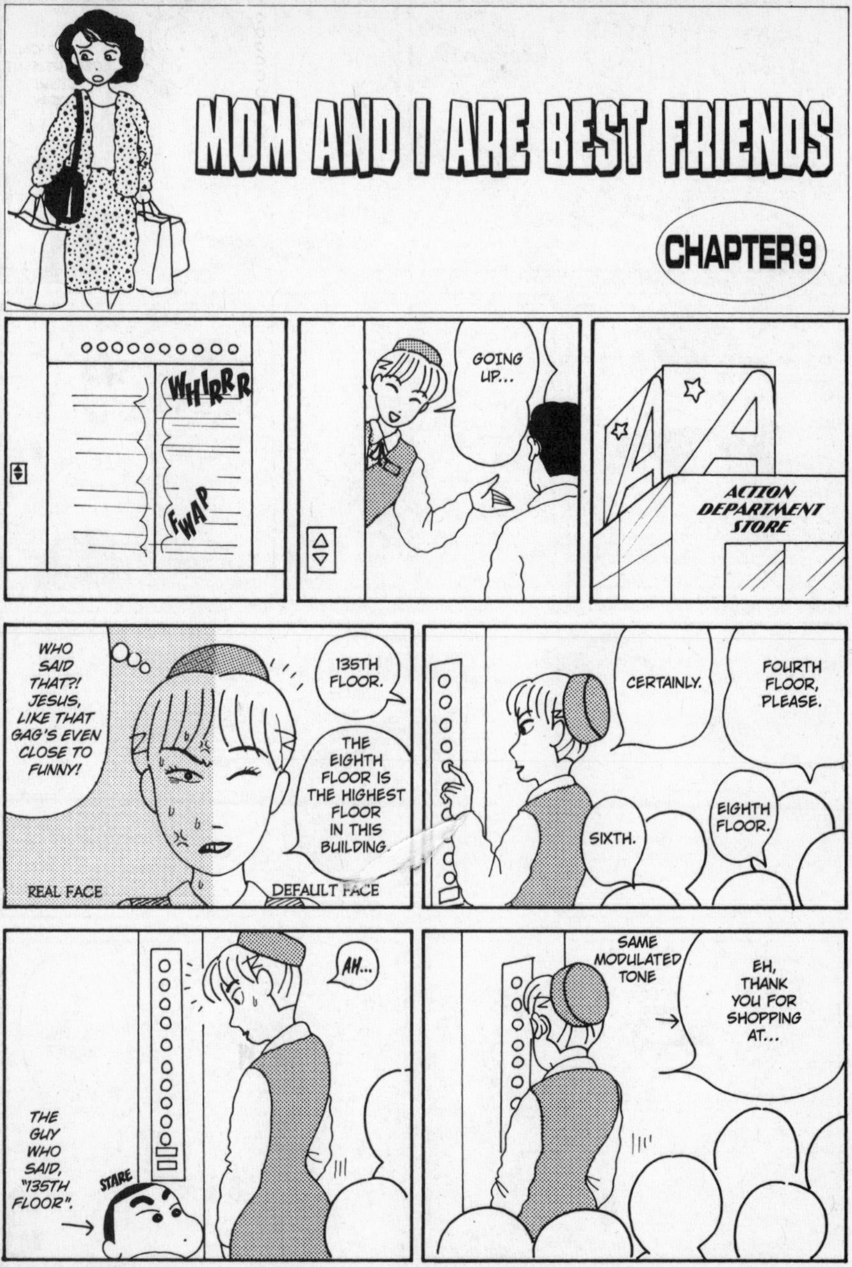
MOM AND I ARE BEST FRIENDS
CHAPTER 9
ACTION DEPARTMENT STORE
GOING UP...
WHIRRR
FWAP
FOURTH FLOOR, PLEASE.
CERTAINLY.
EIGHTH FLOOR.
SIXTH.
135TH FLOOR.
THE EIGHTH FLOOR IS THE HIGHEST FLOOR IN THIS BUILDING.
WHO SAID THAT?! JESUS, LIKE THAT GAG'S EVEN CLOSE TO FUNNY!
REAL FACE
DEFAULT FACE
SAME MODULATED TONE
EH, THANK YOU FOR SHOPPING AT...
AH...
THE GUY WHO SAID, "135TH FLOOR".
STARE

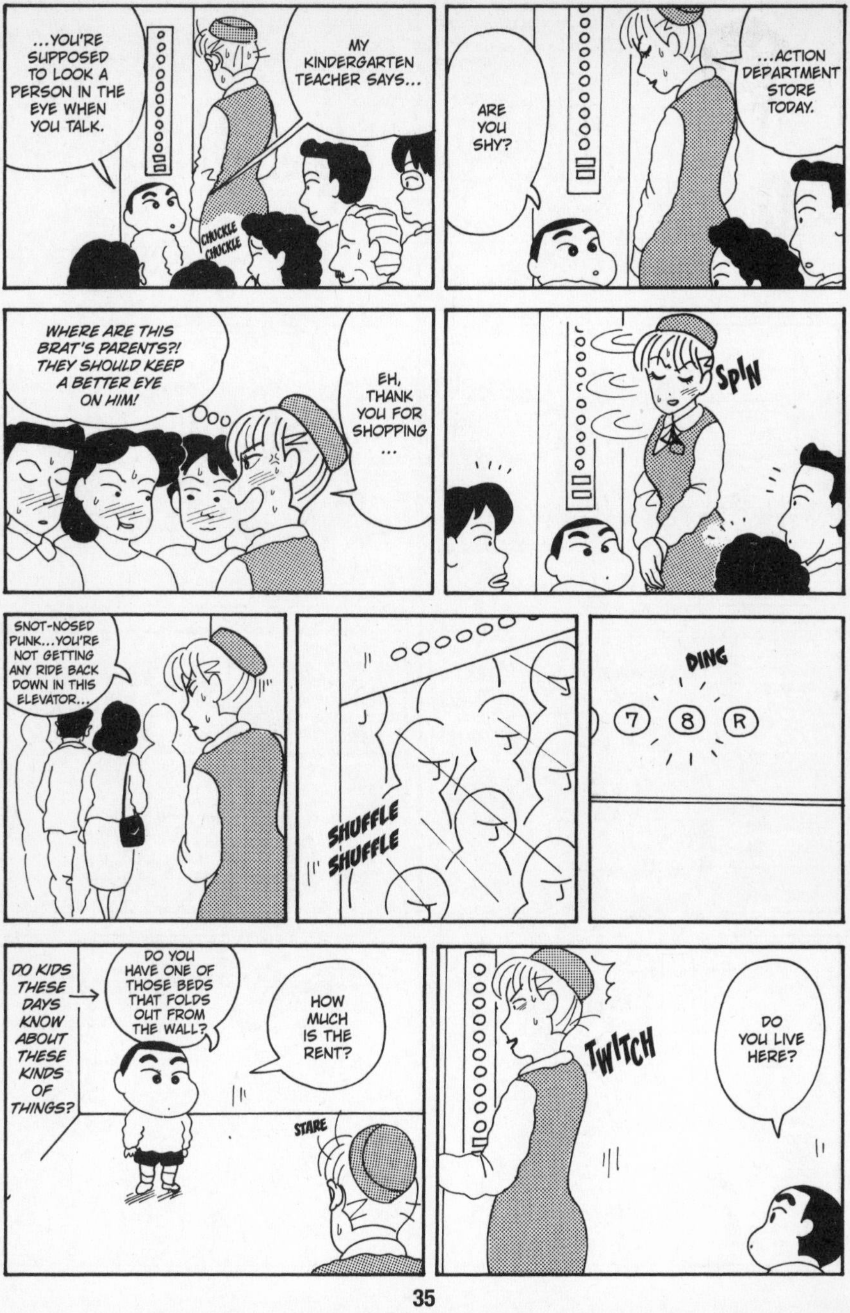
...ACTION DEPARTMENT STORE TODAY.
ARE YOU SHY?
MY KINDERGARTEN TEACHER SAYS...
...YOU'RE SUPPOSED TO LOOK A PERSON IN THE EYE WHEN YOU TALK.
CHUCKLE CHUCKLE
SPIN
EH, THANK YOU FOR SHOPPING ...
WHERE ARE THIS BRAT'S PARENTS?! THEY SHOULD KEEP A BETTER EYE ON HIM!
DING
7 8 R
SHUFFLE SHUFFLE
SNOT-NOSED PUNK...YOU'RE NOT GETTING ANY RIDE BACK DOWN IN THIS ELEVATOR...
DO YOU LIVE HERE?
TWITCH
HOW MUCH IS THE RENT?
DO YOU HAVE ONE OF THOSE BEDS THAT FOLDS OUT FROM THE WALL?
DO KIDS THESE DAYS KNOW ABOUT THESE KINDS OF THINGS?
STARE

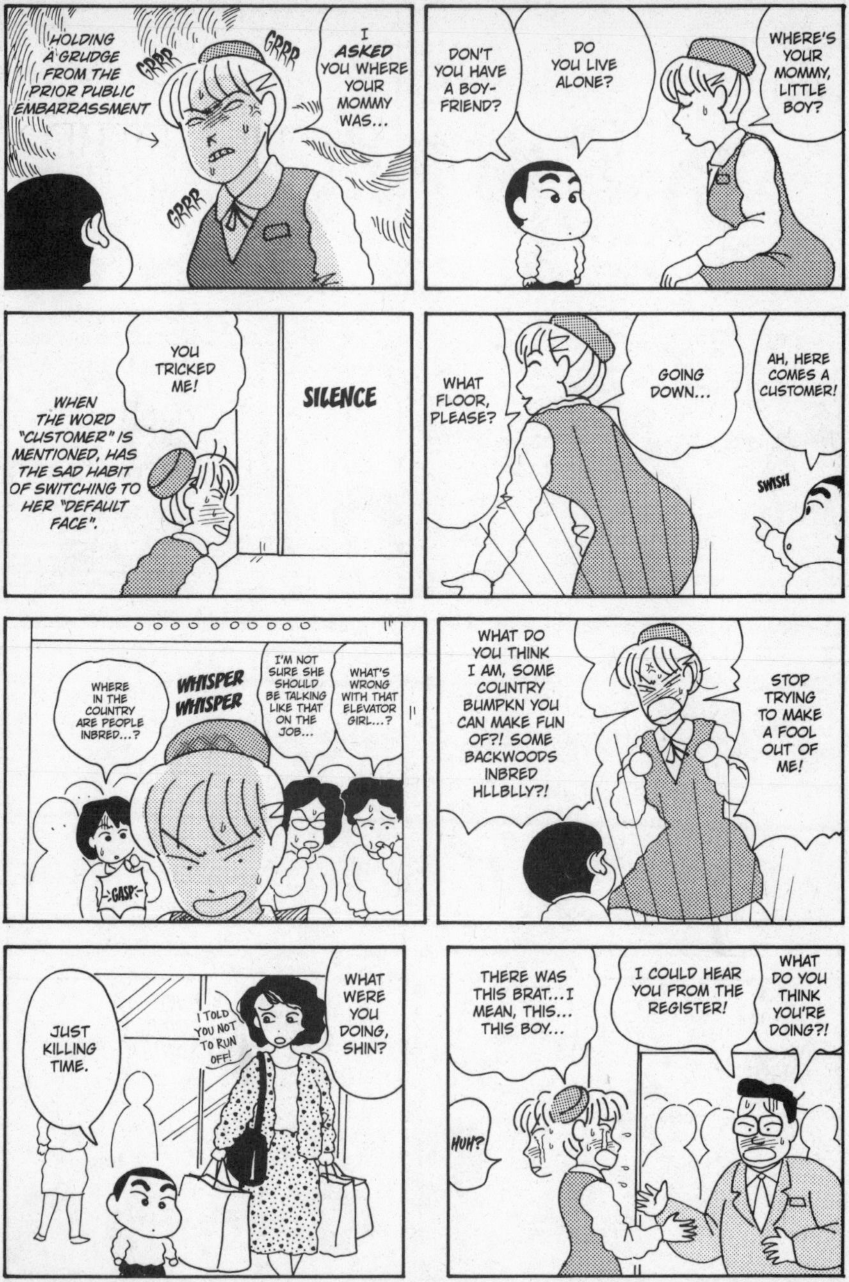

WHERE'S YOUR MOMMY, LITTLE BOY?
DO YOU LIVE ALONE?
DON'T YOU HAVE A BOY-FRIEND?
I ASKED YOU WHERE YOUR MOMMY WAS...
GRRR
GRRR
HOLDING A GRUDGE FROM THE PRIOR PUBLIC EMBARRASSMENT
GRRR
AH, HERE COMES A CUSTOMER!
SWISH
GOING DOWN...
WHAT FLOOR, PLEASE?
SILENCE
YOU TRICKED ME!
WHEN THE WORD "CUSTOMER" IS MENTIONED, HAS THE SAD HABIT OF SWITCHING TO HER "DEFAULT FACE".
STOP TRYING TO MAKE A FOOL OUT OF ME!
WHAT DO YOU THINK I AM, SOME COUNTRY BUMPKN YOU CAN MAKE FUN OF?! SOME BACKWOODS INBRED HLLBLLY?!
WHAT'S WRONG WITH THAT ELEVATOR GIRL...?
I'M NOT SURE SHE SHOULD BE TALKING LIKE THAT ON THE JOB...
WHISPER WHISPER
WHERE IN THE COUNTRY ARE PEOPLE INBRED...?
GASP
WHAT DO YOU THINK YOU'RE DOING?!
I COULD HEAR YOU FROM THE REGISTER!
THERE WAS THIS BRAT...I MEAN, THIS... THIS BOY...
HUH?
WHAT WERE YOU DOING, SHIN?
I TOLD YOU NOT TO RUN OFF!
JUST KILLING TIME.

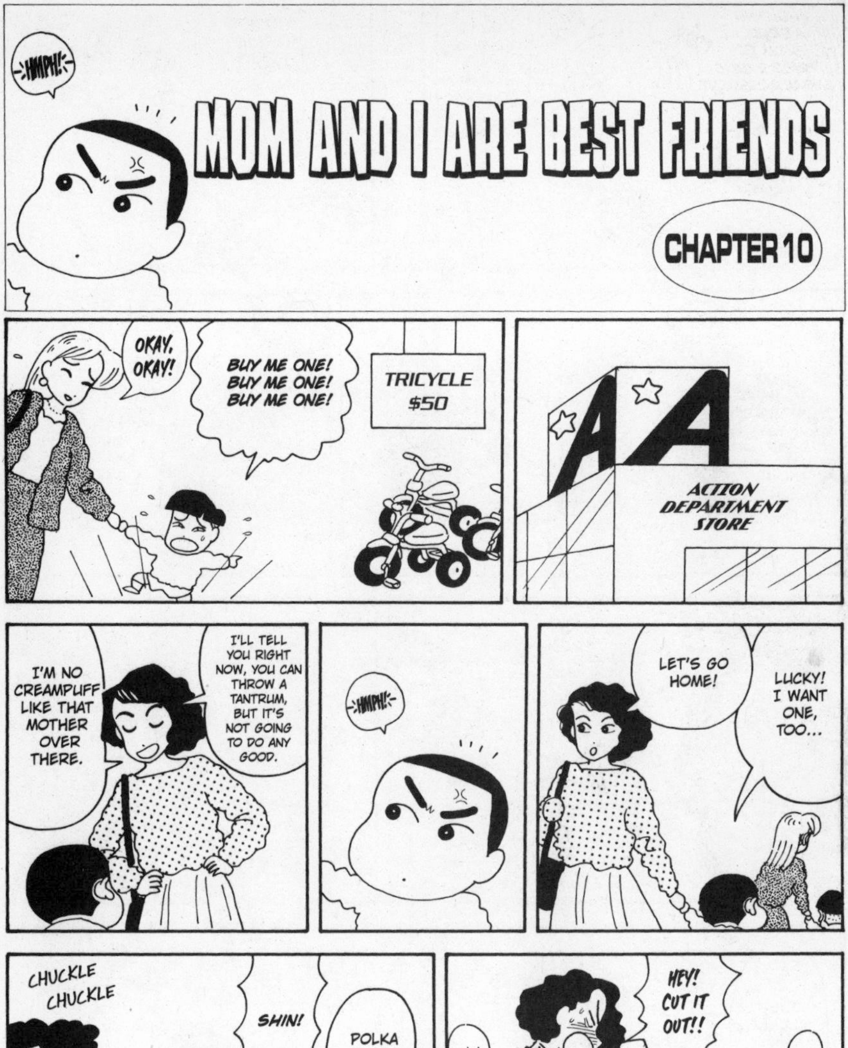
HMPH!
MOM AND I ARE BEST FRIENDS
CHAPTER 10
AA
ACTION DEPARTMENT STORE
TRICYCLE $50
BUY ME ONE! BUY ME ONE! BUY ME ONE!
OKAY, OKAY!
LUCKY! I WANT ONE, TOO...
LET'S GO HOME!
HMPH!
I'LL TELL YOU RIGHT NOW, YOU CAN THROW A TANTRUM, BUT IT'S NOT GOING TO DO ANY GOOD.
I'M NO CREAMPUFF LIKE THAT MOTHER OVER THERE.
HEY! CUT IT OUT!!
SWISH
POLKA DOTS!
SHIN!
CHUCKLE CHUCKLE

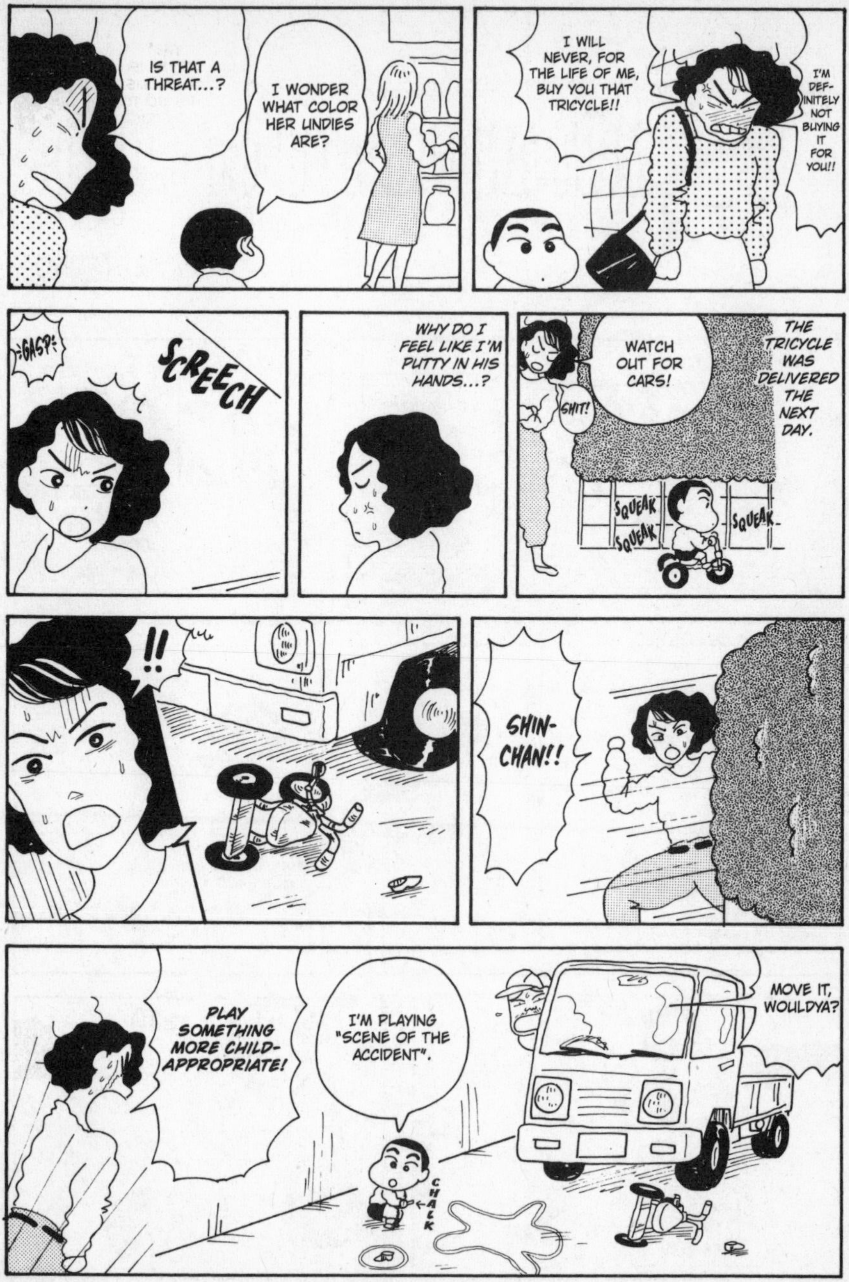
I'M DEFINITELY NOT BUYING IT FOR YOU!!
I WILL NEVER, FOR THE LIFE OF ME, BUY YOU THAT TRICYCLE!!
I WONDER WHAT COLOR HER UNDIES ARE?
IS THAT A THREAT...?
THE TRICYCLE WAS DELIVERED THE NEXT DAY.
WATCH OUT FOR CARS!
SHIT!
SQUEAK
SQUEAK
SQUEAK
WHY DO I FEEL LIKE I'M PUTTY IN HIS HANDS...?
SCREECH
GASP!
SHIN-CHAN!!
!!
MOVE IT, WOULDYA?
I'M PLAYING "SCENE OF THE ACCIDENT".
CHALK
PLAY SOMETHING MORE CHILD-APPROPRIATE!

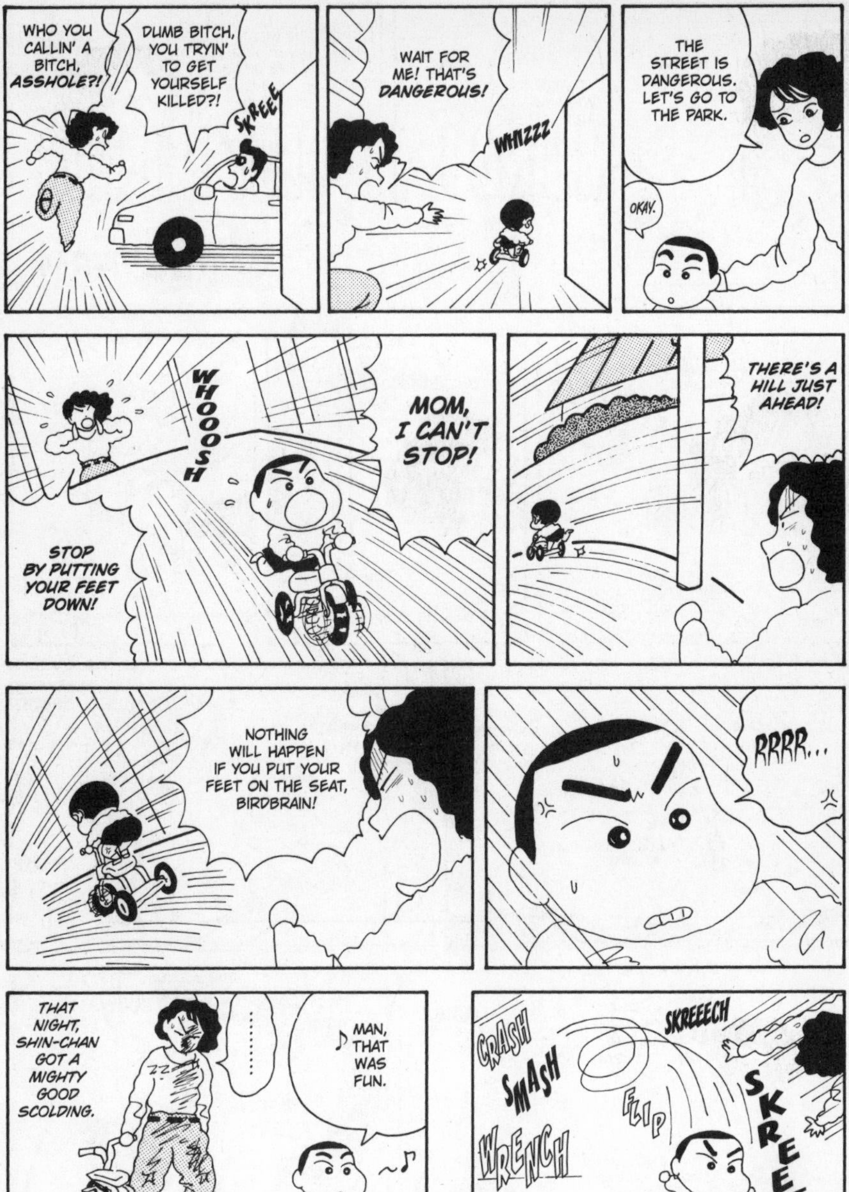
THE STREET IS DANGEROUS. LET'S GO TO THE PARK.
OKAY.
WAIT FOR ME! THAT'S DANGEROUS!
WHIZZZ
SKREEE
DUMB BITCH, YOU TRYIN' TO GET YOURSELF KILLED?!
WHO YOU CALLIN' A BITCH, ASSHOLE?!
THERE'S A HILL JUST AHEAD!
MOM, I CAN'T STOP!
WHOOOSH
STOP BY PUTTING YOUR FEET DOWN!
RRRR...
NOTHING WILL HAPPEN IF YOU PUT YOUR FEET ON THE SEAT, BIRDBRAIN!
SKREEECH
SKREEECH
FLIP
CRASH
SMASH
WRENCH
SNAP
♪ MAN, THAT WAS FUN.
~♪
......
THAT NIGHT, SHIN-CHAN GOT A MIGHTY GOOD SCOLDING.

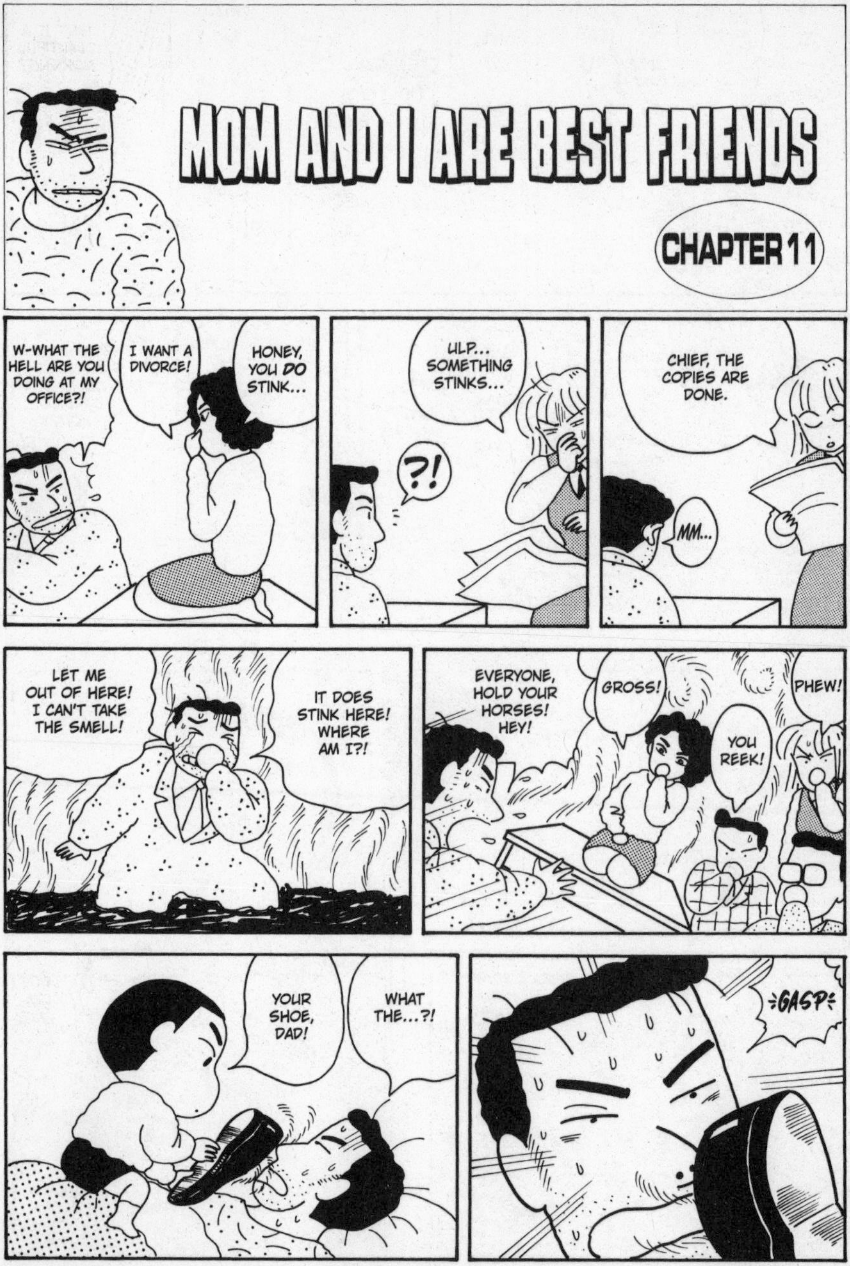
MOM AND I ARE BEST FRIENDS
CHAPTER 11
CHIEF, THE COPIES ARE DONE.
MM...
ULP... SOMETHING STINKS...
?!
HONEY, YOU DO STINK...
I WANT A DIVORCE!
W-WHAT THE HELL ARE YOU DOING AT MY OFFICE?!
PHEW!
GROSS!
YOU REEK!
EVERYONE, HOLD YOUR HORSES! HEY!
IT DOES STINK HERE! WHERE AM I?!
LET ME OUT OF HERE! I CAN'T TAKE THE SMELL!
GASP
WHAT THE...?!
YOUR SHOE, DAD!

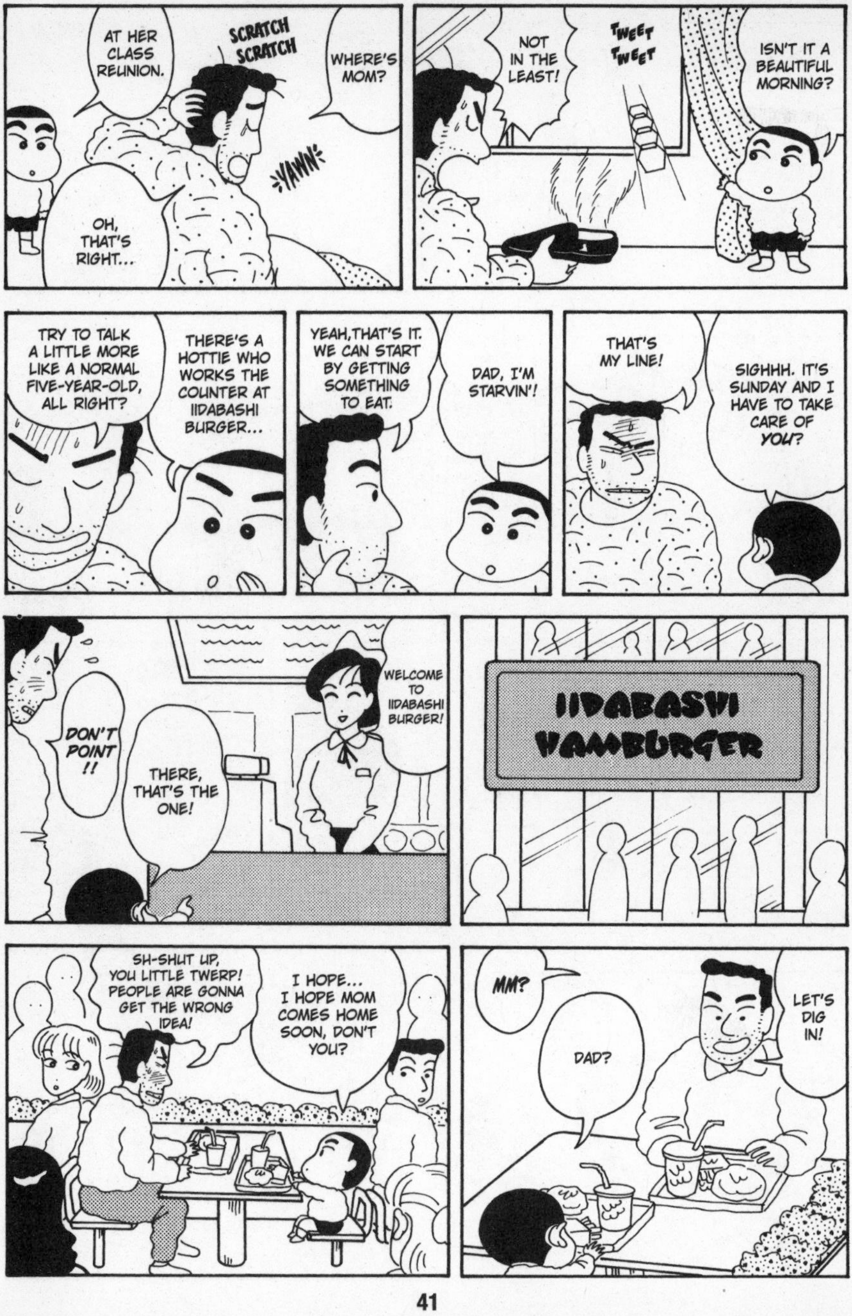
ISN'T IT A BEAUTIFUL MORNING?
TWEET TWEET
NOT IN THE LEAST!
WHERE'S MOM?
SCRATCH SCRATCH
AT HER CLASS REUNION.
YAWN
OH, THAT'S RIGHT...
SIGHHH. IT'S SUNDAY AND I HAVE TO TAKE CARE OF *YOU*?
THAT'S MY LINE!
DAD, I'M STARVIN'!
YEAH, THAT'S IT. WE CAN START BY GETTING SOMETHING TO EAT.
THERE'S A HOTTIE WHO WORKS THE COUNTER AT IIDABASHI BURGER...
TRY TO TALK A LITTLE MORE LIKE A NORMAL FIVE-YEAR-OLD, ALL RIGHT?
IIDABASHI HAMBURGER
WELCOME TO IIDABASHI BURGER!
THERE, THAT'S THE ONE!
DON'T POINT!!
LET'S DIG IN!
DAD?
MM?
I HOPE... I HOPE MOM COMES HOME SOON, DON'T YOU?
SH-SHUT UP, YOU LITTLE TWERP! PEOPLE ARE GONNA GET THE WRONG IDEA!

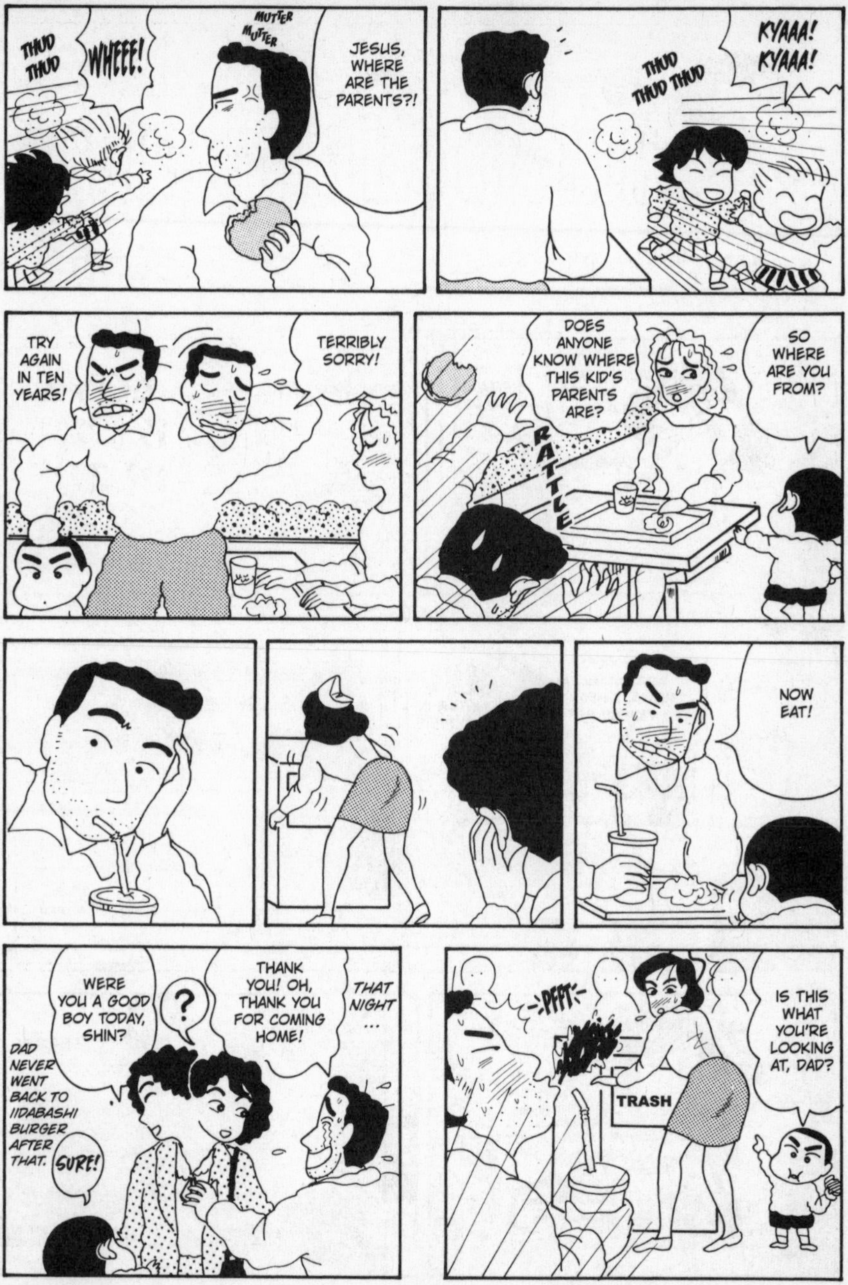
KYAAA! KYAAA!
THUD THUD THUD
JESUS, WHERE ARE THE PARENTS?!
MUTTER MUTTER
WHEEEE!
THUD THUD
SO WHERE ARE YOU FROM?
DOES ANYONE KNOW WHERE THIS KID'S PARENTS ARE?
RATTLE
TERRIBLY SORRY!
TRY AGAIN IN TEN YEARS!
NOW EAT!
IS THIS WHAT YOU'RE LOOKING AT, DAD?
PFFT
THAT NIGHT ...
THANK YOU! OH, THANK YOU FOR COMING HOME!
?
WERE YOU A GOOD BOY TODAY, SHIN?
DAD NEVER WENT BACK TO IIDABASHI BURGER AFTER THAT.
SURE!

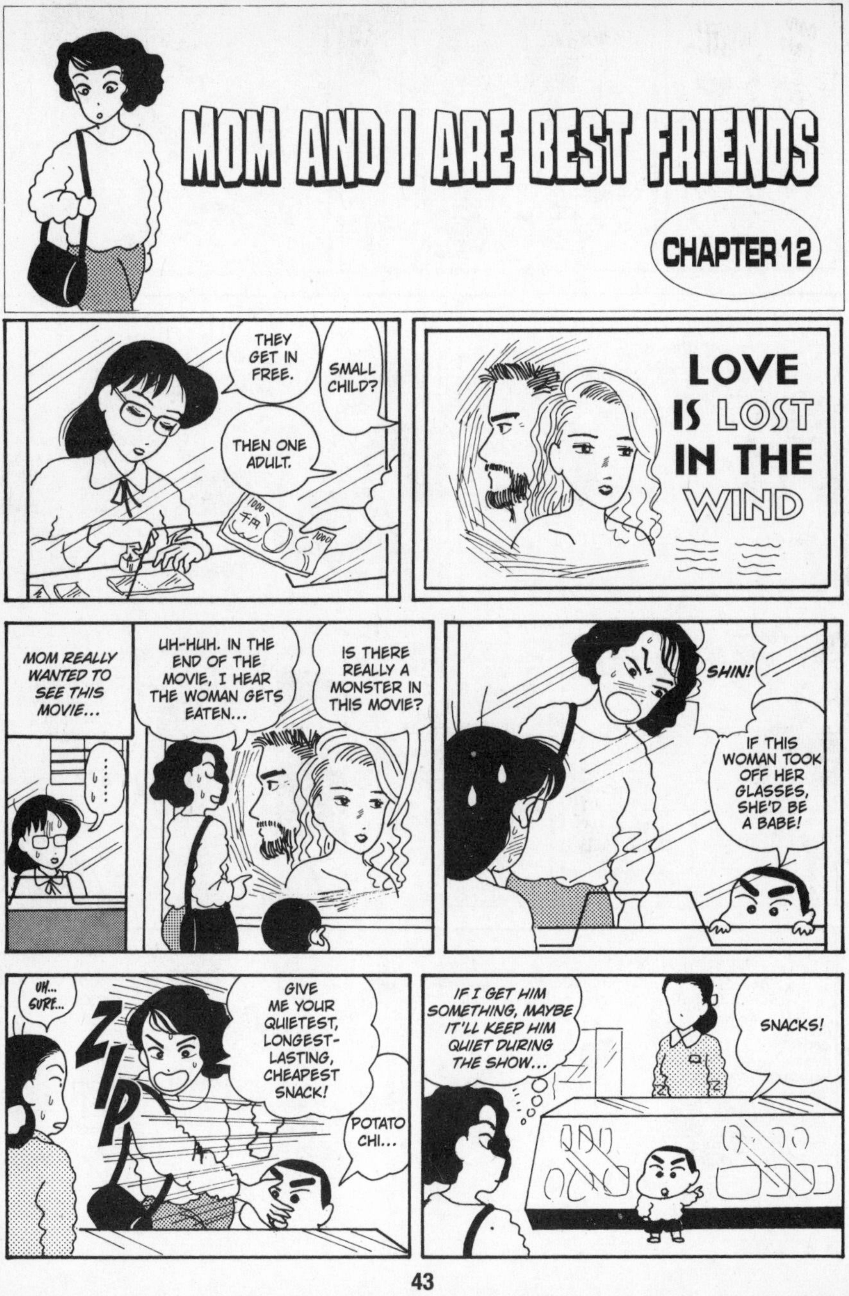
MOM AND I ARE BEST FRIENDS
CHAPTER 12
LOVE IS LOST IN THE WIND
SMALL CHILD?
THEY GET IN FREE.
THEN ONE ADULT.
SHIN!
IF THIS WOMAN TOOK OFF HER GLASSES, SHE'D BE A BABE!
IS THERE REALLY A MONSTER IN THIS MOVIE?
UH-HUH. IN THE END OF THE MOVIE, I HEAR THE WOMAN GETS EATEN...
MOM REALLY WANTED TO SEE THIS MOVIE...
......
SNACKS!
IF I GET HIM SOMETHING, MAYBE IT'LL KEEP HIM QUIET DURING THE SHOW...
GIVE ME YOUR QUIETEST, LONGEST-LASTING, CHEAPEST SNACK!
ZIP
POTATO CHI...
UH... SURE...

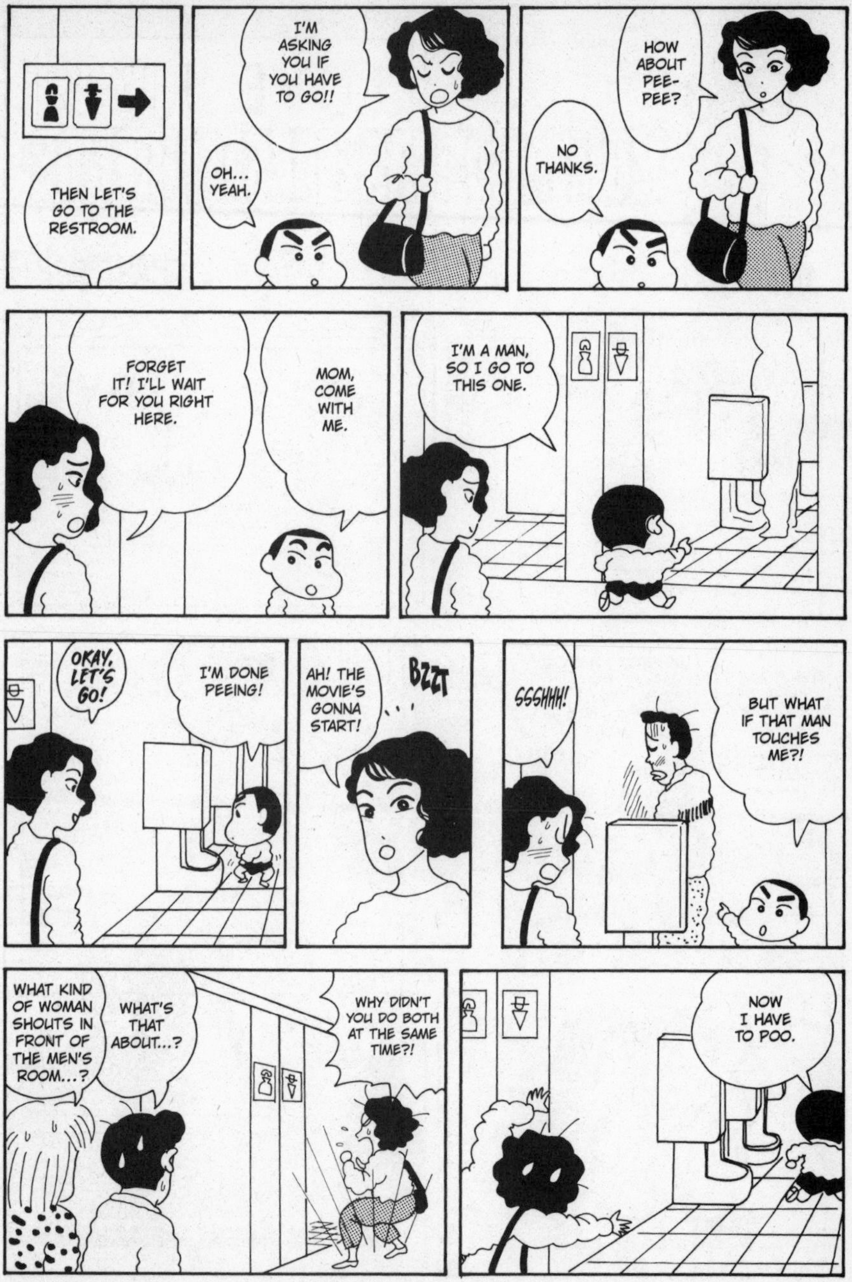
HOW ABOUT PEE-PEE?
NO THANKS.
I'M ASKING YOU IF YOU HAVE TO GO!!
OH... YEAH.
THEN LET'S GO TO THE RESTROOM.
I'M A MAN, SO I GO TO THIS ONE.
MOM, COME WITH ME.
FORGET IT! I'LL WAIT FOR YOU RIGHT HERE.
BUT WHAT IF THAT MAN TOUCHES ME?!
SSSHHH!
BZZT
AH! THE MOVIE'S GONNA START!
I'M DONE PEEING!
OKAY, LET'S GO!
NOW I HAVE TO POO.
WHY DIDN'T YOU DO BOTH AT THE SAME TIME?!
WHAT'S THAT ABOUT...?
WHAT KIND OF WOMAN SHOUTS IN FRONT OF THE MEN'S ROOM...?

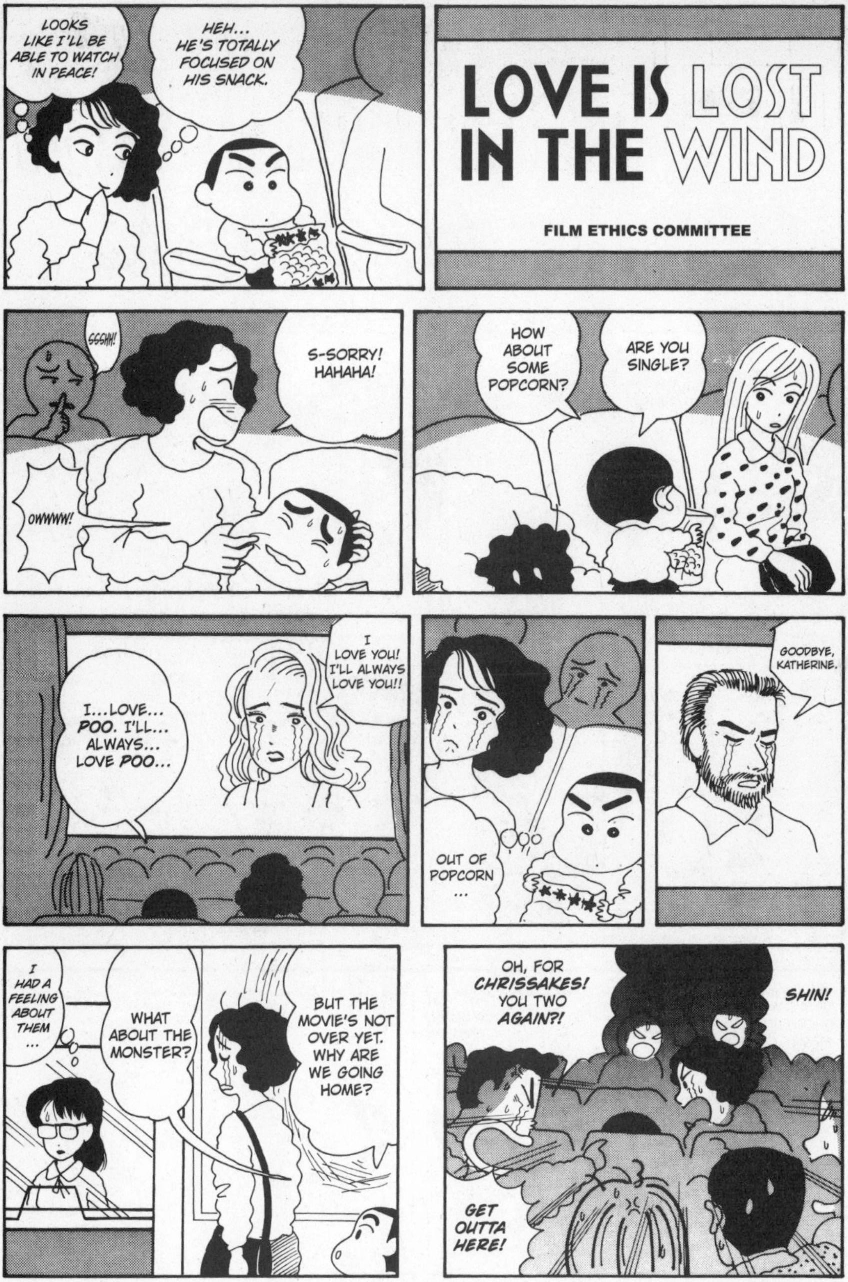
LOVE IS LOST IN THE WIND
FILM ETHICS COMMITTEE
HEH... HE'S TOTALLY FOCUSED ON HIS SNACK.
LOOKS LIKE I'LL BE ABLE TO WATCH IN PEACE!
ARE YOU SINGLE?
HOW ABOUT SOME POPCORN?
S-SORRY! HAHAHA!
SSSHH!
OWWWW!
GOODBYE, KATHERINE.
OUT OF POPCORN ...
I LOVE YOU! I'LL ALWAYS LOVE YOU!!
I...LOVE... POO. I'LL... ALWAYS... LOVE POO...
SHIN!
OH, FOR CHRISSAKES! YOU TWO AGAIN?!
GET OUTTA HERE!
BUT THE MOVIE'S NOT OVER YET. WHY ARE WE GOING HOME?
WHAT ABOUT THE MONSTER?
I HAD A FEELING ABOUT THEM ...

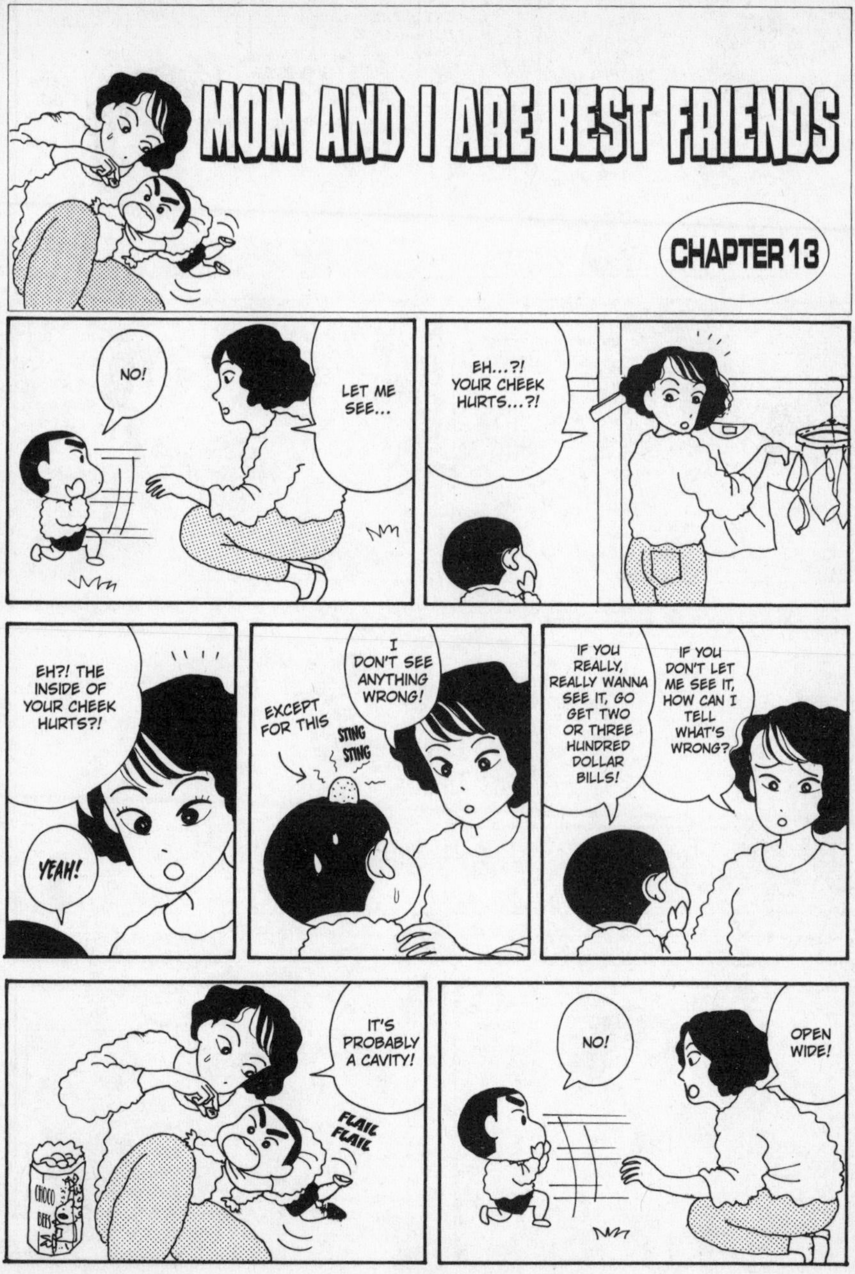
MOM AND I ARE BEST FRIENDS
CHAPTER 13
EH...?! YOUR CHEEK HURTS...?!
LET ME SEE...
NO!
IF YOU DON'T LET ME SEE IT, HOW CAN I TELL WHAT'S WRONG?
IF YOU REALLY, REALLY WANNA SEE IT, GO GET TWO OR THREE HUNDRED DOLLAR BILLS!
I DON'T SEE ANYTHING WRONG!
EXCEPT FOR THIS
STING STING
EH?! THE INSIDE OF YOUR CHEEK HURTS?!
YEAH!
OPEN WIDE!
NO!
IT'S PROBABLY A CAVITY!
FLAIL FLAIL
CHOCO BEES

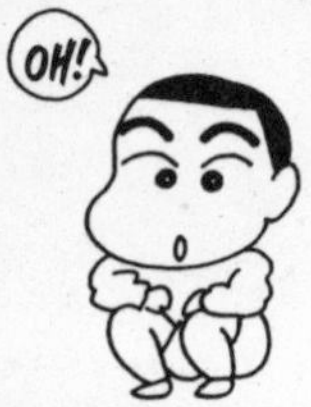
OH!

MOM AND I ARE BEST FRIENDS

CHAPTER 14

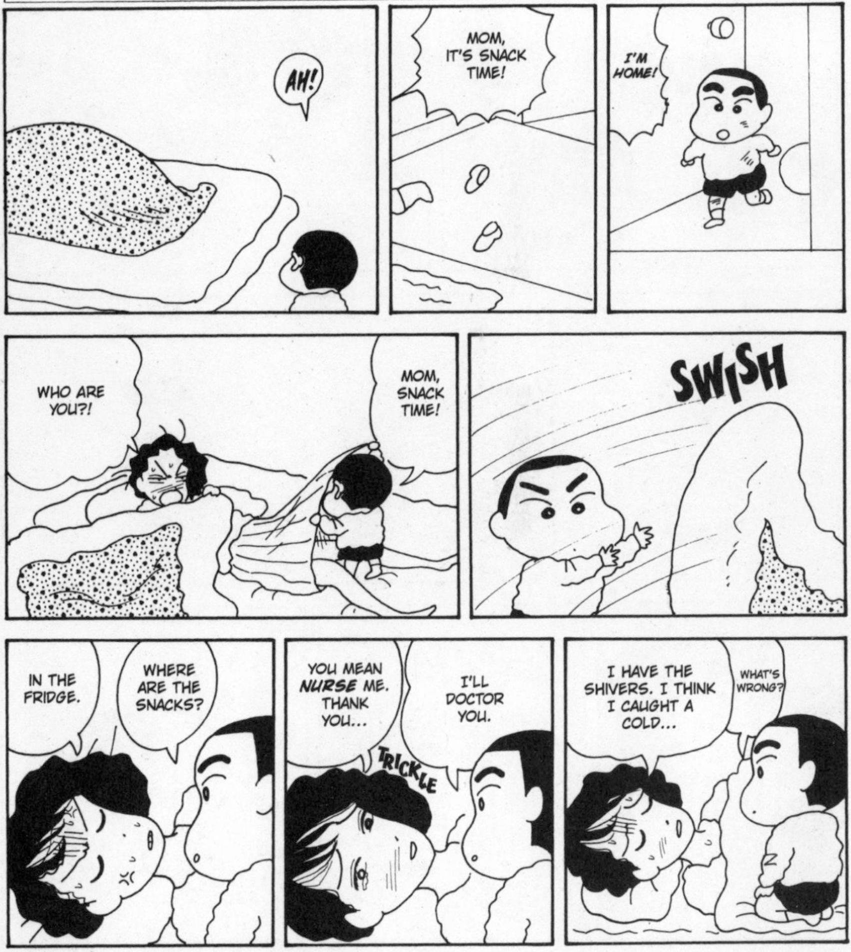
I'M HOME!
MOM, IT'S SNACK TIME!
AH!
SWISH
MOM, SNACK TIME!
WHO ARE YOU?!
WHAT'S WRONG?
I HAVE THE SHIVERS. I THINK I CAUGHT A COLD...
I'LL DOCTOR YOU.
YOU MEAN NURSE ME. THANK YOU...
TRICKLE
WHERE ARE THE SNACKS?
IN THE FRIDGE.

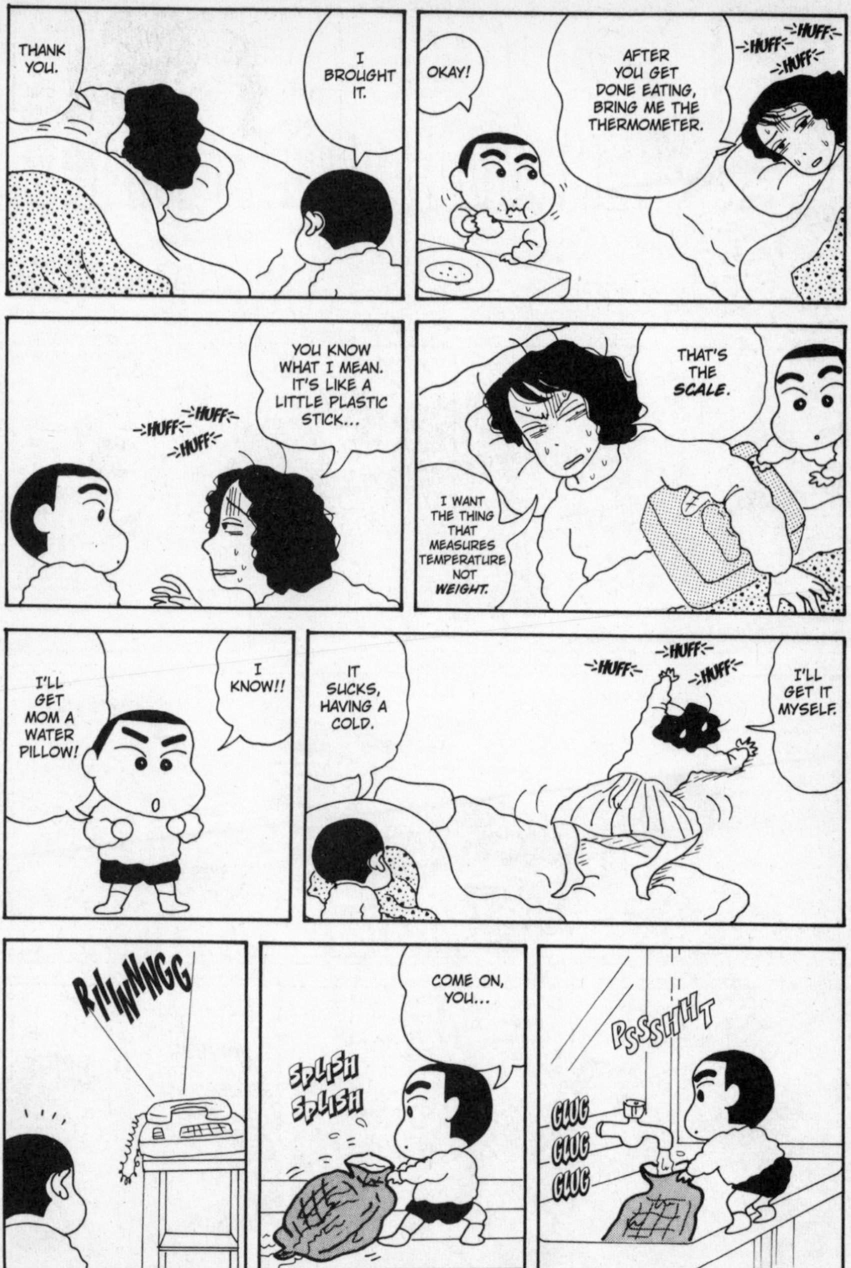
-HUFF- -HUFF- -HUFF-
AFTER YOU GET DONE EATING, BRING ME THE THERMOMETER.
OKAY!
I BROUGHT IT.
THANK YOU.
THAT'S THE *SCALE*.
I WANT THE THING THAT MEASURES TEMPERATURE NOT *WEIGHT*.
YOU KNOW WHAT I MEAN. IT'S LIKE A LITTLE PLASTIC STICK...
-HUFF- -HUFF- -HUFF-
I'LL GET IT MYSELF.
-HUFF- -HUFF- -HUFF-
IT SUCKS, HAVING A COLD.
I KNOW!!
I'LL GET MOM A WATER PILLOW!
PSSSHHT
GLUG GLUG GLUG
COME ON, YOU...
SPLISH SPLISH
RIIINNNGG

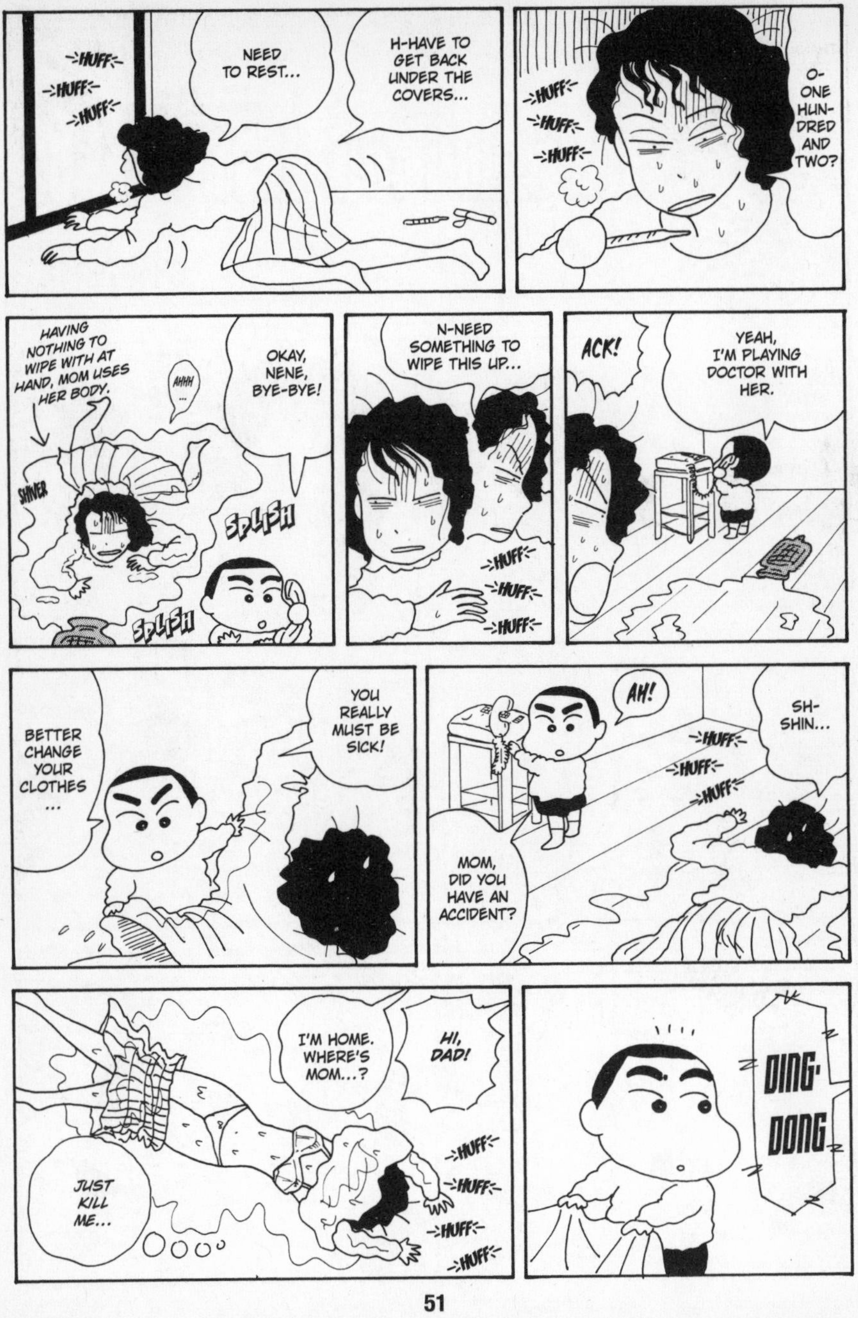
O-ONE HUNDRED AND TWO?
HUFF
HUFF
HUFF
H-HAVE TO GET BACK UNDER THE COVERS...
NEED TO REST...
HUFF
HUFF
HUFF
YEAH, I'M PLAYING DOCTOR WITH HER.
ACK!
N-NEED SOMETHING TO WIPE THIS UP...
HUFF
HUFF
HUFF
OKAY, NENE, BYE-BYE!
AHHH...
HAVING NOTHING TO WIPE WITH AT HAND, MOM USES HER BODY.
SHIVER
SPLISH
SPLISH
SH-SHIN...
AH!
HUFF
HUFF
HUFF
MOM, DID YOU HAVE AN ACCIDENT?
YOU REALLY MUST BE SICK!
BETTER CHANGE YOUR CLOTHES...
DING-DONG
HI, DAD!
I'M HOME. WHERE'S MOM...?
HUFF
HUFF
HUFF
HUFF
JUST KILL ME...

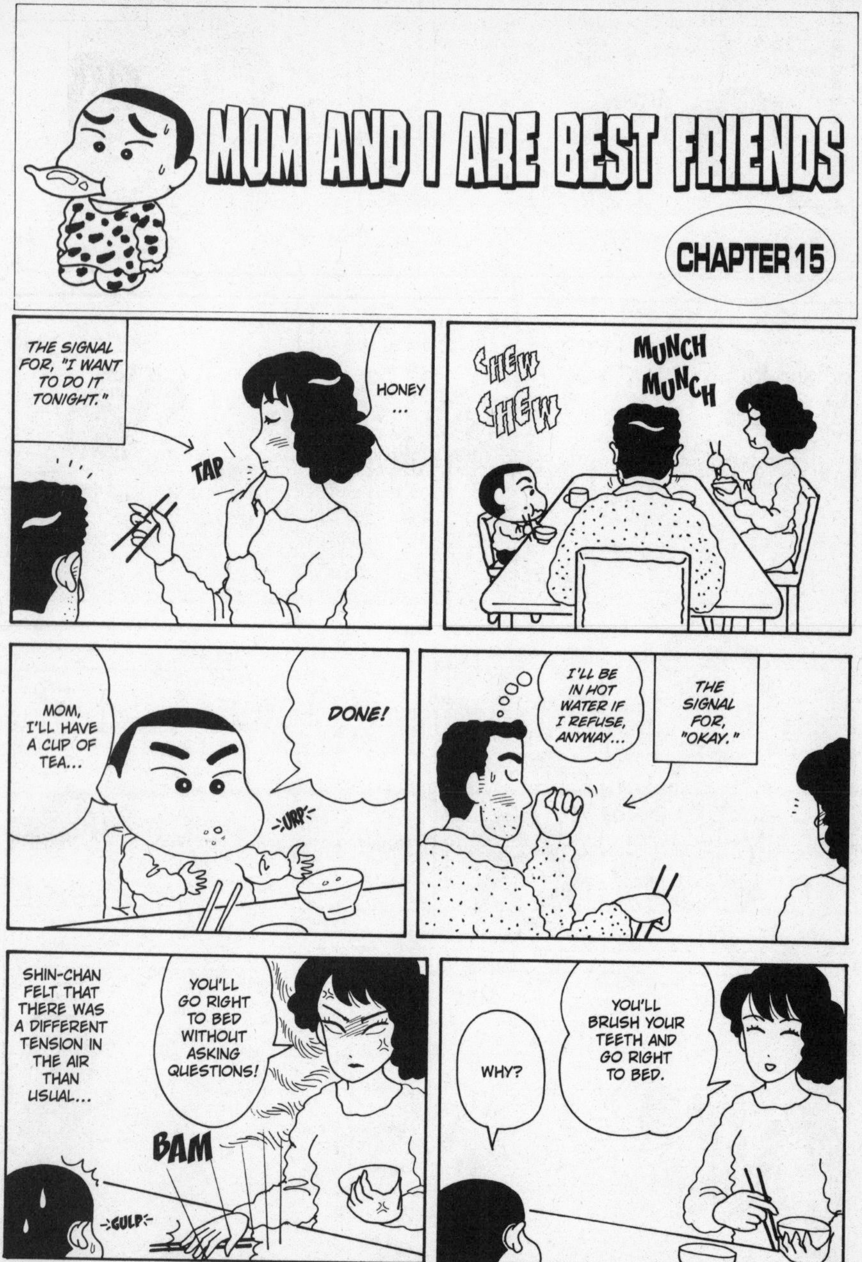
MOM AND I ARE BEST FRIENDS
CHAPTER 15
MUNCH MUNCH
CHEW CHEW
HONEY ...
THE SIGNAL FOR, "I WANT TO DO IT TONIGHT."
TAP
THE SIGNAL FOR, "OKAY."
I'LL BE IN HOT WATER IF I REFUSE, ANYWAY...
DONE!
MOM, I'LL HAVE A CUP OF TEA...
URP
YOU'LL BRUSH YOUR TEETH AND GO RIGHT TO BED.
WHY?
YOU'LL GO RIGHT TO BED WITHOUT ASKING QUESTIONS!
SHIN-CHAN FELT THAT THERE WAS A DIFFERENT TENSION IN THE AIR THAN USUAL...
BAM
GULP

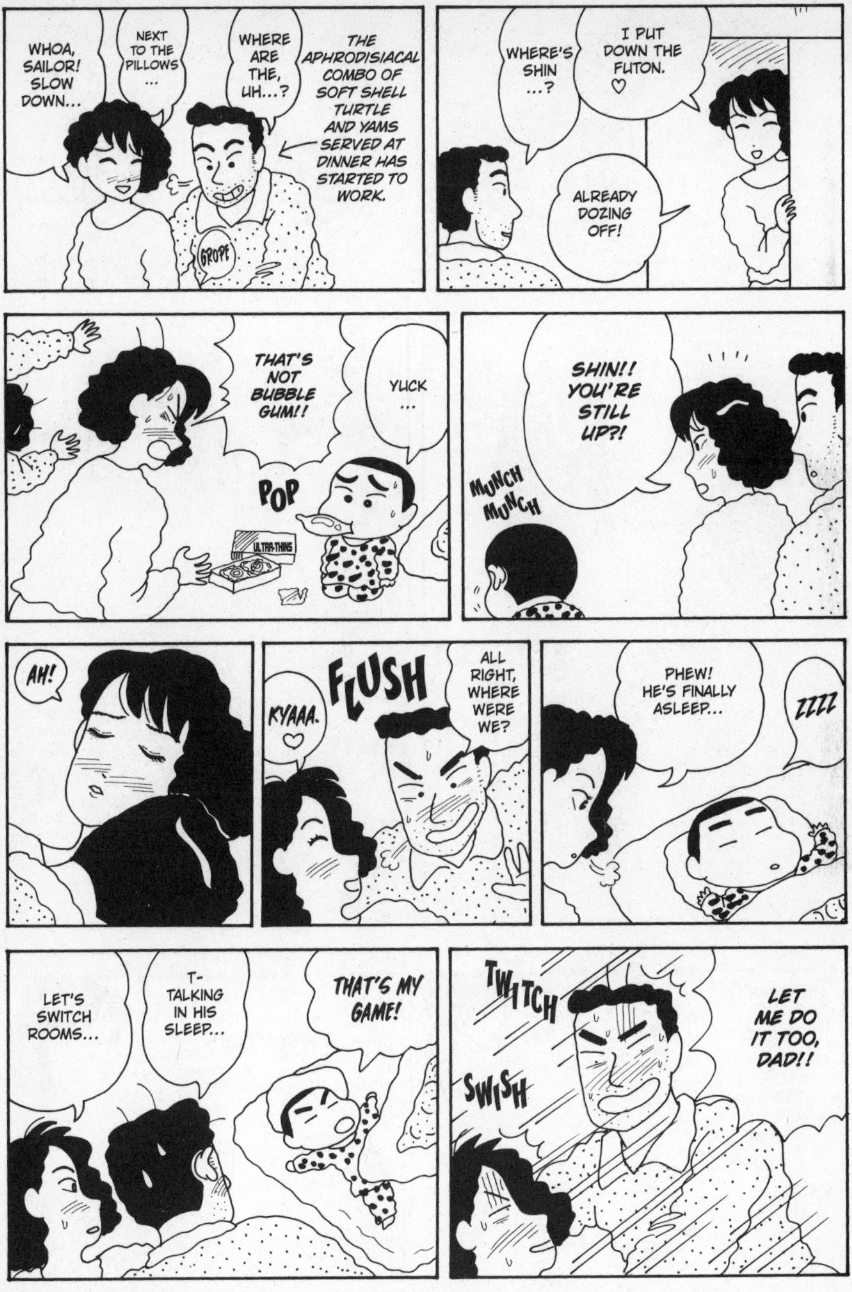
I PUT DOWN THE FUTON. ♡
WHERE'S SHIN ...?
ALREADY DOZING OFF!
THE APHRODISIACAL COMBO OF SOFT SHELL TURTLE AND YAMS SERVED AT DINNER HAS STARTED TO WORK.
WHERE ARE THE, UH...?
NEXT TO THE PILLOWS ...
WHOA, SAILOR! SLOW DOWN...
GROPE
SHIN!! YOU'RE STILL UP?!
MUNCH MUNCH
YUCK ...
THAT'S NOT BUBBLE GUM!!
POP
ULTRA-THINS
ZZZZ
PHEW! HE'S FINALLY ASLEEP...
ALL RIGHT, WHERE WERE WE?
FLUSH
KYAAA. ♡
AH!
LET ME DO IT TOO, DAD!!
TWITCH
SWISH
THAT'S MY GAME!
T- TALKING IN HIS SLEEP...
LET'S SWITCH ROOMS...

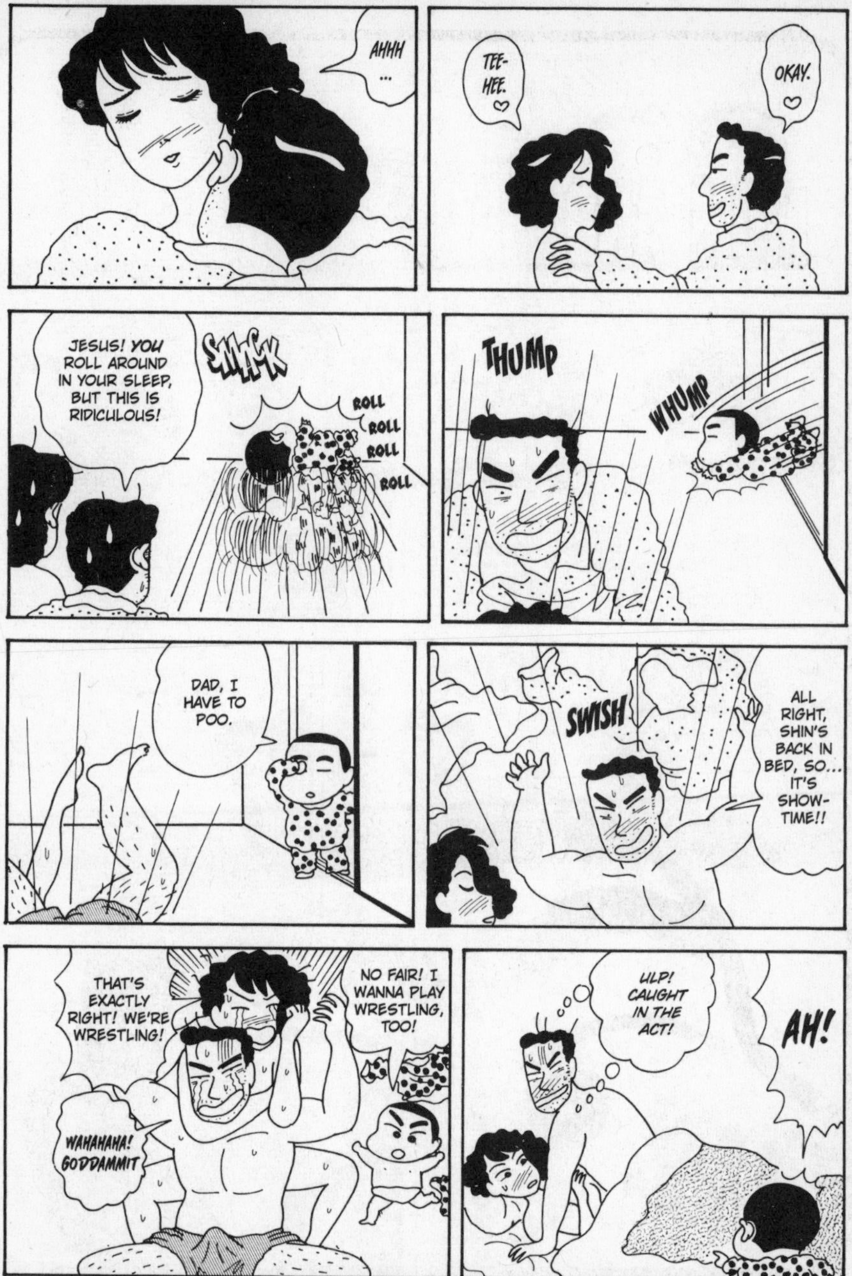
OKAY. ♡
TEE-HEE. ♡
AHHH ...
THUMP
WHUMP
JESUS! YOU ROLL AROUND IN YOUR SLEEP, BUT THIS IS RIDICULOUS!
SMACK
ROLL
ROLL
ROLL
ROLL
ALL RIGHT, SHIN'S BACK IN BED, SO... IT'S SHOW-TIME!!
SWISH
DAD, I HAVE TO POO.
AH!
ULP! CAUGHT IN THE ACT!
NO FAIR! I WANNA PLAY WRESTLING, TOO!
THAT'S EXACTLY RIGHT! WE'RE WRESTLING!
WAHAHAHA! GODDAMMIT

THE "WRESTLING SAVE" WORKED BUT MOM AND DAD WERE FORCED TO ROUGHHOUSE TILL MIDNIGHT.

MOM AND I ARE BEST FRIENDS

PART2

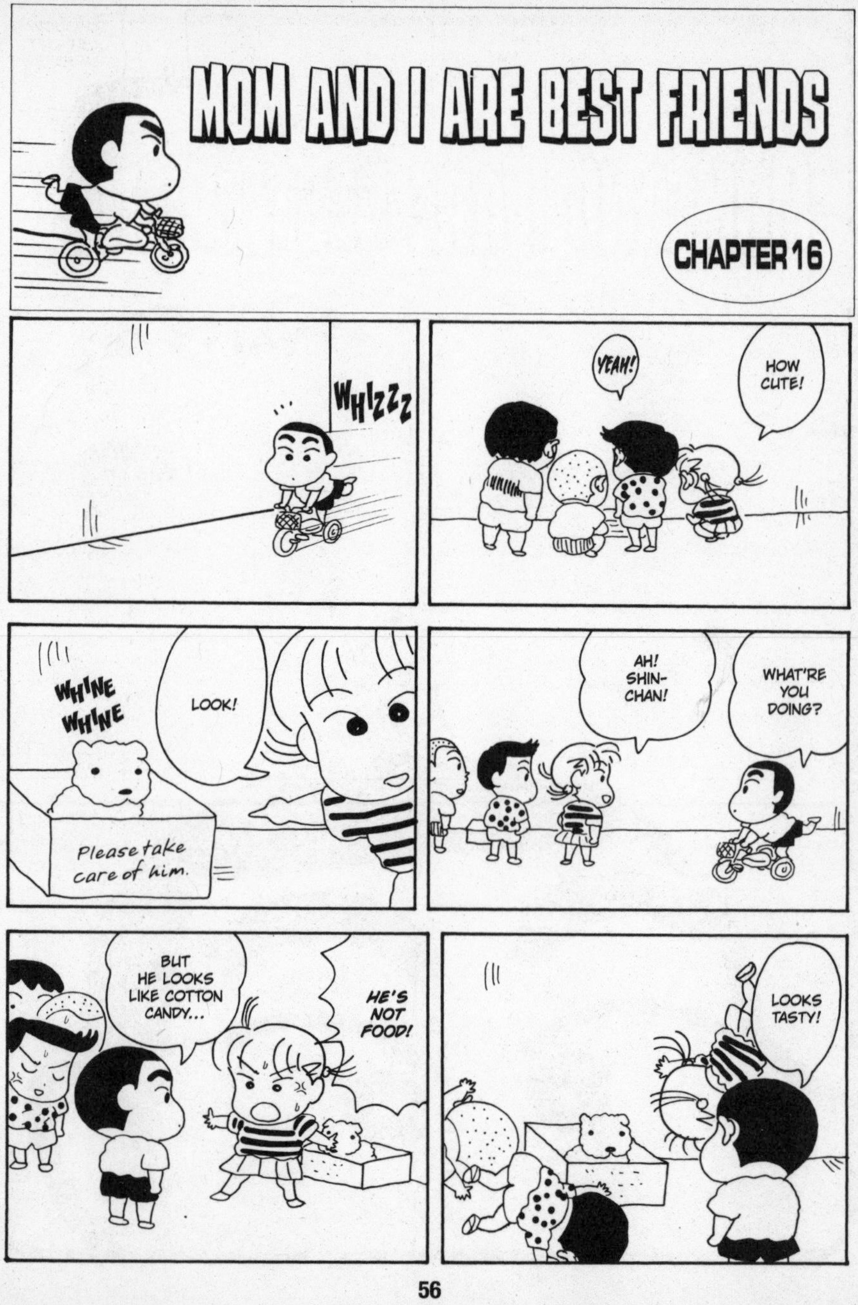
MOM AND I ARE BEST FRIENDS
CHAPTER 16
HOW CUTE!
YEAH!
WHIZZZ
WHAT'RE YOU DOING?
AH! SHIN-CHAN!
LOOK!
WHINE WHINE
Please take care of him.
LOOKS TASTY!
HE'S NOT FOOD!
BUT HE LOOKS LIKE COTTON CANDY...

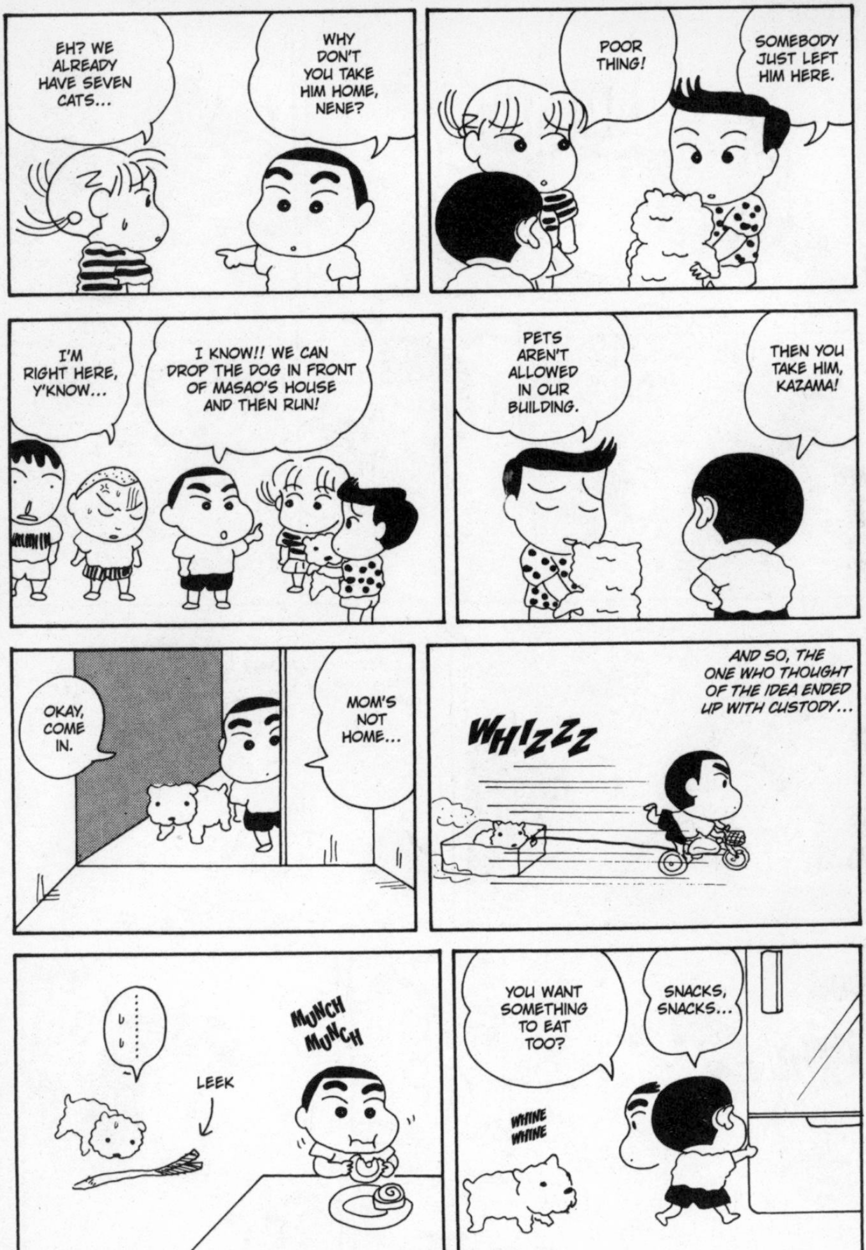
SOMEBODY JUST LEFT HIM HERE.
POOR THING!
WHY DON'T YOU TAKE HIM HOME, NENE?
EH? WE ALREADY HAVE SEVEN CATS...
THEN YOU TAKE HIM, KAZAMA!
PETS AREN'T ALLOWED IN OUR BUILDING.
I KNOW!! WE CAN DROP THE DOG IN FRONT OF MASAO'S HOUSE AND THEN RUN!
I'M RIGHT HERE, Y'KNOW...
AND SO, THE ONE WHO THOUGHT OF THE IDEA ENDED UP WITH CUSTODY...
WHIZZZ
MOM'S NOT HOME...
OKAY, COME IN.
SNACKS, SNACKS...
YOU WANT SOMETHING TO EAT TOO?
WHINE WHINE
MUNCH MUNCH
LEEK
......

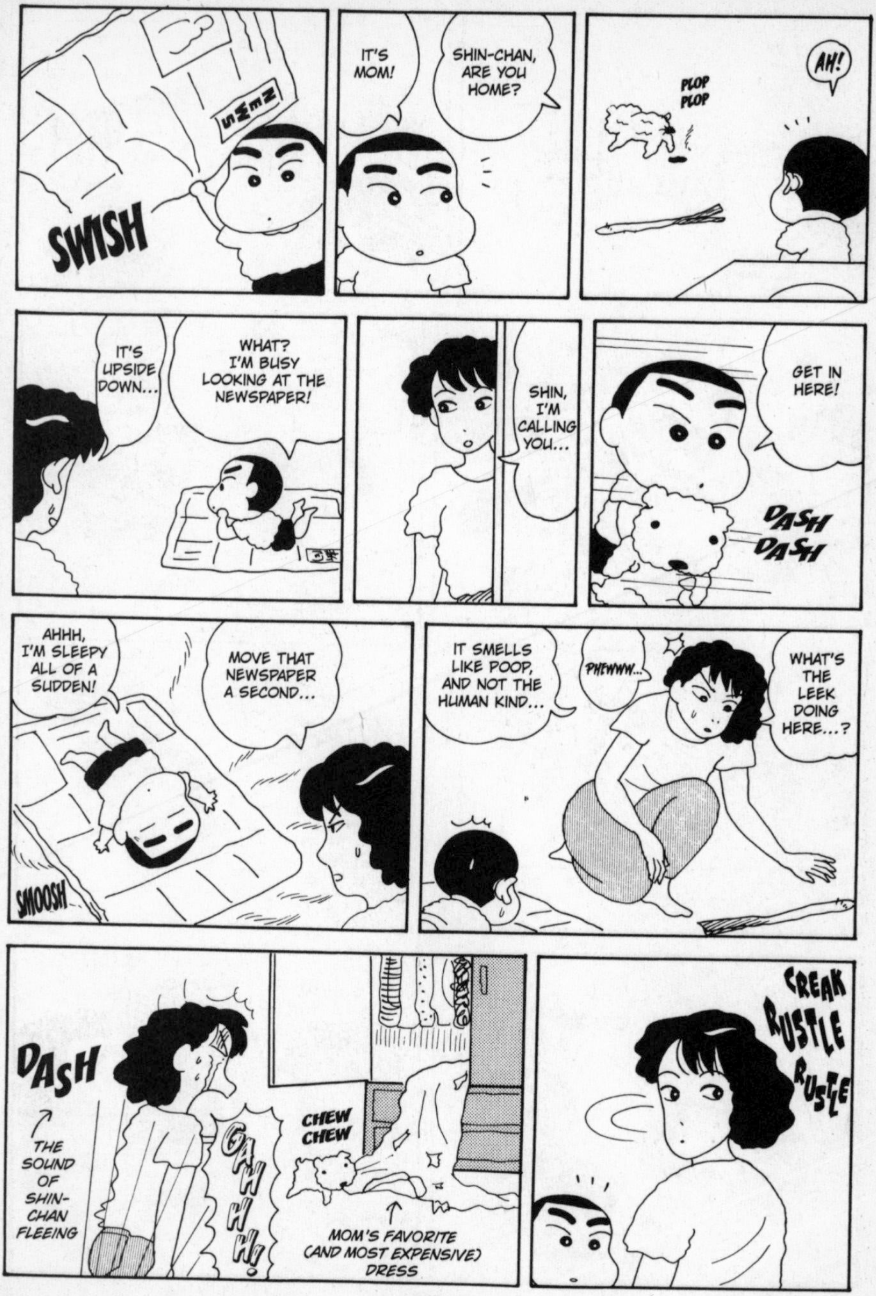
AH!
PLOP PLOP
SHIN-CHAN, ARE YOU HOME?
IT'S MOM!
SWISH
GET IN HERE!
DASH DASH
SHIN, I'M CALLING YOU...
WHAT? I'M BUSY LOOKING AT THE NEWSPAPER!
IT'S UPSIDE DOWN...
WHAT'S THE LEEK DOING HERE...?
PHEWWW...
IT SMELLS LIKE POOP, AND NOT THE HUMAN KIND...
MOVE THAT NEWSPAPER A SECOND...
AHHH, I'M SLEEPY ALL OF A SUDDEN!
SMOOSH
CREAK
RUSTLE RUSTLE
CHEW CHEW
MOM'S FAVORITE (AND MOST EXPENSIVE) DRESS
GAHHHH!
DASH
THE SOUND OF SHIN-CHAN FLEEING

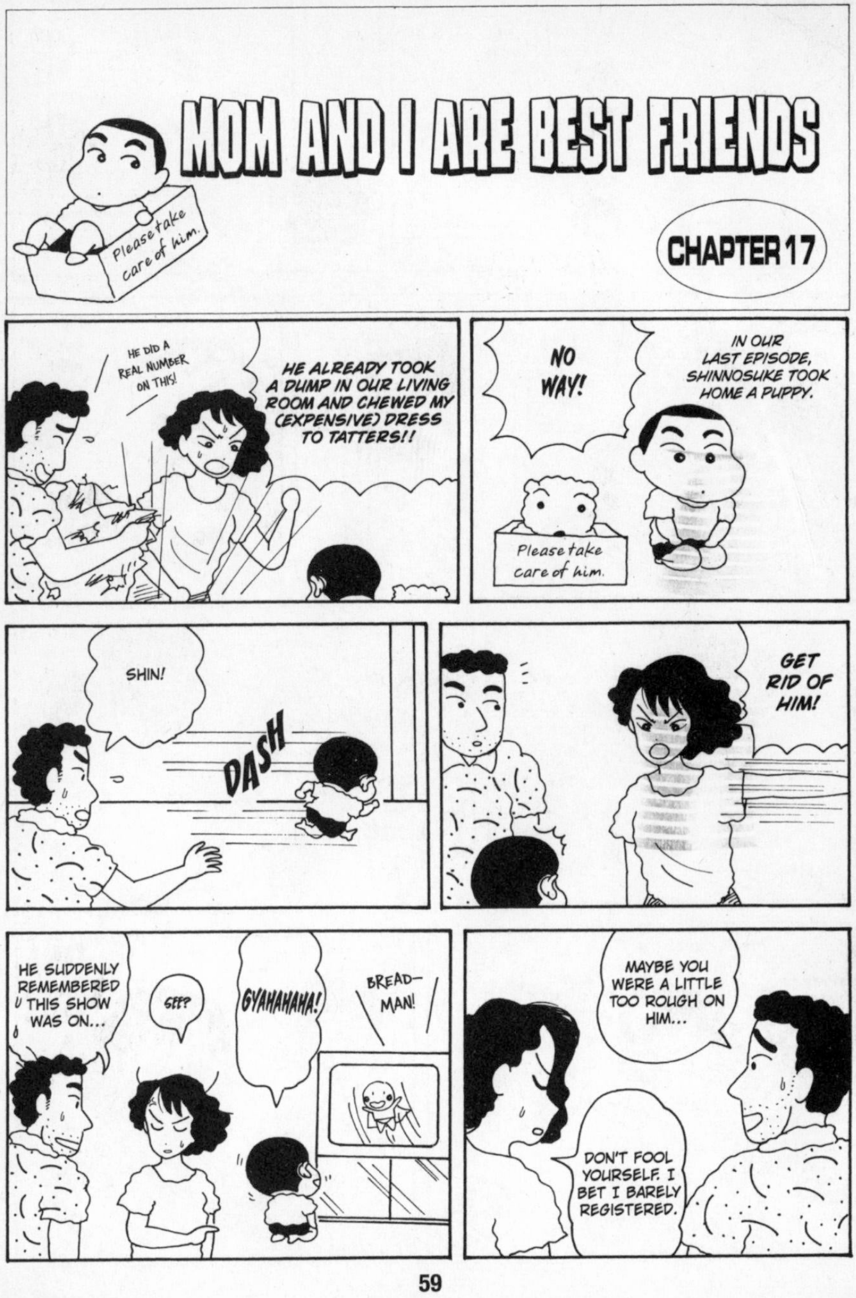
MOM AND I ARE BEST FRIENDS
CHAPTER 17
Please take care of him.
IN OUR LAST EPISODE, SHINNOSUKE TOOK HOME A PUPPY.
NO WAY!
Please take care of him.
HE ALREADY TOOK A DUMP IN OUR LIVING ROOM AND CHEWED MY (EXPENSIVE) DRESS TO TATTERS!!
HE DID A REAL NUMBER ON THIS!
GET RID OF HIM!
SHIN!
DASH
MAYBE YOU WERE A LITTLE TOO ROUGH ON HIM...
DON'T FOOL YOURSELF. I BET I BARELY REGISTERED.
BREAD-MAN!
GYAHAHAHA!
SEE?
HE SUDDENLY REMEMBERED THIS SHOW WAS ON...

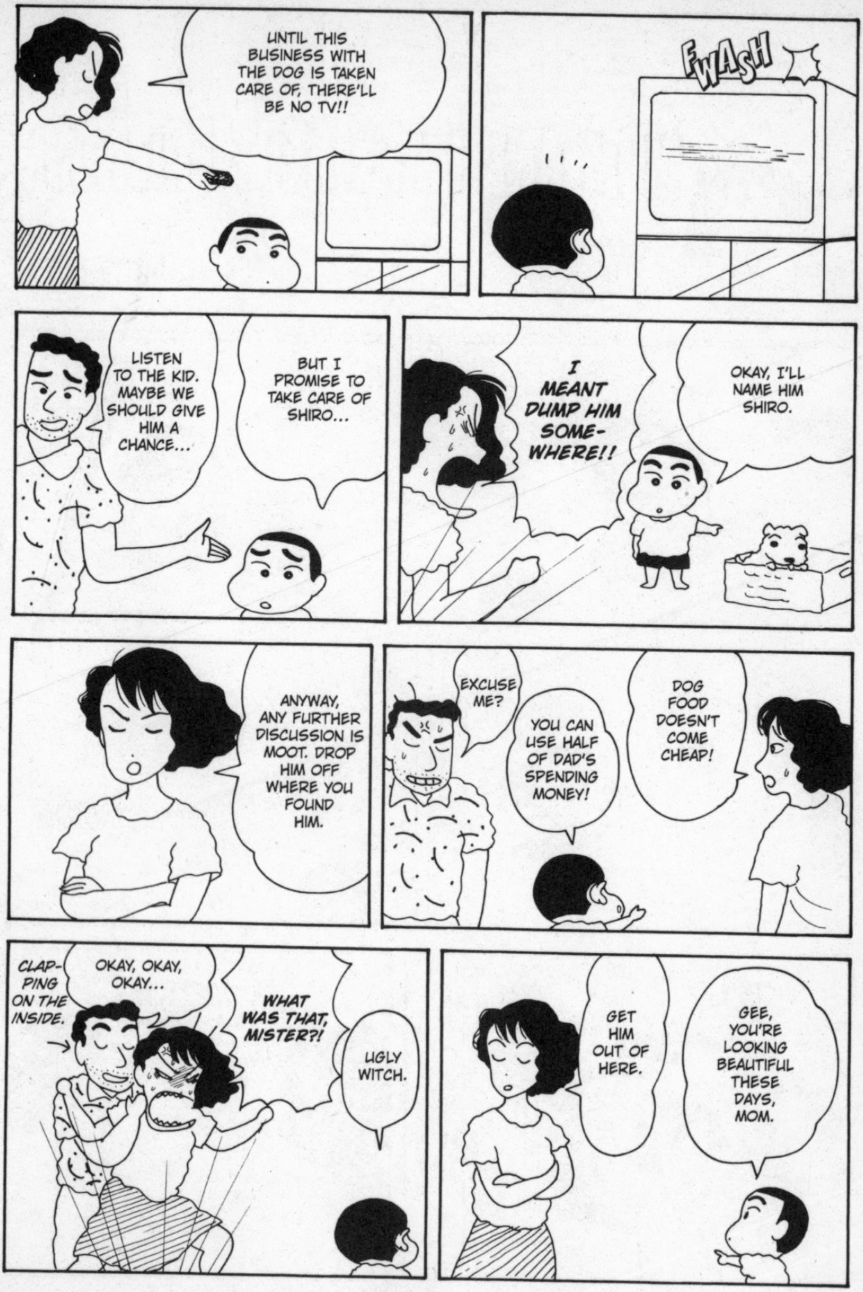
FWASH
UNTIL THIS BUSINESS WITH THE DOG IS TAKEN CARE OF, THERE'LL BE NO TV!!
OKAY, I'LL NAME HIM SHIRO.
I MEANT DUMP HIM SOME-WHERE!!
BUT I PROMISE TO TAKE CARE OF SHIRO...
LISTEN TO THE KID. MAYBE WE SHOULD GIVE HIM A CHANCE...
DOG FOOD DOESN'T COME CHEAP!
YOU CAN USE HALF OF DAD'S SPENDING MONEY!
EXCUSE ME?
ANYWAY, ANY FURTHER DISCUSSION IS MOOT. DROP HIM OFF WHERE YOU FOUND HIM.
GEE, YOU'RE LOOKING BEAUTIFUL THESE DAYS, MOM.
GET HIM OUT OF HERE.
UGLY WITCH.
WHAT WAS THAT, MISTER?!
OKAY, OKAY, OKAY...
CLAP-PING ON THE INSIDE.

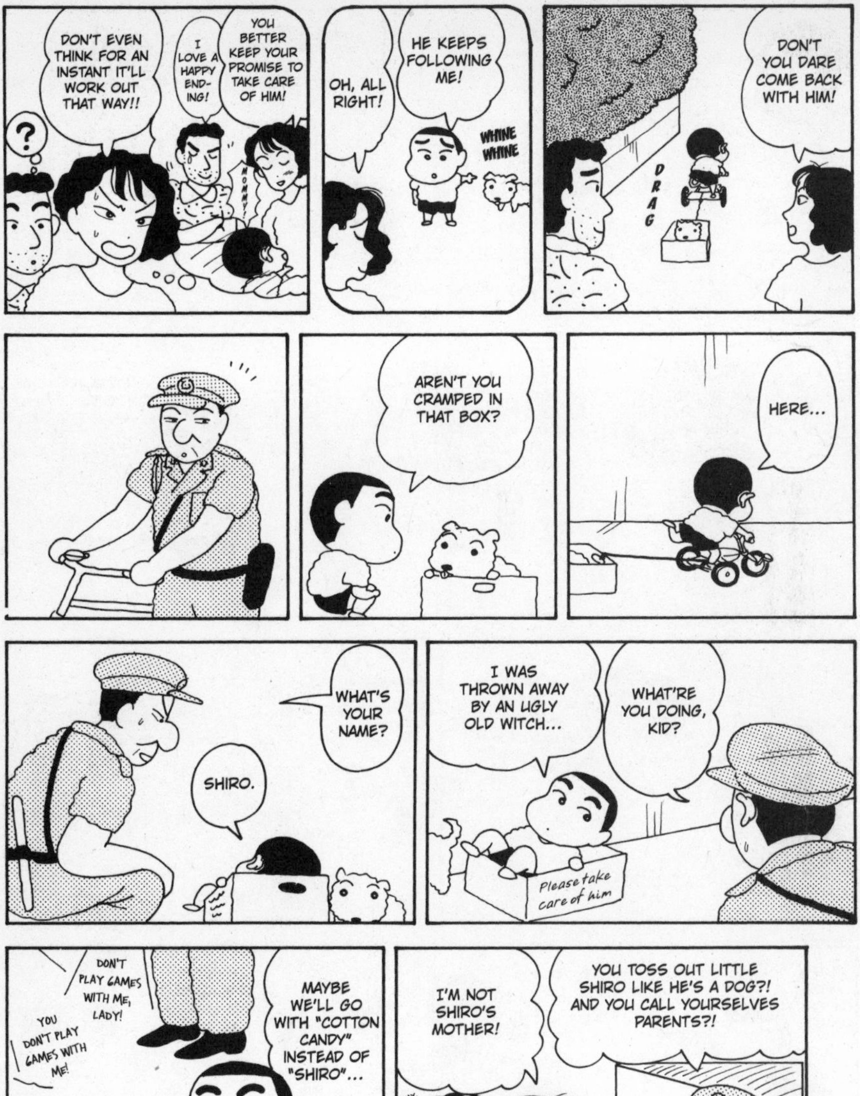
DON'T YOU DARE COME BACK WITH HIM!
DRAG
HE KEEPS FOLLOWING ME!
WHINE WHINE
OH, ALL RIGHT!
YOU BETTER KEEP YOUR PROMISE TO TAKE CARE OF HIM!
I LOVE A HAPPY ENDING!
MOMMY!
DON'T EVEN THINK FOR AN INSTANT IT'LL WORK OUT THAT WAY!!
?
HERE...
AREN'T YOU CRAMPED IN THAT BOX?
WHAT'RE YOU DOING, KID?
I WAS THROWN AWAY BY AN UGLY OLD WITCH...
Please take care of him
WHAT'S YOUR NAME?
SHIRO.
YOU TOSS OUT LITTLE SHIRO LIKE HE'S A DOG?! AND YOU CALL YOURSELVES PARENTS?!
I'M NOT SHIRO'S MOTHER!
OKAY, OKAY...
MAYBE WE'LL GO WITH "COTTON CANDY" INSTEAD OF "SHIRO"...
DON'T PLAY GAMES WITH ME, LADY!
YOU DON'T PLAY GAMES WITH ME!
OKAY, OKAY...

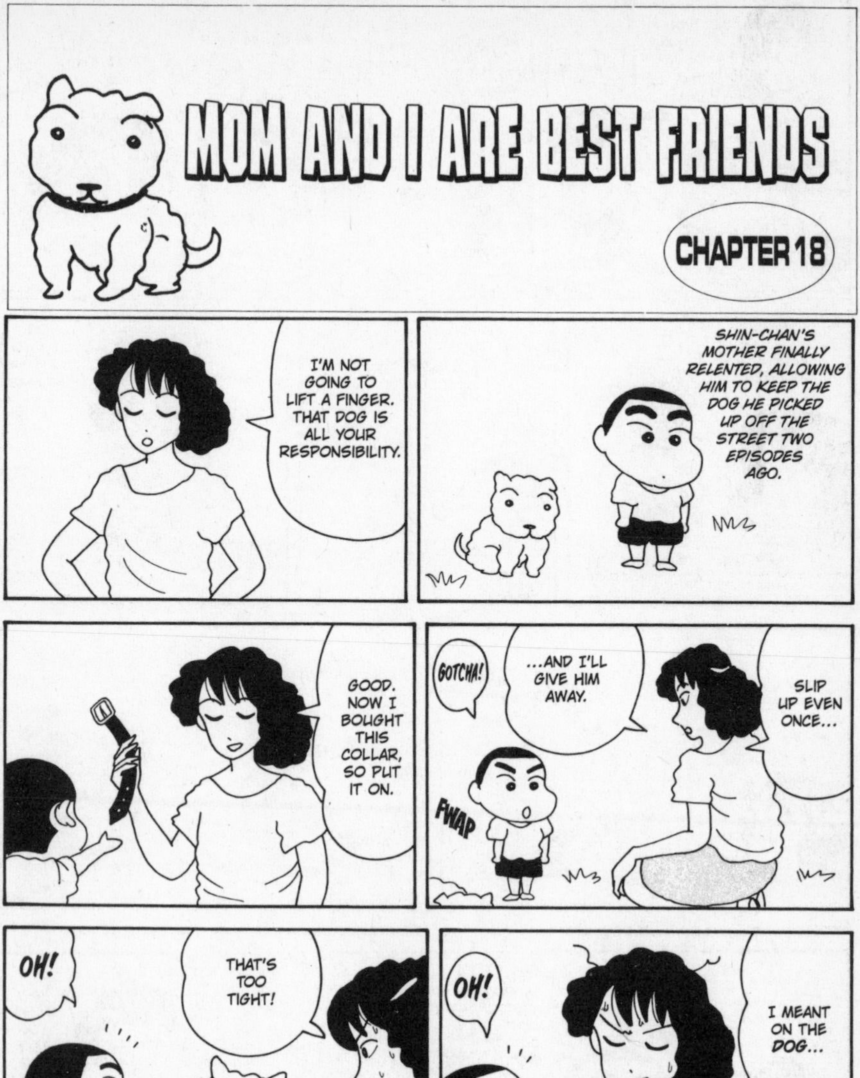
MOM AND I ARE BEST FRIENDS
CHAPTER 18
SHIN-CHAN'S MOTHER FINALLY RELENTED, ALLOWING HIM TO KEEP THE DOG HE PICKED UP OFF THE STREET TWO EPISODES AGO.
I'M NOT GOING TO LIFT A FINGER. THAT DOG IS ALL YOUR RESPONSIBILITY.
SLIP UP EVEN ONCE...
...AND I'LL GIVE HIM AWAY.
GOTCHA!
FWAP
GOOD. NOW I BOUGHT THIS COLLAR, SO PUT IT ON.
I MEANT ON THE *DOG*...
OH!
THAT'S TOO TIGHT!
OH!

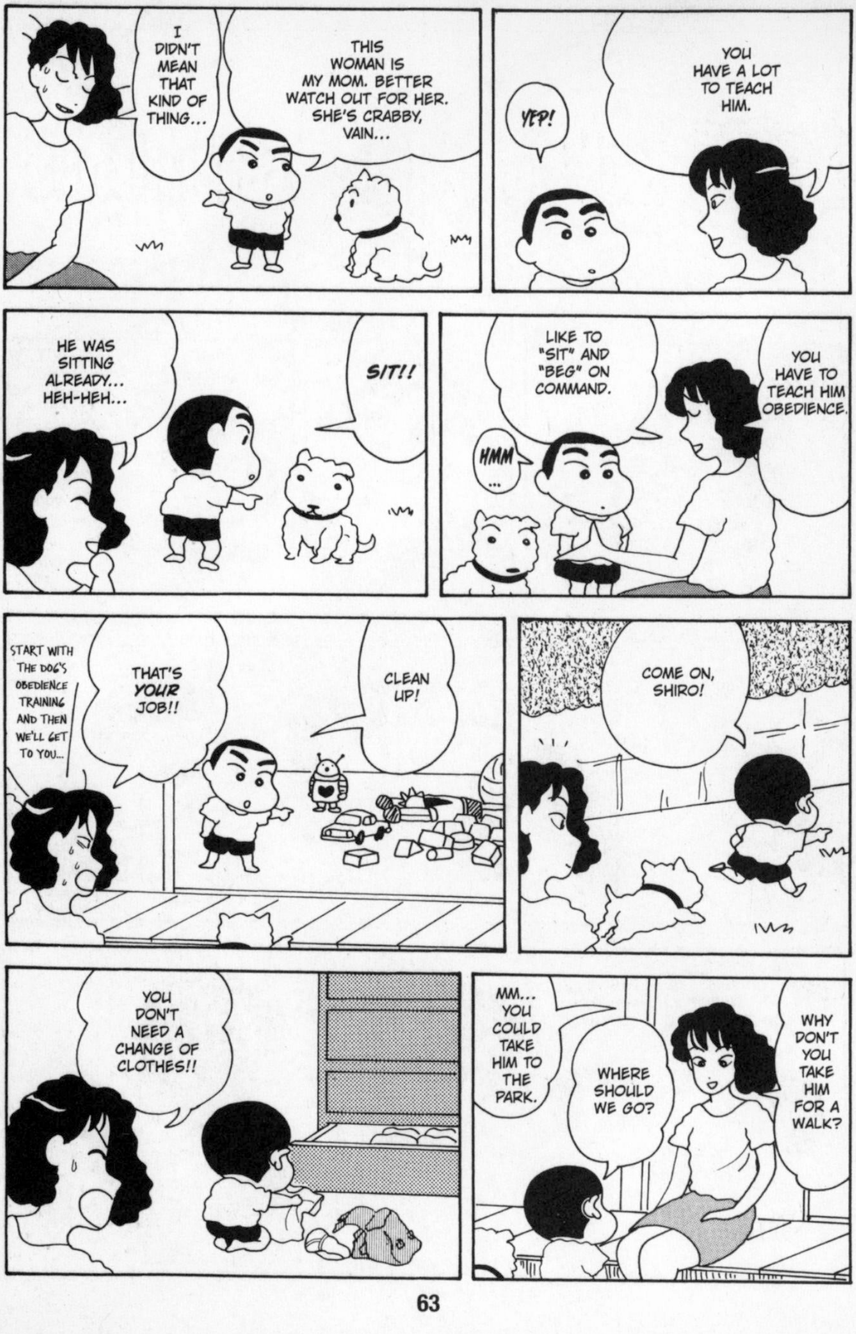
YOU HAVE A LOT TO TEACH HIM.
YEP!
THIS WOMAN IS MY MOM. BETTER WATCH OUT FOR HER. SHE'S CRABBY, VAIN...
I DIDN'T MEAN THAT KIND OF THING...
YOU HAVE TO TEACH HIM OBEDIENCE.
LIKE TO "SIT" AND "BEG" ON COMMAND.
HMM...
SIT!!
HE WAS SITTING ALREADY... HEH-HEH...
COME ON, SHIRO!
CLEAN UP!
THAT'S *YOUR* JOB!!
START WITH THE DOG'S OBEDIENCE TRAINING AND THEN WE'LL GET TO YOU...
WHY DON'T YOU TAKE HIM FOR A WALK?
WHERE SHOULD WE GO?
MM... YOU COULD TAKE HIM TO THE PARK.
YOU DON'T NEED A CHANGE OF CLOTHES!!

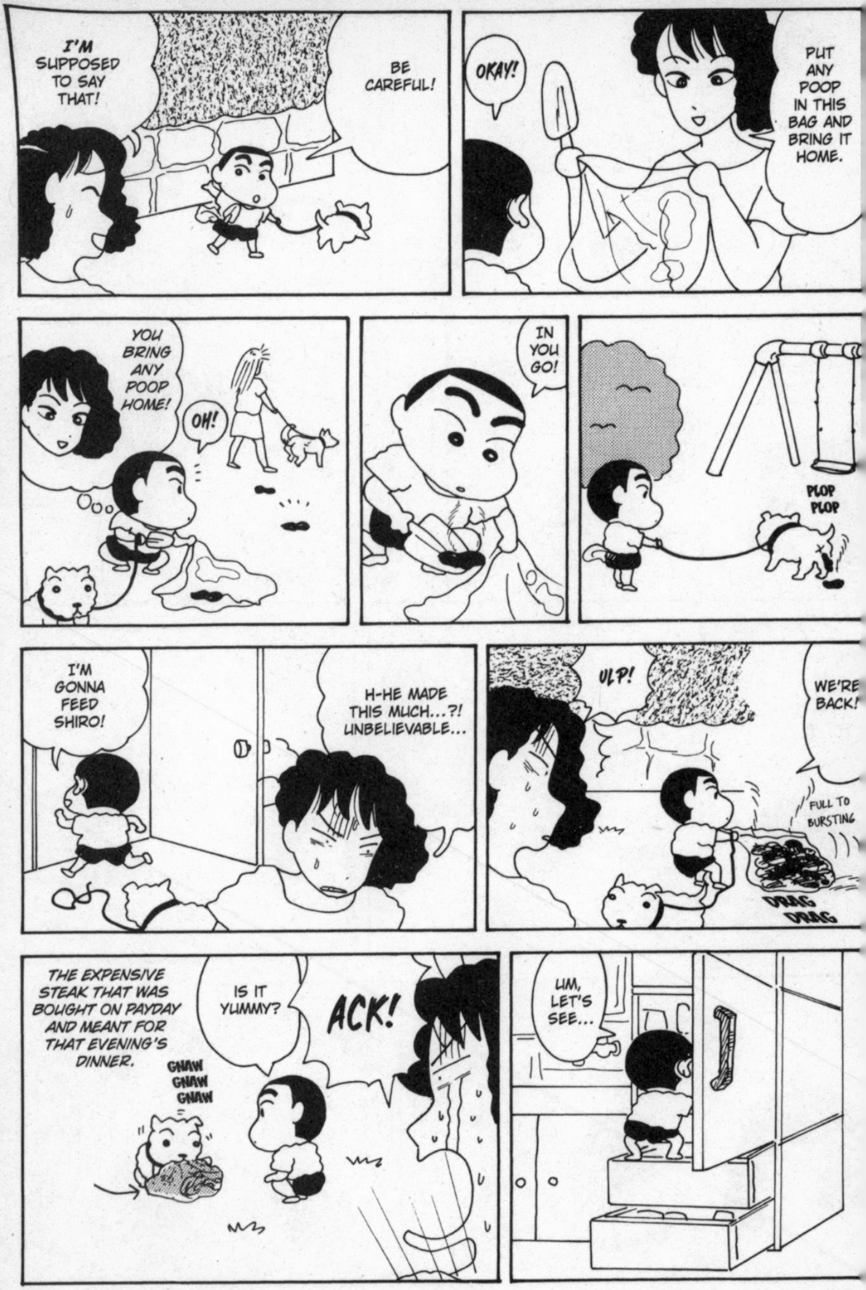
PUT ANY POOP IN THIS BAG AND BRING IT HOME.
OKAY!
BE CAREFUL!
I'M SUPPOSED TO SAY THAT!
PLOP PLOP
IN YOU GO!
YOU BRING ANY POOP HOME!
OH!
WE'RE BACK!
ULP!
FULL TO BURSTING
DRAG DRAG
H-HE MADE THIS MUCH...?! UNBELIEVABLE...
I'M GONNA FEED SHIRO!
UM, LET'S SEE...
ACK!
IS IT YUMMY?
THE EXPENSIVE STEAK THAT WAS BOUGHT ON PAYDAY AND MEANT FOR THAT EVENING'S DINNER.
GNAW GNAW GNAW

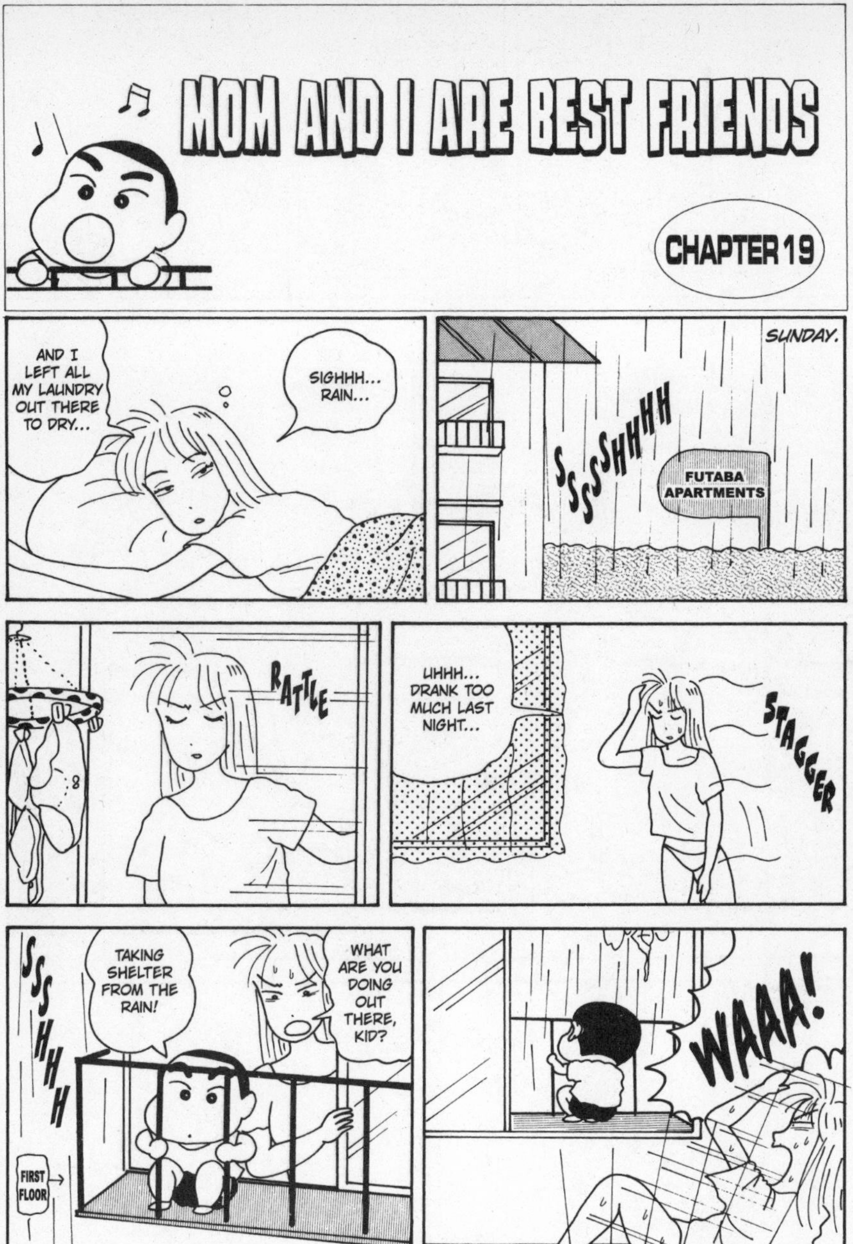
MOM AND I ARE BEST FRIENDS
CHAPTER 19
SUNDAY.
SSSSHHHHH
FUTABA APARTMENTS
SIGHHH... RAIN...
AND I LEFT ALL MY LAUNDRY OUT THERE TO DRY...
STAGGER
UHHH... DRANK TOO MUCH LAST NIGHT...
RATTLE
WAAA!
WHAT ARE YOU DOING OUT THERE, KID?
TAKING SHELTER FROM THE RAIN!
SSSHHHH
FIRST FLOOR

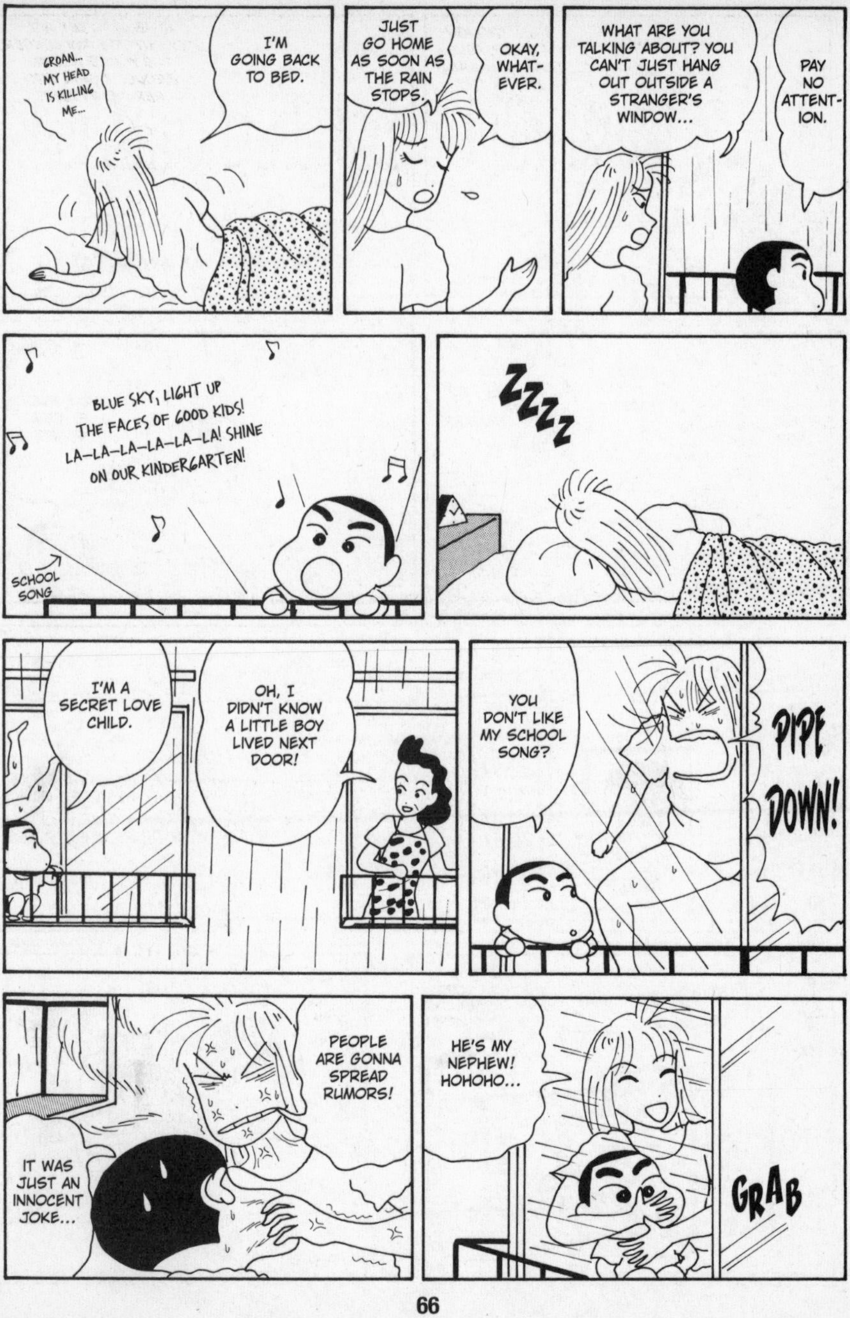
PAY NO ATTENTION.
WHAT ARE YOU TALKING ABOUT? YOU CAN'T JUST HANG OUT OUTSIDE A STRANGER'S WINDOW...
OKAY, WHAT-EVER.
JUST GO HOME AS SOON AS THE RAIN STOPS.
I'M GOING BACK TO BED.
GROAN... MY HEAD IS KILLING ME...
ZZZZ
BLUE SKY, LIGHT UP THE FACES OF GOOD KIDS! LA-LA-LA-LA-LA-LA! SHINE ON OUR KINDERGARTEN!
SCHOOL SONG
PIPE DOWN!
YOU DON'T LIKE MY SCHOOL SONG?
OH, I DIDN'T KNOW A LITTLE BOY LIVED NEXT DOOR!
I'M A SECRET LOVE CHILD.
GRAB
HE'S MY NEPHEW! HOHOHO...
PEOPLE ARE GONNA SPREAD RUMORS!
IT WAS JUST AN INNOCENT JOKE...

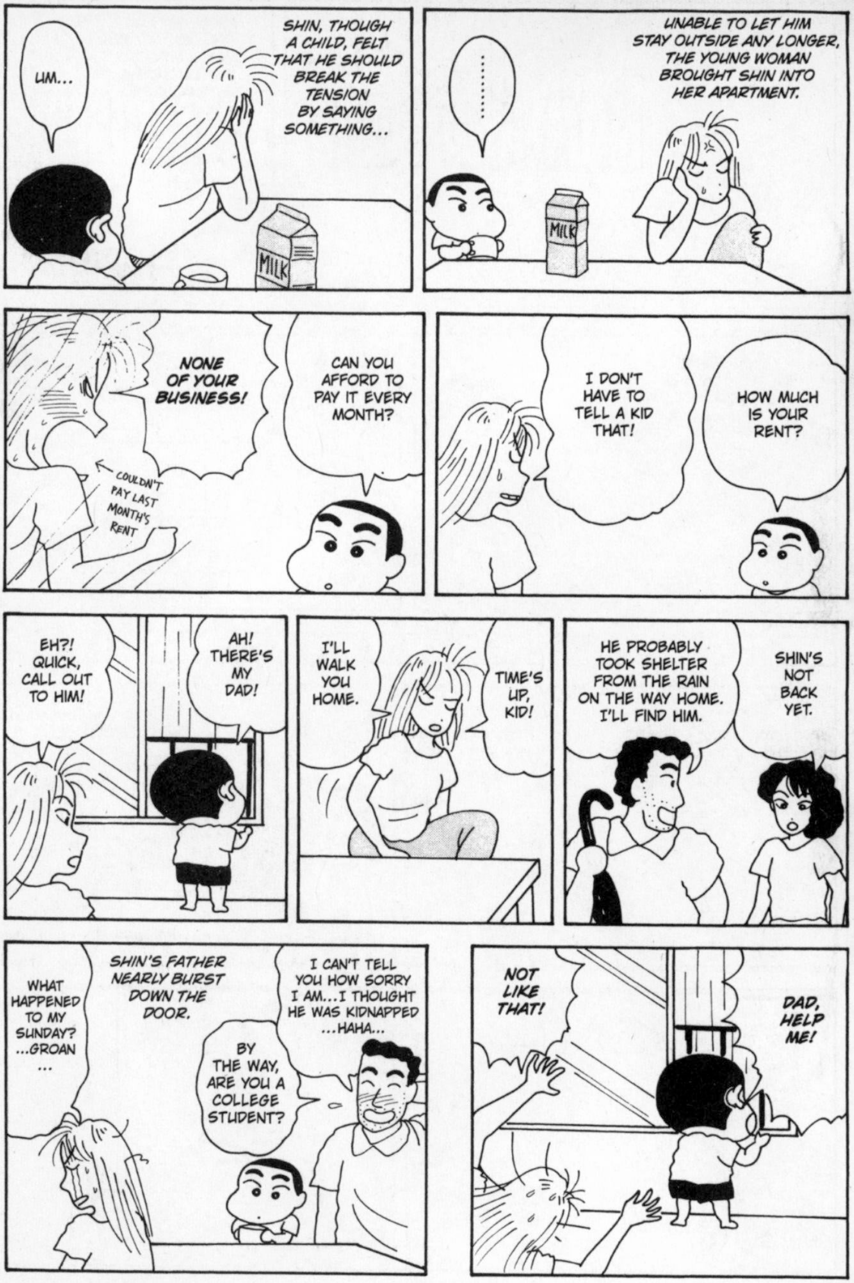
UNABLE TO LET HIM STAY OUTSIDE ANY LONGER, THE YOUNG WOMAN BROUGHT SHIN INTO HER APARTMENT.
......
MILK
SHIN, THOUGH A CHILD, FELT THAT HE SHOULD BREAK THE TENSION BY SAYING SOMETHING...
UM...
MILK
HOW MUCH IS YOUR RENT?
I DON'T HAVE TO TELL A KID THAT!
CAN YOU AFFORD TO PAY IT EVERY MONTH?
NONE OF YOUR BUSINESS!
COULDN'T PAY LAST MONTH'S RENT
SHIN'S NOT BACK YET.
HE PROBABLY TOOK SHELTER FROM THE RAIN ON THE WAY HOME. I'LL FIND HIM.
TIME'S UP, KID!
I'LL WALK YOU HOME.
AH! THERE'S MY DAD!
EH?! QUICK, CALL OUT TO HIM!
DAD, HELP ME!
NOT LIKE THAT!
I CAN'T TELL YOU HOW SORRY I AM...I THOUGHT HE WAS KIDNAPPED ...HAHA...
BY THE WAY, ARE YOU A COLLEGE STUDENT?
SHIN'S FATHER NEARLY BURST DOWN THE DOOR.
WHAT HAPPENED TO MY SUNDAY? ...GROAN ...

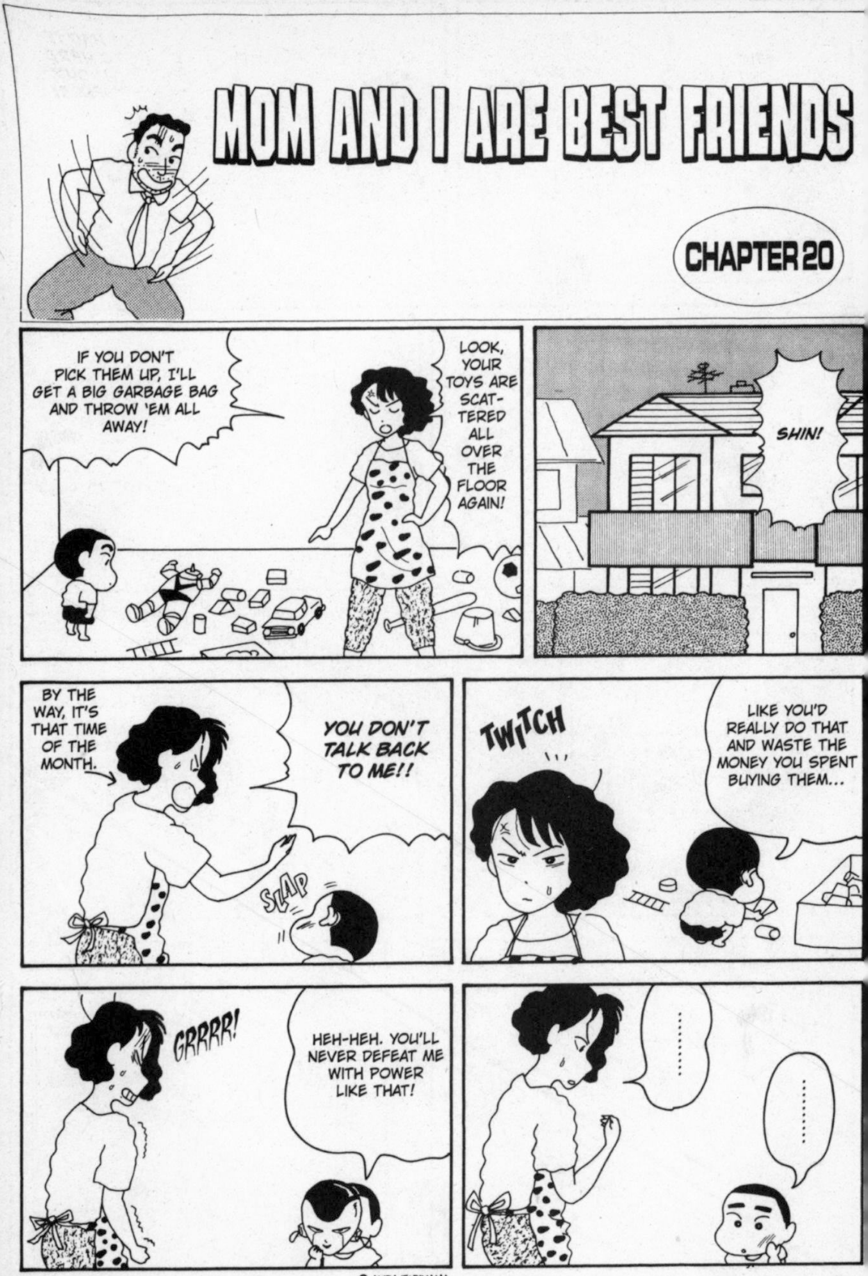
MOM AND I ARE BEST FRIENDS
CHAPTER 20
SHIN!
LOOK, YOUR TOYS ARE SCATTERED ALL OVER THE FLOOR AGAIN!
IF YOU DON'T PICK THEM UP, I'LL GET A BIG GARBAGE BAG AND THROW 'EM ALL AWAY!
LIKE YOU'D REALLY DO THAT AND WASTE THE MONEY YOU SPENT BUYING THEM...
TWITCH
YOU DON'T TALK BACK TO ME!!
BY THE WAY, IT'S THAT TIME OF THE MONTH.
SLAP
......
......
HEH-HEH. YOU'LL NEVER DEFEAT ME WITH POWER LIKE THAT!
GRRRR!

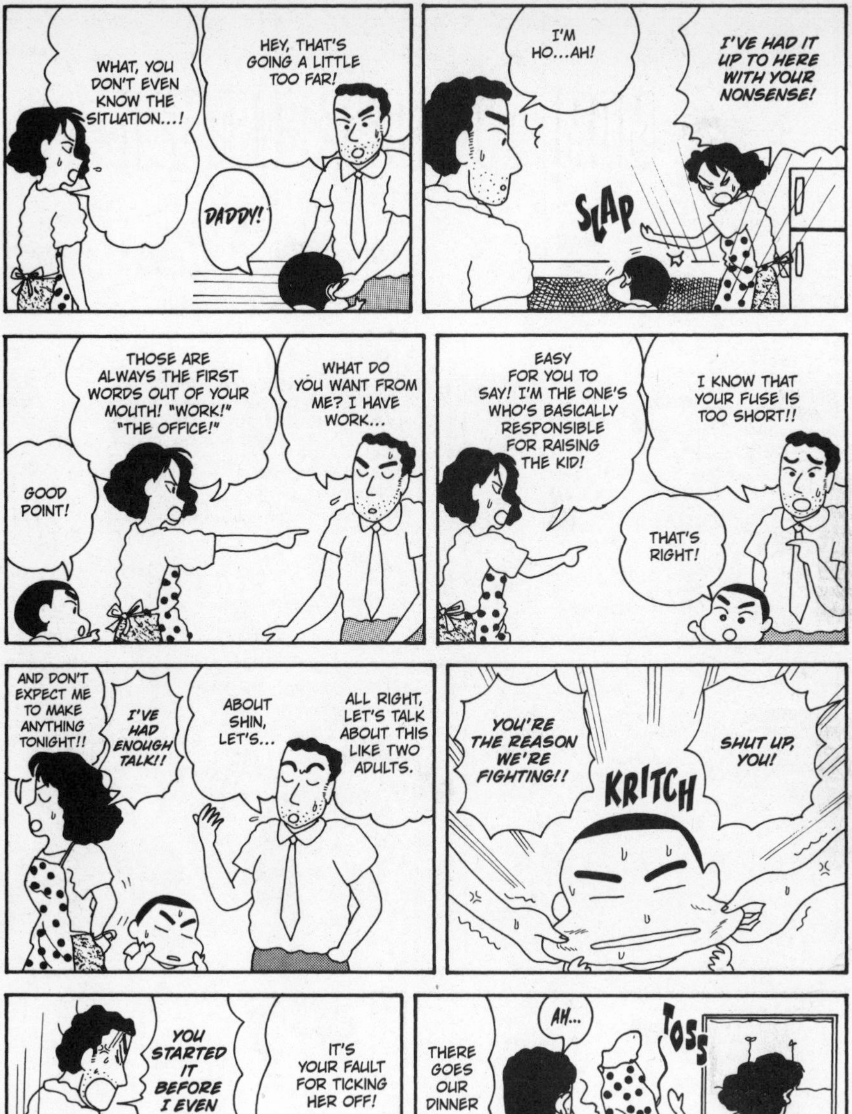
WHAT, YOU DON'T EVEN KNOW THE SITUATION...!
HEY, THAT'S GOING A LITTLE TOO FAR!
DADDY!
I'M HO...AH!
I'VE HAD IT UP TO HERE WITH YOUR NONSENSE!
SLAP
THOSE ARE ALWAYS THE FIRST WORDS OUT OF YOUR MOUTH! "WORK!" "THE OFFICE!"
WHAT DO YOU WANT FROM ME? I HAVE WORK...
GOOD POINT!
EASY FOR YOU TO SAY! I'M THE ONE'S WHO'S BASICALLY RESPONSIBLE FOR RAISING THE KID!
I KNOW THAT YOUR FUSE IS TOO SHORT!!
THAT'S RIGHT!
AND DON'T EXPECT ME TO MAKE ANYTHING TONIGHT!!
I'VE HAD ENOUGH TALK!!
ABOUT SHIN, LET'S...
ALL RIGHT, LET'S TALK ABOUT THIS LIKE TWO ADULTS.
YOU'RE THE REASON WE'RE FIGHTING!!
KRITCH
SHUT UP, YOU!
YOU STARTED IT BEFORE I EVEN GOT HOME!!
IT'S YOUR FAULT FOR TICKING HER OFF!
THERE GOES OUR DINNER ...
AH...
TOSS

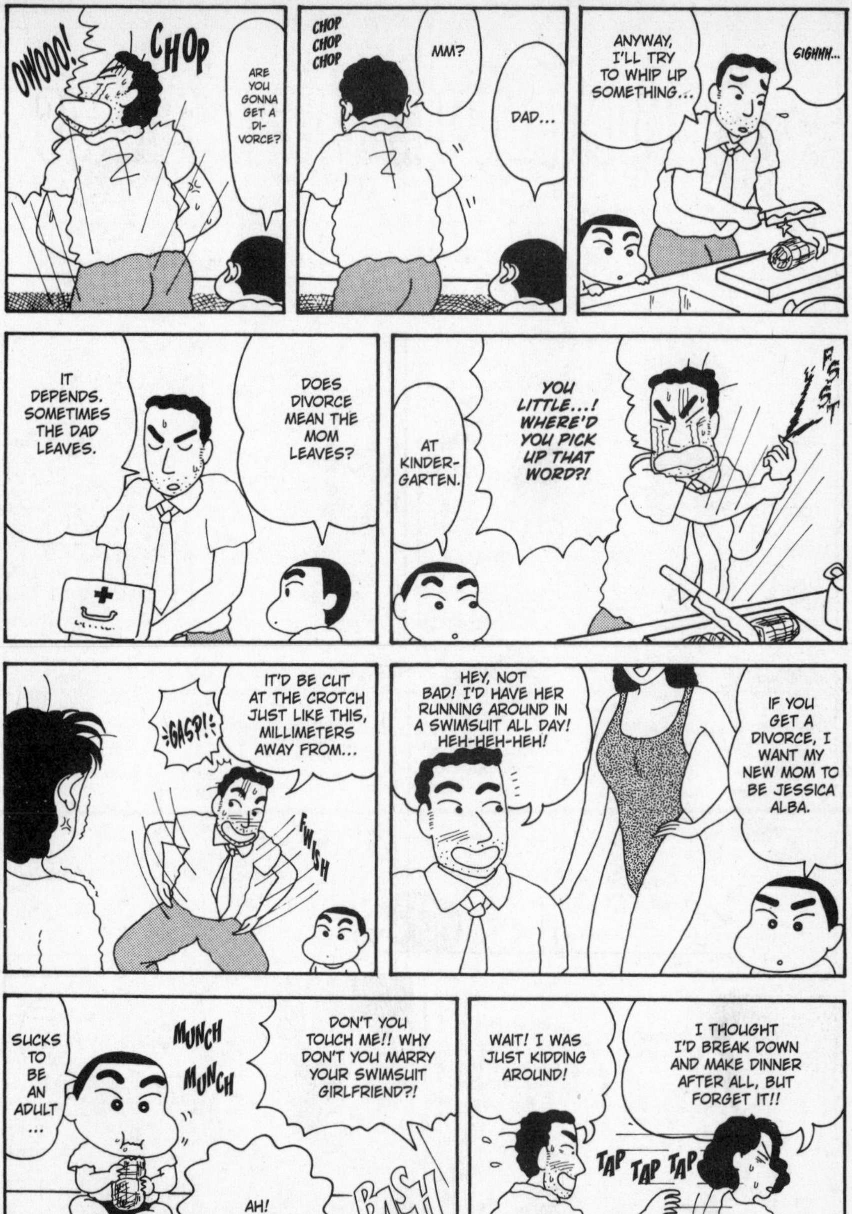
SIGHHH...
ANYWAY, I'LL TRY TO WHIP UP SOMETHING...
DAD...
MM?
CHOP CHOP CHOP
ARE YOU GONNA GET A DI-VORCE?
CHOP
OWOOO!
FSST
YOU LITTLE...! WHERE'D YOU PICK UP THAT WORD?!
AT KINDER-GARTEN.
DOES DIVORCE MEAN THE MOM LEAVES?
IT DEPENDS. SOMETIMES THE DAD LEAVES.
IF YOU GET A DIVORCE, I WANT MY NEW MOM TO BE JESSICA ALBA.
HEY, NOT BAD! I'D HAVE HER RUNNING AROUND IN A SWIMSUIT ALL DAY! HEH-HEH-HEH!
IT'D BE CUT AT THE CROTCH JUST LIKE THIS, MILLIMETERS AWAY FROM...
GASP?!
FWISH
I THOUGHT I'D BREAK DOWN AND MAKE DINNER AFTER ALL, BUT FORGET IT!!
WAIT! I WAS JUST KIDDING AROUND!
TAP TAP TAP
DON'T YOU TOUCH ME!! WHY DON'T YOU MARRY YOUR SWIMSUIT GIRLFRIEND?!
MUNCH MUNCH
SUCKS TO BE AN ADULT ...
BASH
AH! YOU HIT ME!

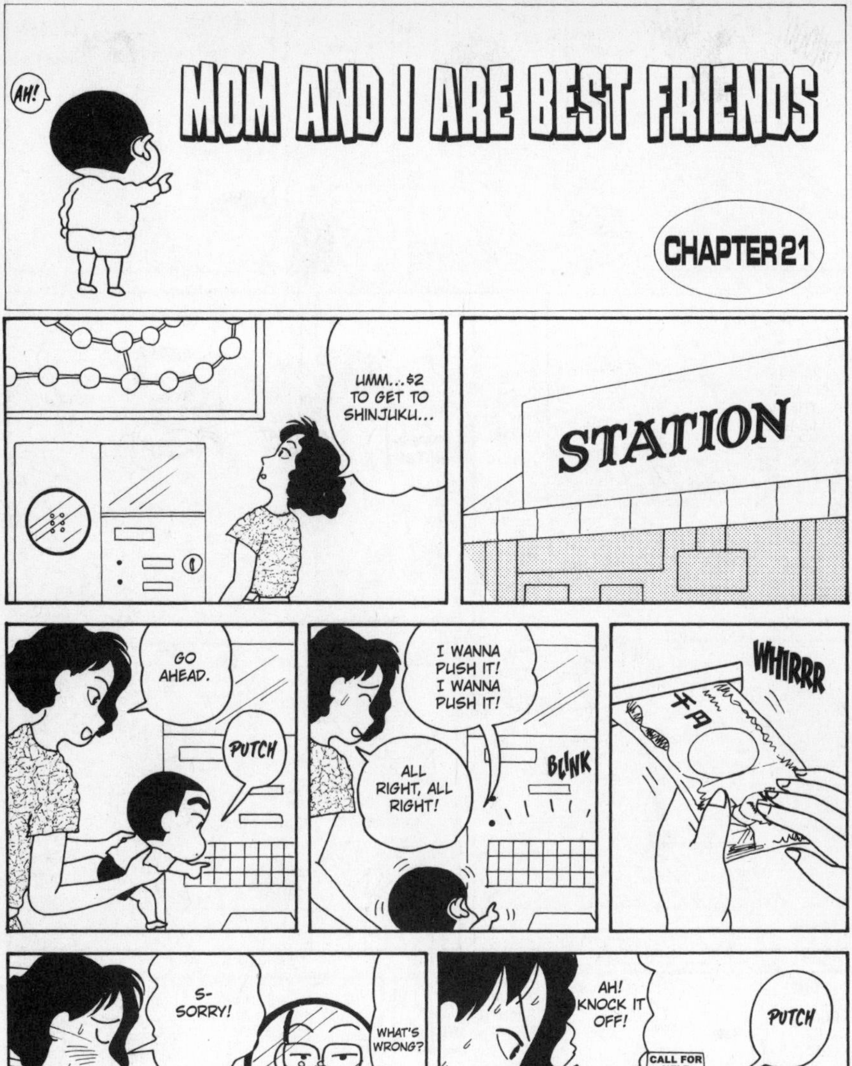

MOM AND I ARE BEST FRIENDS
CHAPTER 21
AH!
STATION
UMM...$2 TO GET TO SHINJUKU...
WHIRRR
I WANNA PUSH IT! I WANNA PUSH IT!
BLINK
ALL RIGHT, ALL RIGHT!
GO AHEAD.
PUTCH
AH! KNOCK IT OFF!
PUTCH
CALL FOR HELP
S-SORRY!
WHAT'S WRONG?
DO YOU LIVE IN THERE?

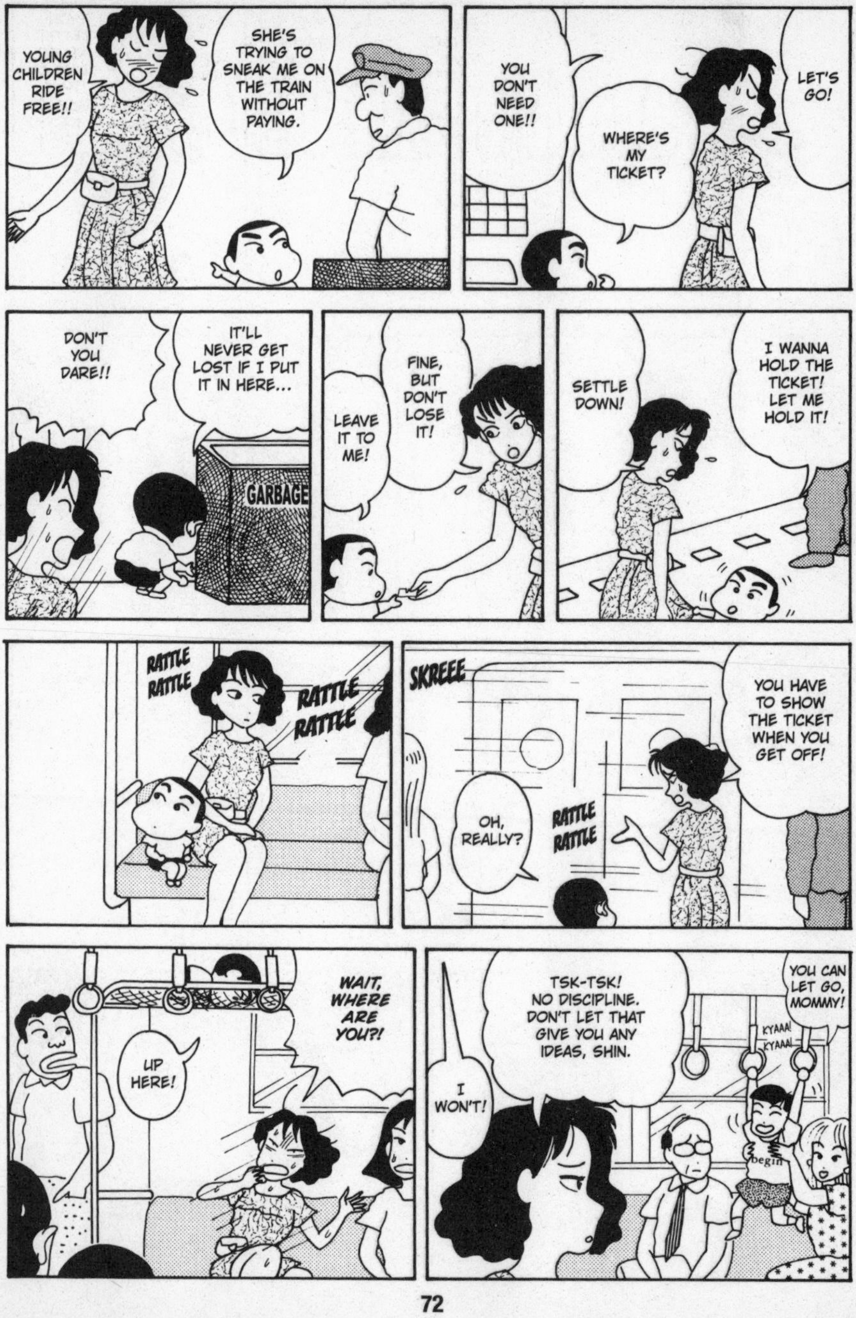

LET'S GO!
WHERE'S MY TICKET?
YOU DON'T NEED ONE!!
SHE'S TRYING TO SNEAK ME ON THE TRAIN WITHOUT PAYING.
YOUNG CHILDREN RIDE FREE!!
I WANNA HOLD THE TICKET! LET ME HOLD IT!
SETTLE DOWN!
FINE, BUT DON'T LOSE IT!
LEAVE IT TO ME!
IT'LL NEVER GET LOST IF I PUT IT IN HERE...
DON'T YOU DARE!!
GARBAGE
SKREEE
YOU HAVE TO SHOW THE TICKET WHEN YOU GET OFF!
RATTLE RATTLE
OH, REALLY?
RATTLE RATTLE
RATTLE RATTLE
YOU CAN LET GO, MOMMY!
KYAAA! KYAAA!
TSK-TSK! NO DISCIPLINE. DON'T LET THAT GIVE YOU ANY IDEAS, SHIN.
I WON'T!
begin
WAIT, WHERE ARE YOU?!
UP HERE!

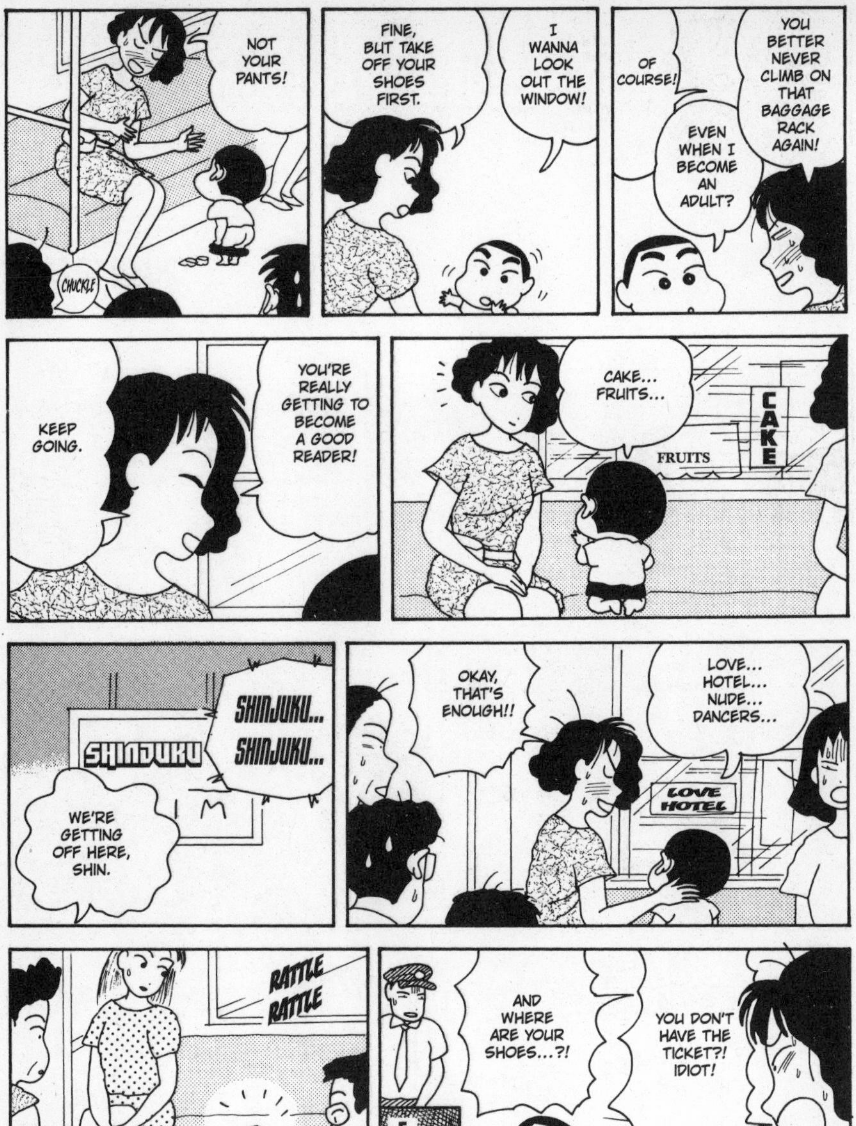

YOU BETTER NEVER CLIMB ON THAT BAGGAGE RACK AGAIN!
OF COURSE!
EVEN WHEN I BECOME AN ADULT?
I WANNA LOOK OUT THE WINDOW!
FINE, BUT TAKE OFF YOUR SHOES FIRST.
NOT YOUR PANTS!
CHUCKLE
CAKE... FRUITS...
CAKE
FRUITS
YOU'RE REALLY GETTING TO BECOME A GOOD READER!
KEEP GOING.
LOVE... HOTEL... NUDE... DANCERS...
LOVE HOTEL
OKAY, THAT'S ENOUGH!!
SHINJUKU... SHINJUKU...
SHINJUKU
WE'RE GETTING OFF HERE, SHIN.
YOU DON'T HAVE THE TICKET?! IDIOT!
AND WHERE ARE YOUR SHOES...?!
EXIT
RATTLE RATTLE

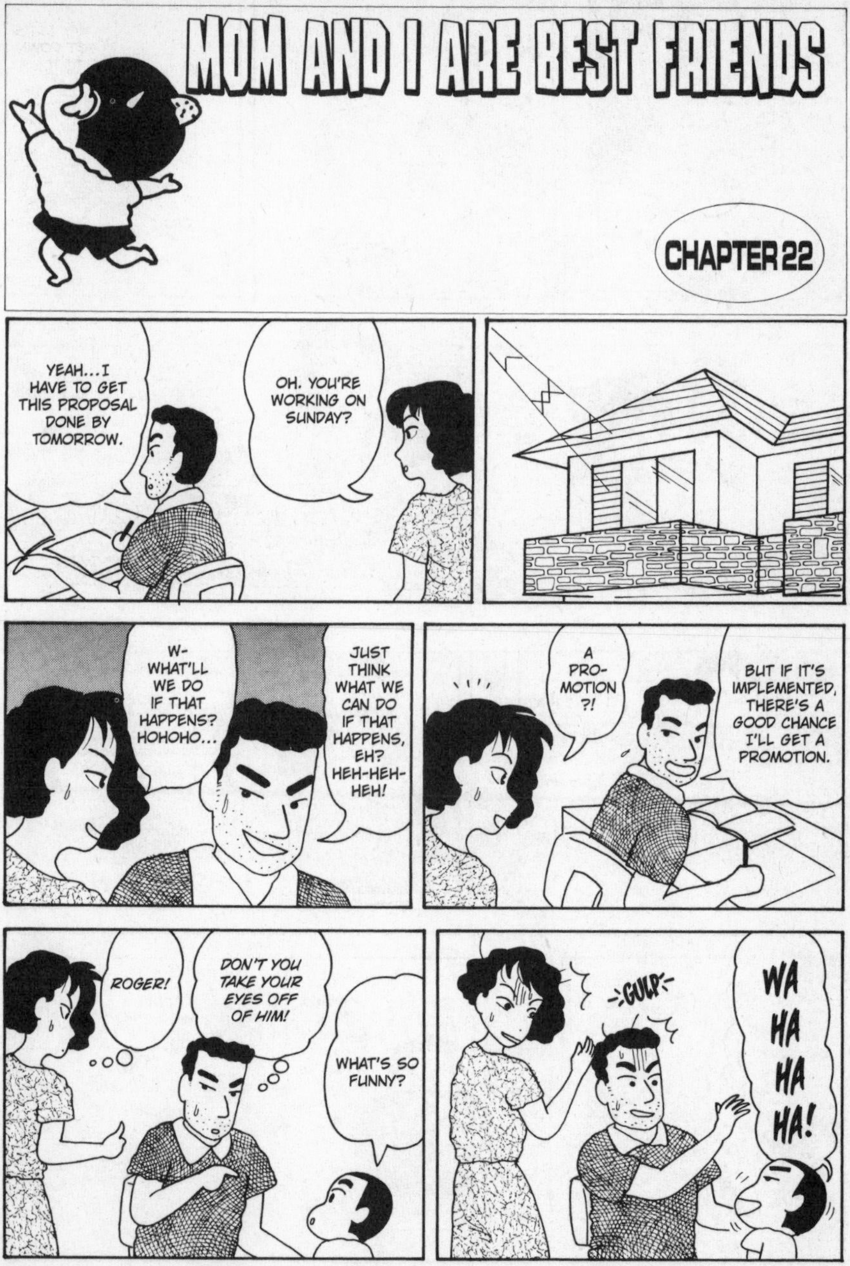
MOM AND I ARE BEST FRIENDS
CHAPTER 22
OH. YOU'RE WORKING ON SUNDAY?
YEAH...I HAVE TO GET THIS PROPOSAL DONE BY TOMORROW.
BUT IF IT'S IMPLEMENTED, THERE'S A GOOD CHANCE I'LL GET A PROMOTION.
A PRO-MOTION?!
JUST THINK WHAT WE CAN DO IF THAT HAPPENS, EH? HEH-HEH-HEH!
W-WHAT'LL WE DO IF THAT HAPPENS? HOHOHO...
WA HA HA HA!
GULP
WHAT'S SO FUNNY?
DON'T YOU TAKE YOUR EYES OFF OF HIM!
ROGER!

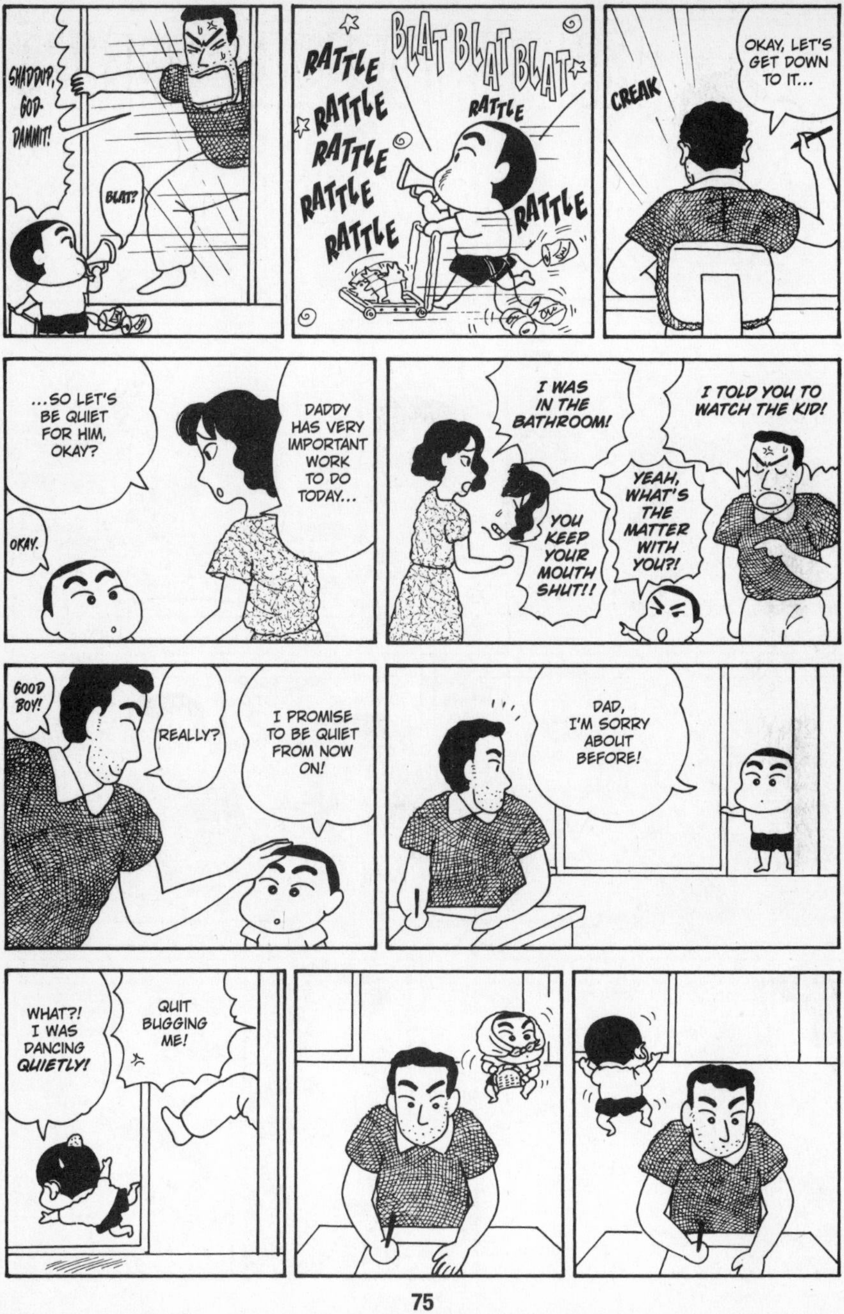
CREAK
OKAY, LET'S GET DOWN TO IT...
BLAT BLAT BLAT
RATTLE
RATTLE RATTLE RATTLE RATTLE RATTLE
RATTLE
SHADDUP, GOD-DAMMIT!
BLAT?
I TOLD YOU TO WATCH THE KID!
I WAS IN THE BATHROOM!
YEAH, WHAT'S THE MATTER WITH YOU?!
YOU KEEP YOUR MOUTH SHUT!!
DADDY HAS VERY IMPORTANT WORK TO DO TODAY...
...SO LET'S BE QUIET FOR HIM, OKAY?
OKAY.
DAD, I'M SORRY ABOUT BEFORE!
I PROMISE TO BE QUIET FROM NOW ON!
REALLY?
GOOD BOY!
QUIT BUGGING ME!
WHAT?! I WAS DANCING *QUIETLY!*

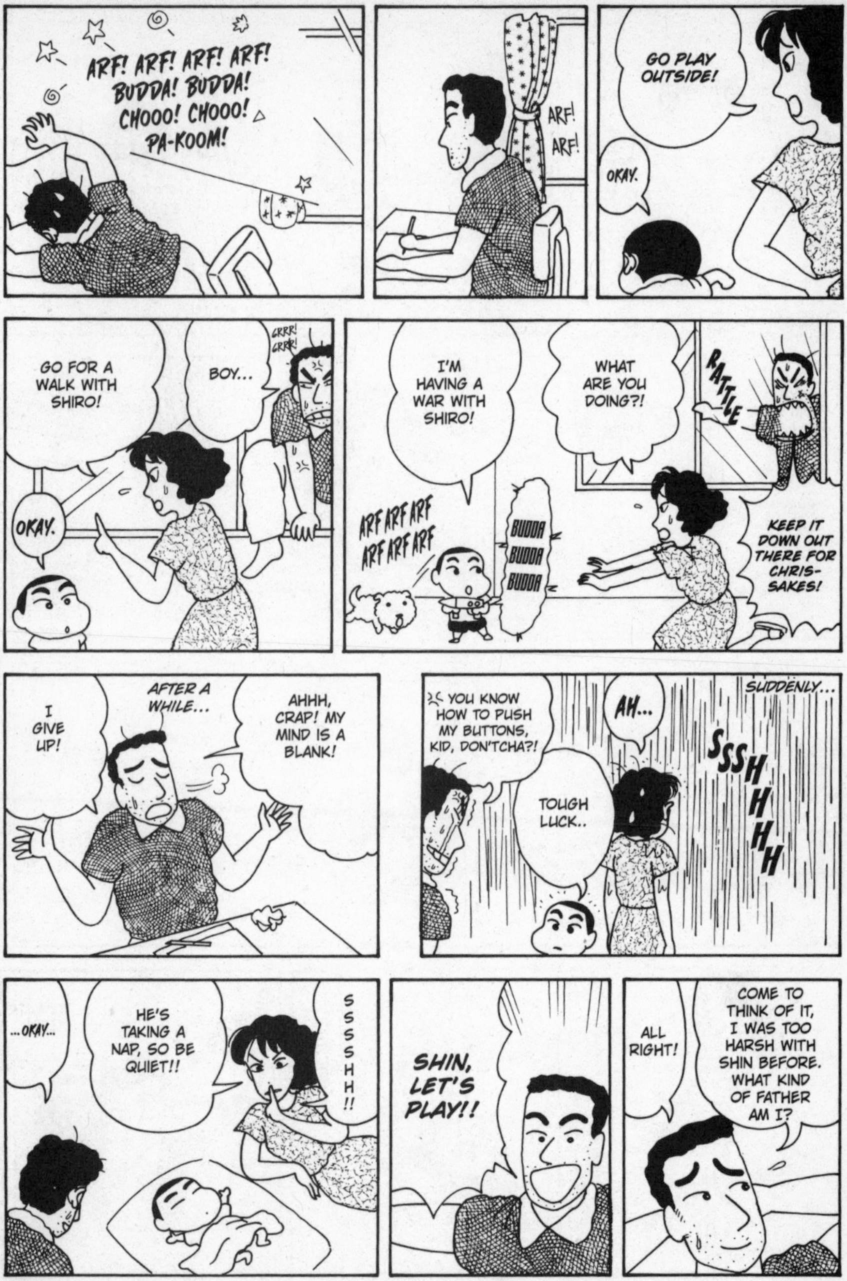
GO PLAY OUTSIDE!
OKAY.
ARF! ARF!
ARF! ARF! ARF! ARF! BUDDA! BUDDA! CHOOO! CHOOO! PA-KOOM!
RATTLE
WHAT ARE YOU DOING?!
KEEP IT DOWN OUT THERE FOR CHRIS-SAKES!
I'M HAVING A WAR WITH SHIRO!
BUDDA BUDDA BUDDA
ARF ARF ARF ARF ARF ARF
GRRR! GRRR!
BOY...
GO FOR A WALK WITH SHIRO!
OKAY.
SUDDENLY...
SSSHHHHH
AH...
TOUGH LUCK..
YOU KNOW HOW TO PUSH MY BUTTONS, KID, DON'TCHA?!
AFTER A WHILE...
AHHH, CRAP! MY MIND IS A BLANK!
I GIVE UP!
COME TO THINK OF IT, I WAS TOO HARSH WITH SHIN BEFORE. WHAT KIND OF FATHER AM I?
ALL RIGHT!
SHIN, LET'S PLAY!!
SSSSHH!!
HE'S TAKING A NAP, SO BE QUIET!!
...OKAY...

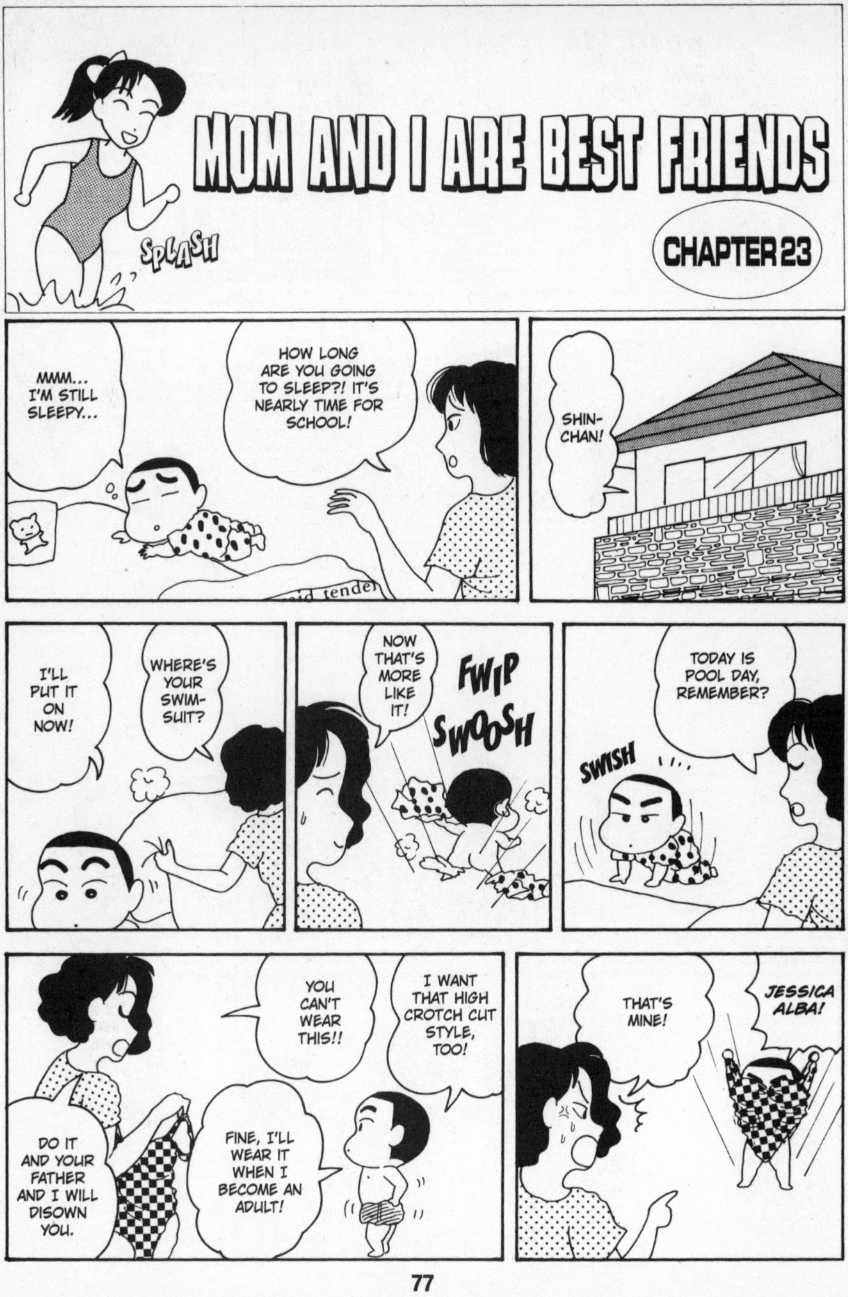
MOM AND I ARE BEST FRIENDS
CHAPTER 23
SPLASH
SHIN-CHAN!
HOW LONG ARE YOU GOING TO SLEEP?! IT'S NEARLY TIME FOR SCHOOL!
MMM... I'M STILL SLEEPY...
TODAY IS POOL DAY, REMEMBER?
SWISH
FWIP
SWOOSH
NOW THAT'S MORE LIKE IT!
WHERE'S YOUR SWIM-SUIT?
I'LL PUT IT ON NOW!
JESSICA ALBA!
THAT'S MINE!
I WANT THAT HIGH CROTCH CUT STYLE, TOO!
YOU CAN'T WEAR THIS!!
FINE, I'LL WEAR IT WHEN I BECOME AN ADULT!
DO IT AND YOUR FATHER AND I WILL DISOWN YOU.

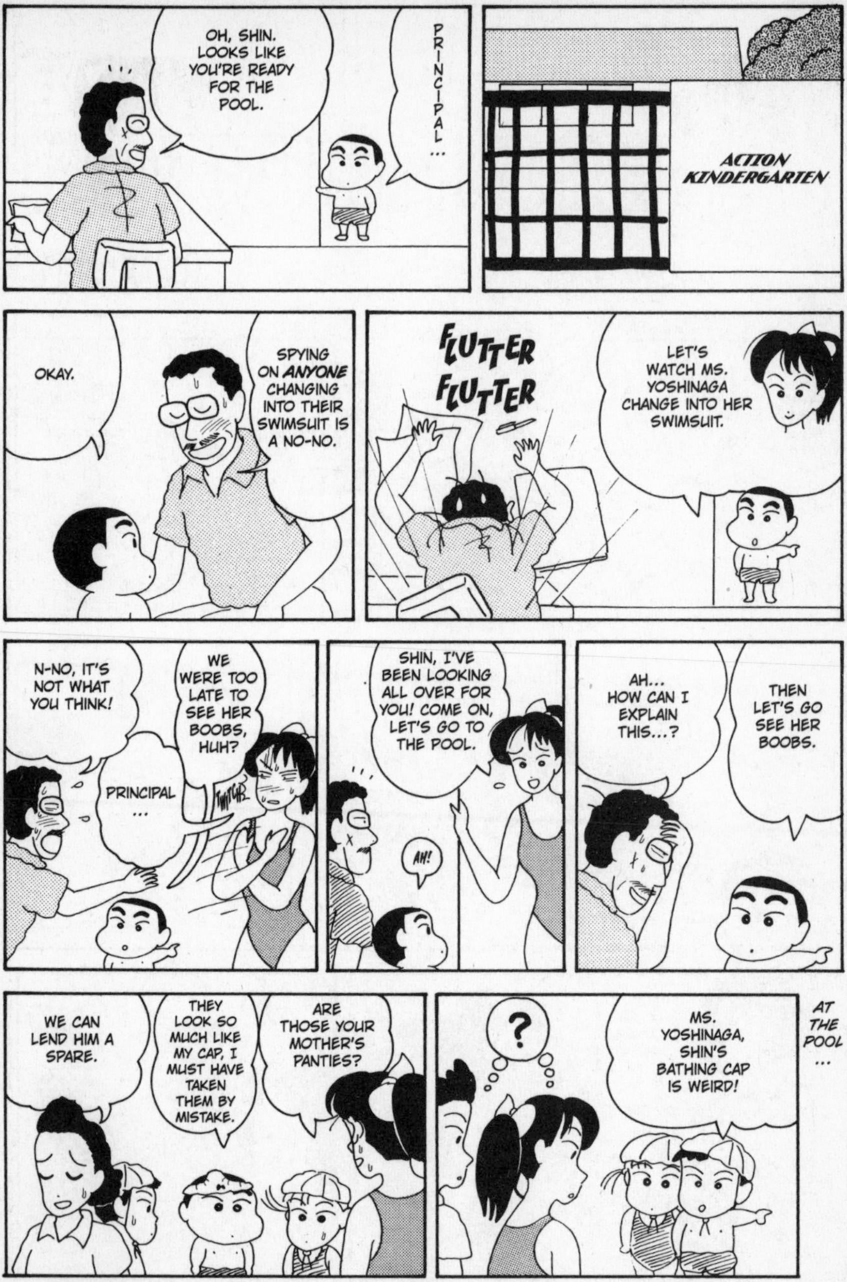
ACTION KINDERGARTEN
PRINCIPAL...
OH, SHIN. LOOKS LIKE YOU'RE READY FOR THE POOL.
LET'S WATCH MS. YOSHINAGA CHANGE INTO HER SWIMSUIT.
FLUTTER FLUTTER
SPYING ON ANYONE CHANGING INTO THEIR SWIMSUIT IS A NO-NO.
OKAY.
THEN LET'S GO SEE HER BOOBS.
AH... HOW CAN I EXPLAIN THIS...?
SHIN, I'VE BEEN LOOKING ALL OVER FOR YOU! COME ON, LET'S GO TO THE POOL.
AH!
WE WERE TOO LATE TO SEE HER BOOBS, HUH?
N-NO, IT'S NOT WHAT YOU THINK!
PRINCIPAL...
AT THE POOL...
MS. YOSHINAGA, SHIN'S BATHING CAP IS WEIRD!
?
ARE THOSE YOUR MOTHER'S PANTIES?
THEY LOOK SO MUCH LIKE MY CAP, I MUST HAVE TAKEN THEM BY MISTAKE.
WE CAN LEND HIM A SPARE.

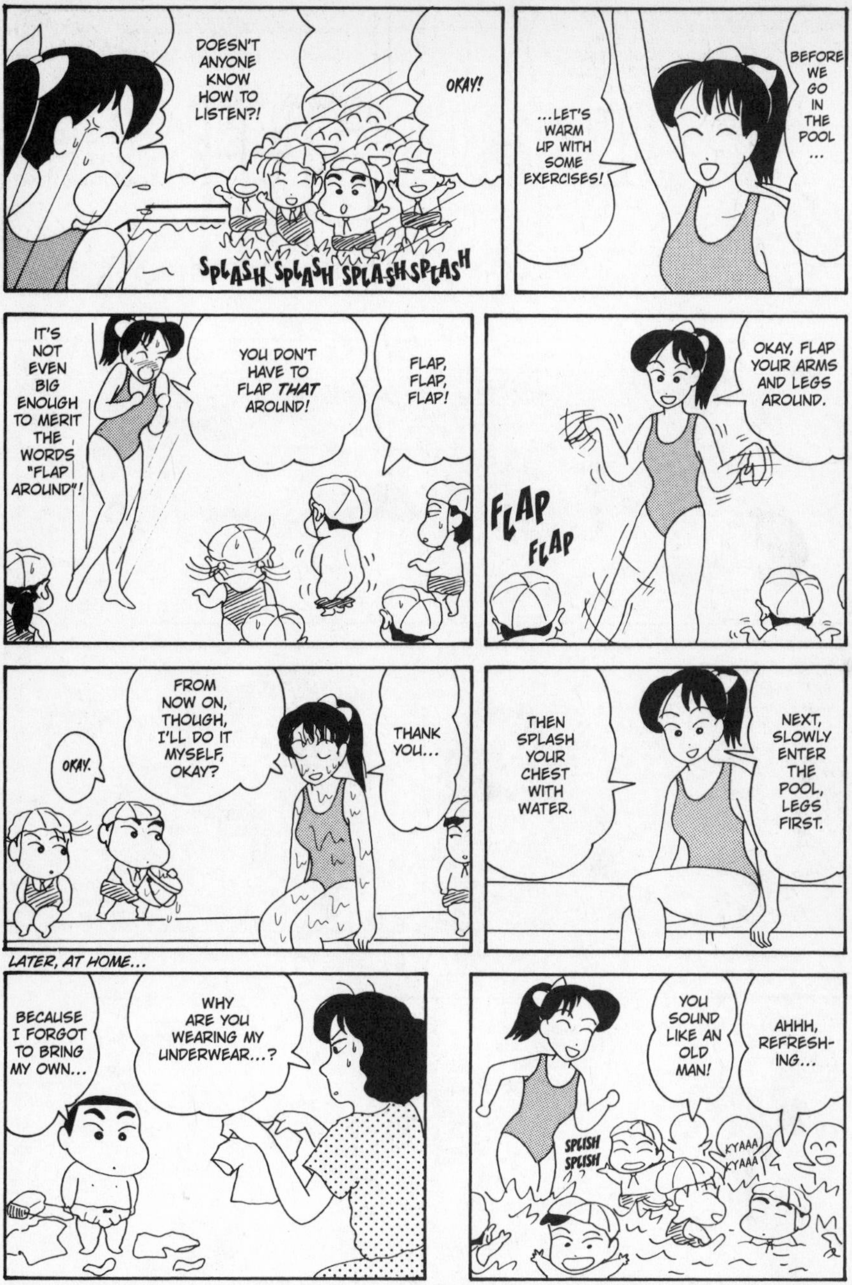
BEFORE WE GO IN THE POOL...
...LET'S WARM UP WITH SOME EXERCISES!
OKAY!
DOESN'T ANYONE KNOW HOW TO LISTEN?!
SPLASH SPLASH SPLASH SPLASH
OKAY, FLAP YOUR ARMS AND LEGS AROUND.
FLAP FLAP
FLAP, FLAP, FLAP!
YOU DON'T HAVE TO FLAP *THAT* AROUND!
IT'S NOT EVEN BIG ENOUGH TO MERIT THE WORDS "FLAP AROUND"!
NEXT, SLOWLY ENTER THE POOL, LEGS FIRST.
THEN SPLASH YOUR CHEST WITH WATER.
THANK YOU...
FROM NOW ON, THOUGH, I'LL DO IT MYSELF, OKAY?
OKAY.
AHHH, REFRESHING...
YOU SOUND LIKE AN OLD MAN!
KYAAA KYAAA
SPLISH SPLISH
LATER, AT HOME...
WHY ARE YOU WEARING MY UNDERWEAR...?
BECAUSE I FORGOT TO BRING MY OWN...

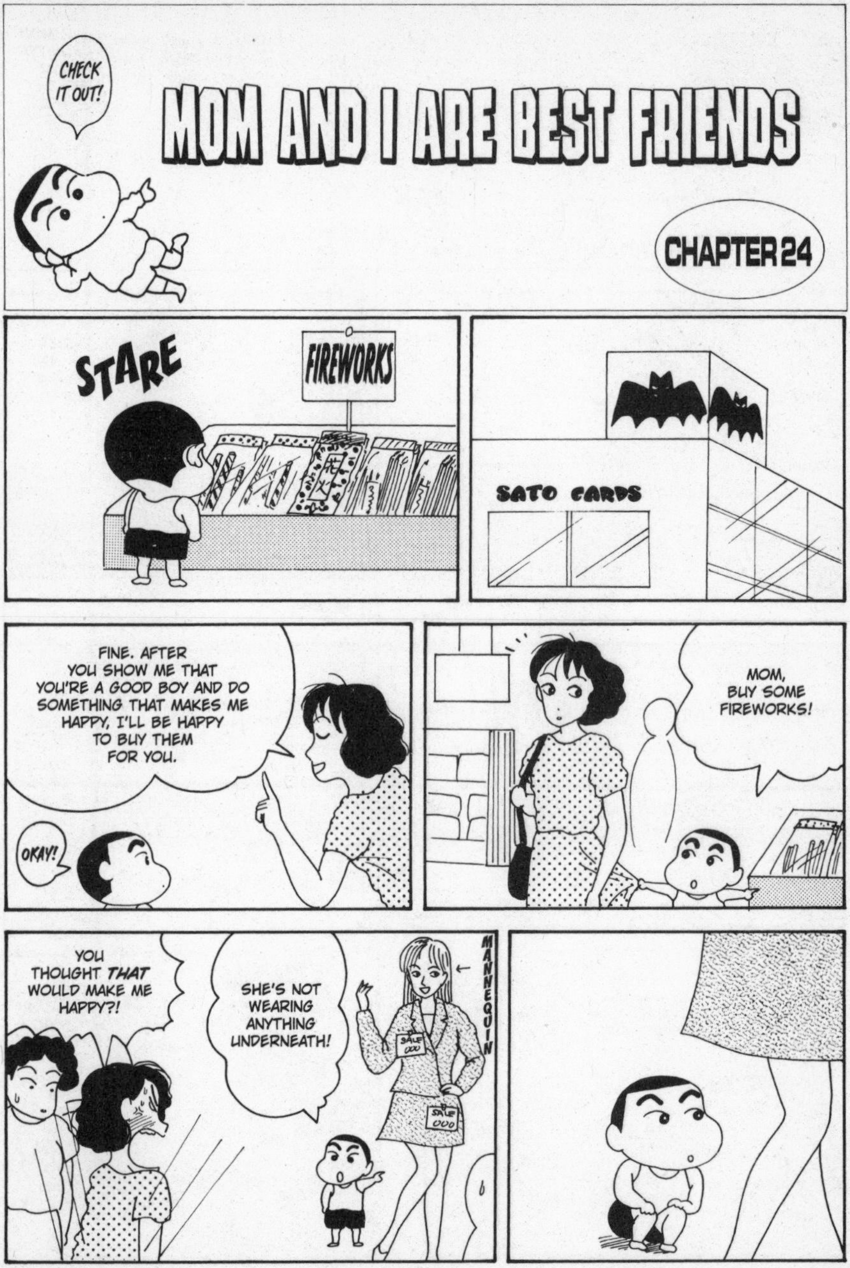
MOM AND I ARE BEST FRIENDS
CHECK IT OUT!
CHAPTER 24
SATO CARDS
FIREWORKS
STARE
MOM, BUY SOME FIREWORKS!
FINE. AFTER YOU SHOW ME THAT YOU'RE A GOOD BOY AND DO SOMETHING THAT MAKES ME HAPPY, I'LL BE HAPPY TO BUY THEM FOR YOU.
OKAY!
MANNEQUIN
SALE OOO
SHE'S NOT WEARING ANYTHING UNDERNEATH!
YOU THOUGHT *THAT* WOULD MAKE ME HAPPY?!

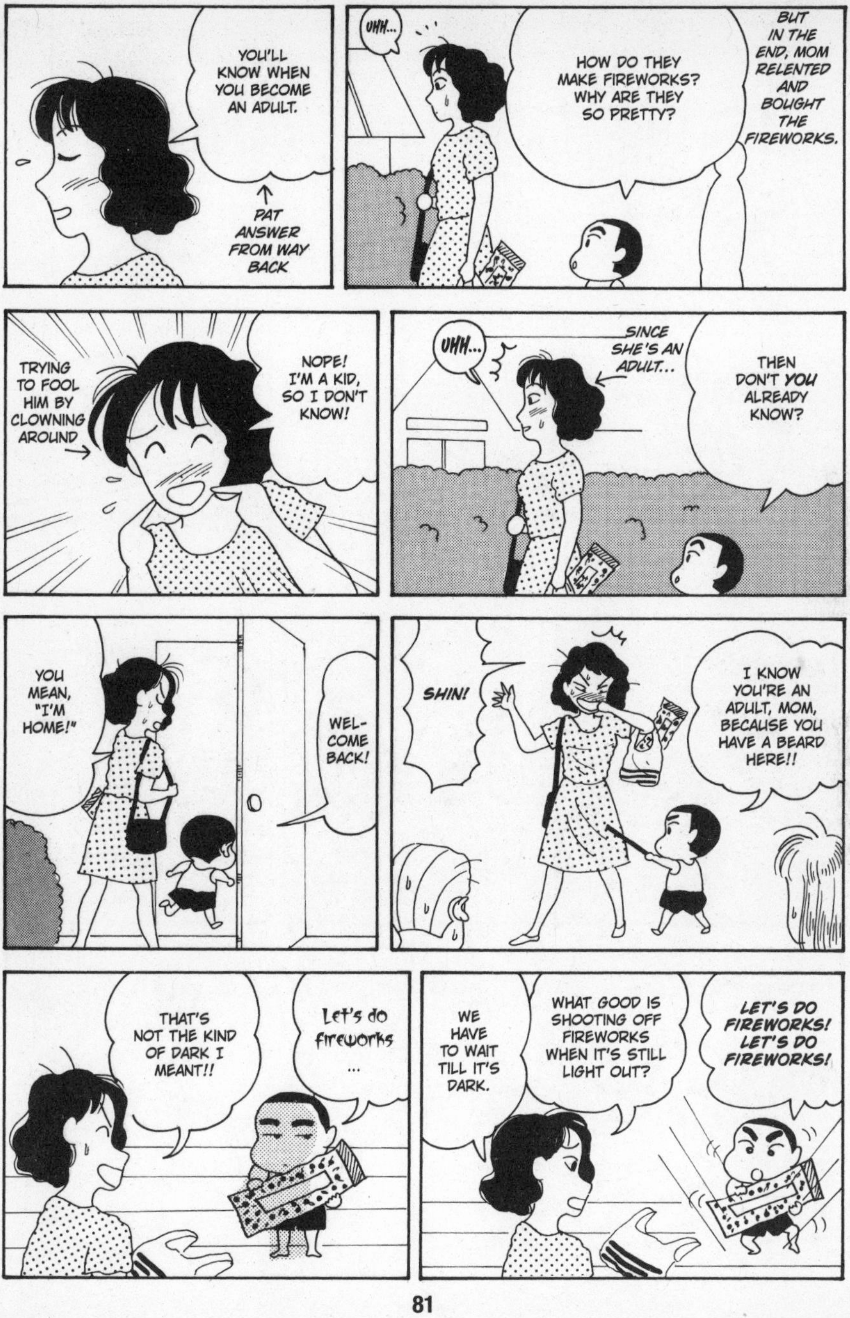
BUT IN THE END, MOM RELENTED AND BOUGHT THE FIREWORKS.
HOW DO THEY MAKE FIREWORKS? WHY ARE THEY SO PRETTY?
UHH...
YOU'LL KNOW WHEN YOU BECOME AN ADULT.
PAT ANSWER FROM WAY BACK
THEN DON'T *YOU* ALREADY KNOW?
SINCE SHE'S AN ADULT...
UHH...
NOPE! I'M A KID, SO I DON'T KNOW!
TRYING TO FOOL HIM BY CLOWNING AROUND
I KNOW YOU'RE AN ADULT, MOM, BECAUSE YOU HAVE A BEARD HERE!!
SHIN!
WEL-COME BACK!
YOU MEAN, "I'M HOME!"
LET'S DO FIREWORKS! LET'S DO FIREWORKS!
WHAT GOOD IS SHOOTING OFF FIREWORKS WHEN IT'S STILL LIGHT OUT?
WE HAVE TO WAIT TILL IT'S DARK.
Let's do fireworks ...
THAT'S NOT THE KIND OF DARK I MEANT!!

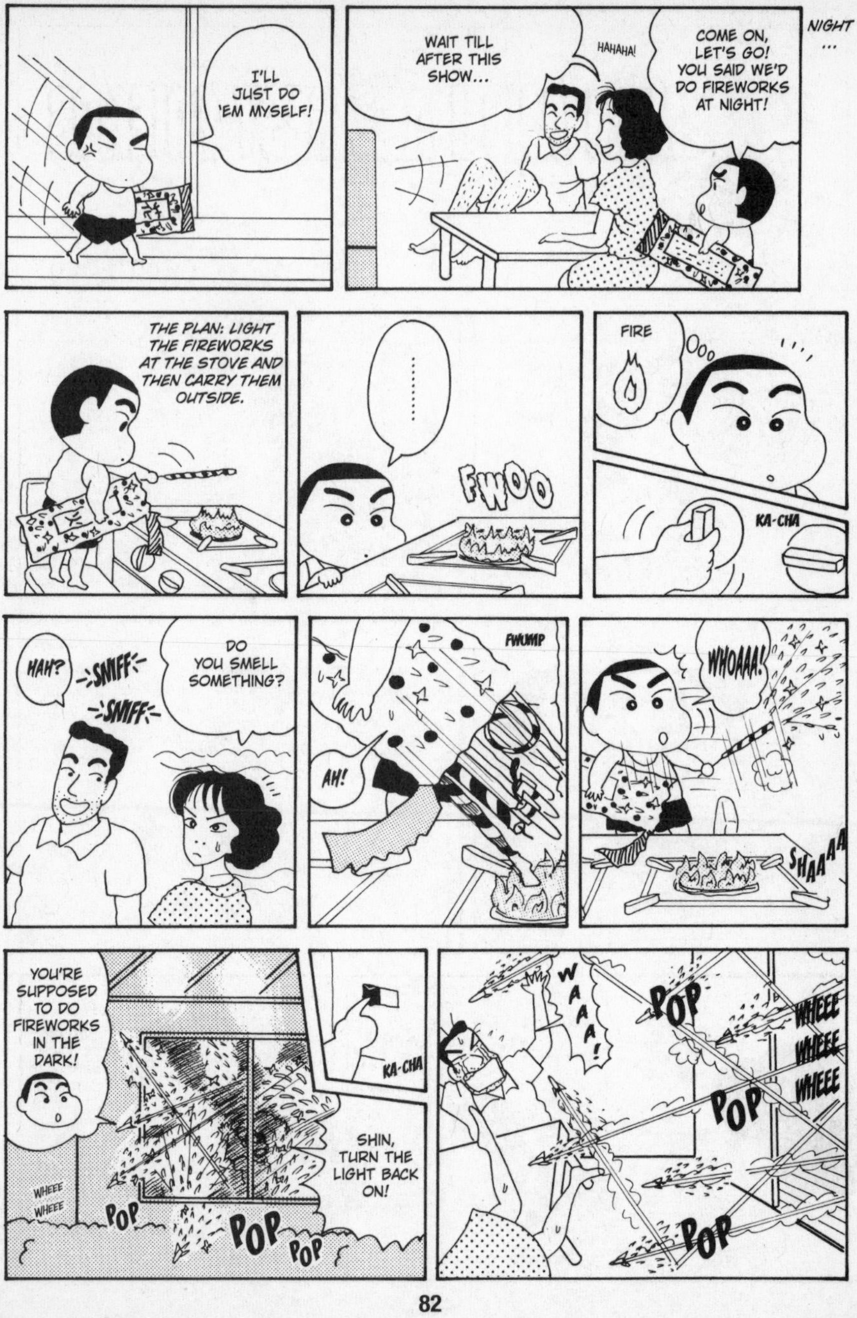
NIGHT...
COME ON, LET'S GO! YOU SAID WE'D DO FIREWORKS AT NIGHT!
HAHAHA!
WAIT TILL AFTER THIS SHOW...
I'LL JUST DO 'EM MYSELF!
FIRE
Ooo
KA-CHA
......
FWOO
THE PLAN: LIGHT THE FIREWORKS AT THE STOVE AND THEN CARRY THEM OUTSIDE.
WHOAAA!
SHAAAA
FWUMP
AH!
DO YOU SMELL SOMETHING?
SNIFF
SNIFF
HAH?
WAAAA!
POP
WHEEE
WHEEE
WHEEE
POP
POP
KA-CHA
SHIN, TURN THE LIGHT BACK ON!
YOU'RE SUPPOSED TO DO FIREWORKS IN THE DARK!
WHEEE
WHEEE
POP
POP
POP

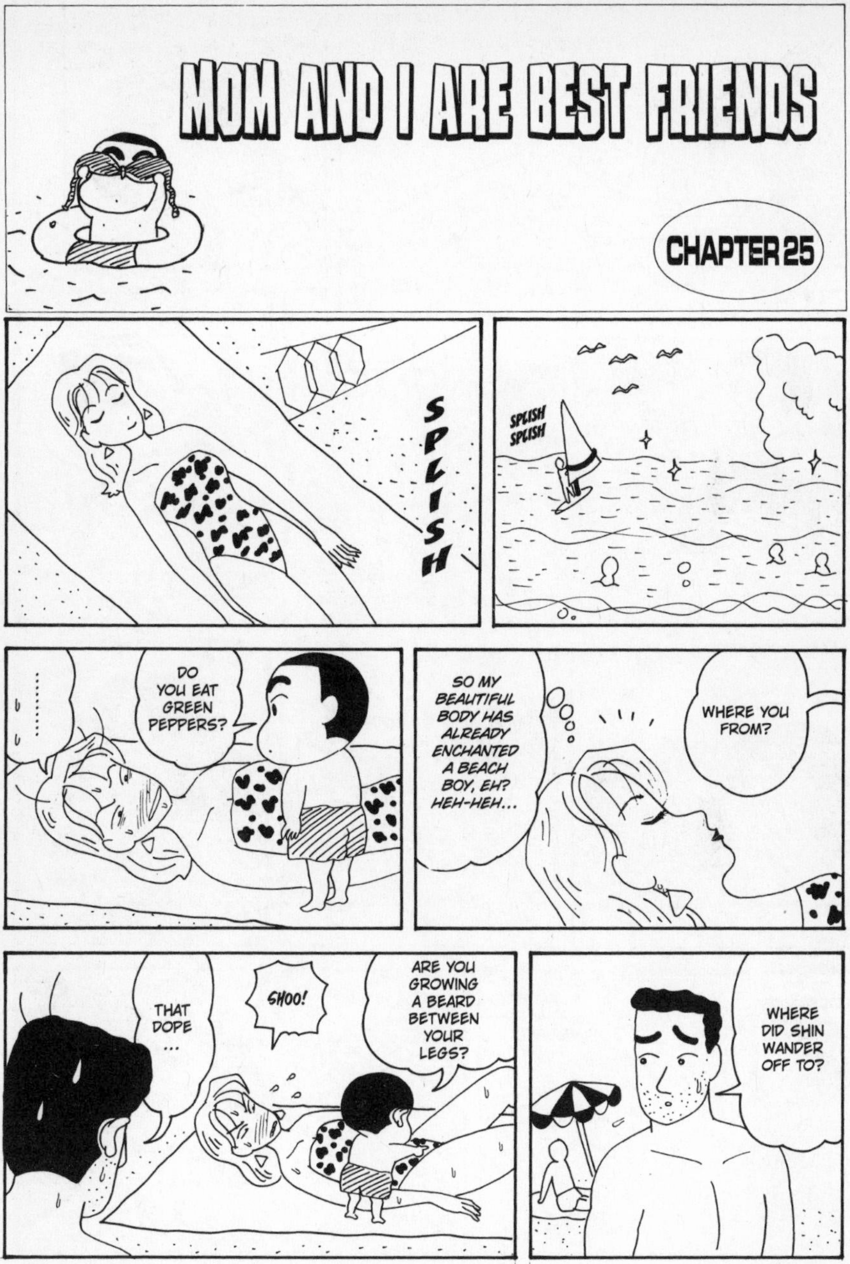
MOM AND I ARE BEST FRIENDS
CHAPTER 25
SPLISH SPLISH
SPLISH
WHERE YOU FROM?
SO MY BEAUTIFUL BODY HAS ALREADY ENCHANTED A BEACH BOY, EH? HEH-HEH...
DO YOU EAT GREEN PEPPERS?
......
WHERE DID SHIN WANDER OFF TO?
ARE YOU GROWING A BEARD BETWEEN YOUR LEGS?
SHOO!
THAT DOPE ...

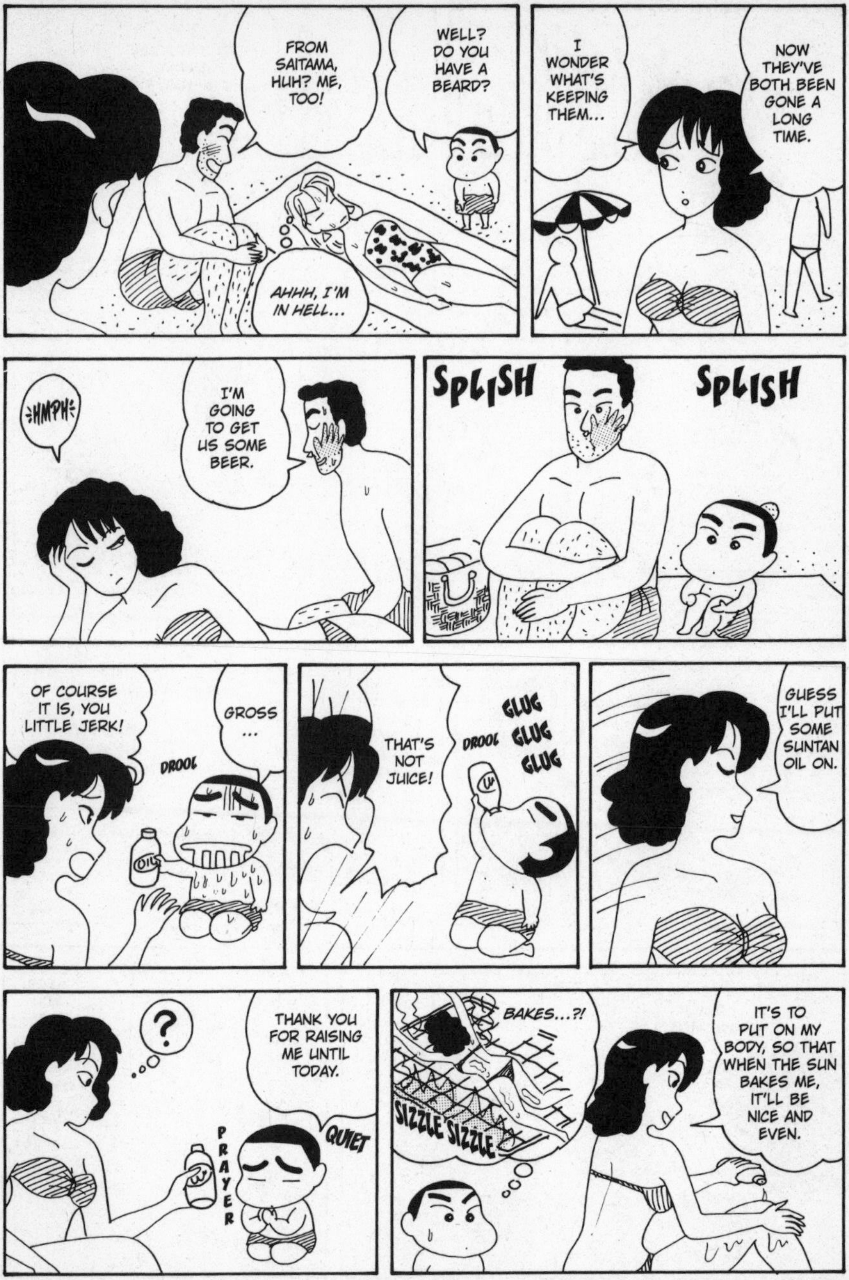
NOW THEY'VE BOTH BEEN GONE A LONG TIME.
I WONDER WHAT'S KEEPING THEM...
WELL? DO YOU HAVE A BEARD?
FROM SAITAMA, HUH? ME, TOO!
AHHH, I'M IN HELL...
SPLISH
SPLISH
I'M GOING TO GET US SOME BEER.
HMPH
GUESS I'LL PUT SOME SUNTAN OIL ON.
GLUG GLUG GLUG
DROOL
THAT'S NOT JUICE!
GROSS...
DROOL
OF COURSE IT IS, YOU LITTLE JERK!
IT'S TO PUT ON MY BODY, SO THAT WHEN THE SUN BAKES ME, IT'LL BE NICE AND EVEN.
BAKES...?!
SIZZLE SIZZLE
THANK YOU FOR RAISING ME UNTIL TODAY.
QUIET
PRAYER
?

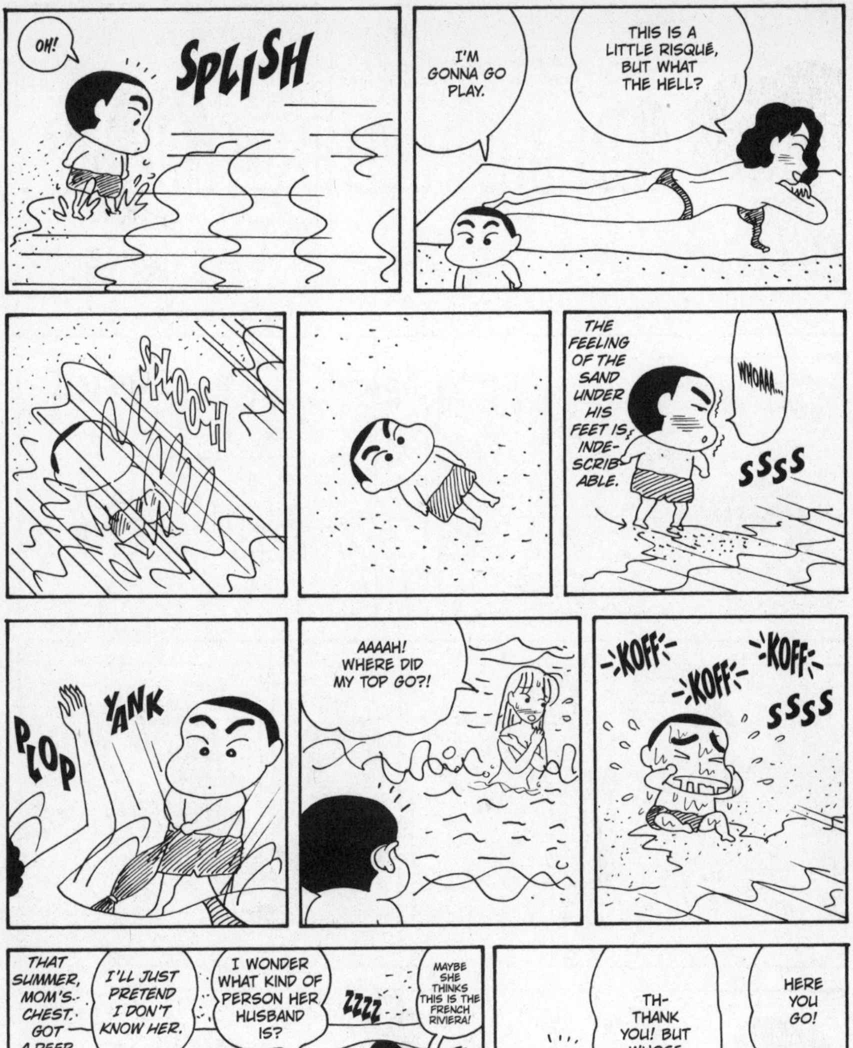
THIS IS A LITTLE RISQUÉ, BUT WHAT THE HELL?
I'M GONNA GO PLAY.
OH!
SPLISH
WHOAAA...
THE FEELING OF THE SAND UNDER HIS FEET IS INDESCRIBABLE.
SSSS
SPLOOSH
-KOFF- -KOFF- -KOFF-
SSSS
AAAAH! WHERE DID MY TOP GO?!
YANK
PLOP
HERE YOU GO!
TH-THANK YOU! BUT WHOSE IS IT...?
MAYBE SHE THINKS THIS IS THE FRENCH RIVIERA!
ZZZZ
I WONDER WHAT KIND OF PERSON HER HUSBAND IS?
I'LL JUST PRETEND I DON'T KNOW HER.
THAT SUMMER, MOM'S CHEST GOT A DEEP, ALL-OVER TAN.
BUZZ
BUZZ

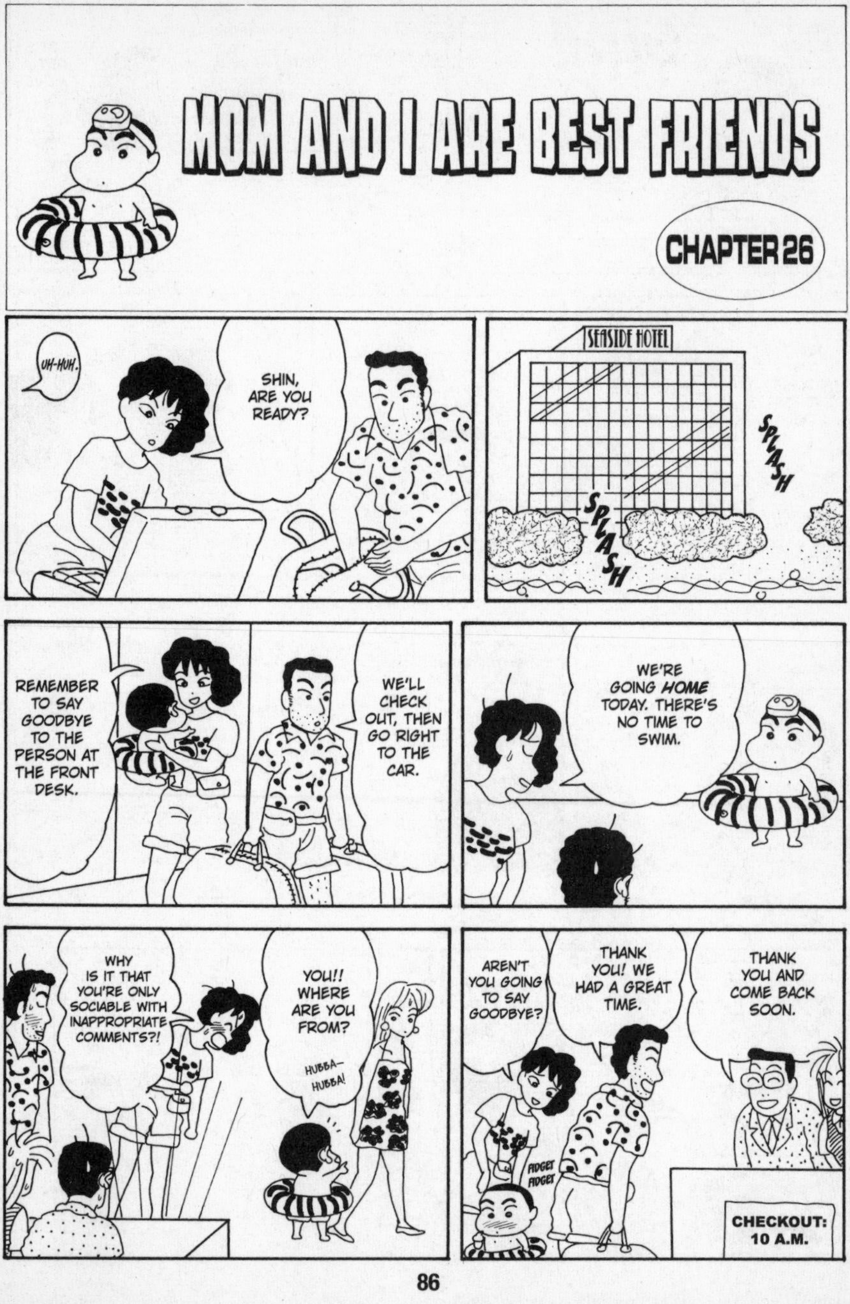
MOM AND I ARE BEST FRIENDS
CHAPTER 26
SEASIDE HOTEL
SPLASH
SPLASH
SPLASH
SHIN, ARE YOU READY?
UH-HUH.
WE'RE GOING HOME TODAY. THERE'S NO TIME TO SWIM.
WE'LL CHECK OUT, THEN GO RIGHT TO THE CAR.
REMEMBER TO SAY GOODBYE TO THE PERSON AT THE FRONT DESK.
THANK YOU AND COME BACK SOON.
THANK YOU! WE HAD A GREAT TIME.
AREN'T YOU GOING TO SAY GOODBYE?
FIDGET FIDGET
CHECKOUT: 10 A.M.
YOU!! WHERE ARE YOU FROM?
HUBBA-HUBBA!
WHY IS IT THAT YOU'RE ONLY SOCIABLE WITH INAPPROPRIATE COMMENTS?!

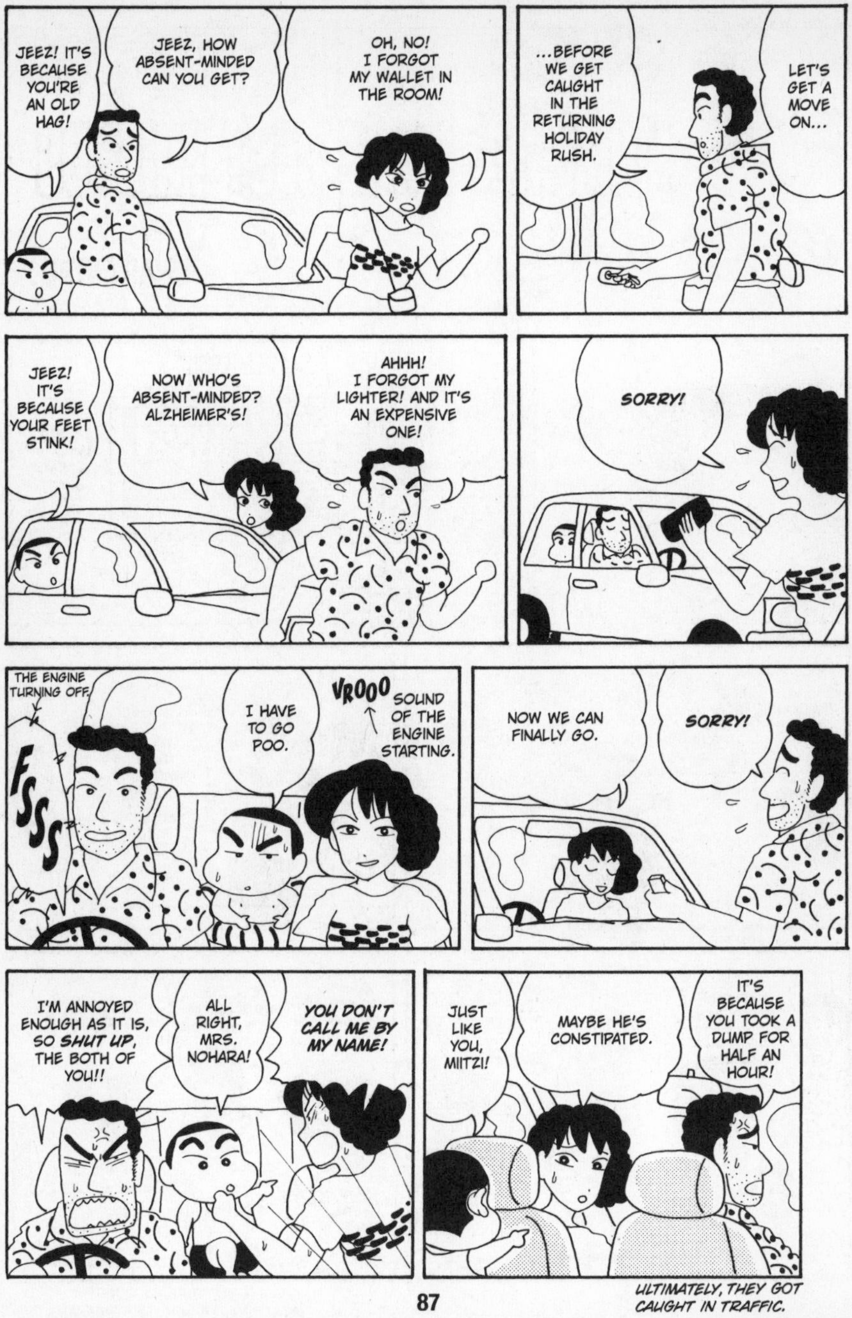
LET'S GET A MOVE ON...
...BEFORE WE GET CAUGHT IN THE RETURNING HOLIDAY RUSH.
OH, NO! I FORGOT MY WALLET IN THE ROOM!
JEEZ, HOW ABSENT-MINDED CAN YOU GET?
JEEZ! IT'S BECAUSE YOU'RE AN OLD HAG!
SORRY!
AHHH! I FORGOT MY LIGHTER! AND IT'S AN EXPENSIVE ONE!
NOW WHO'S ABSENT-MINDED? ALZHEIMER'S!
JEEZ! IT'S BECAUSE YOUR FEET STINK!
SORRY!
NOW WE CAN FINALLY GO.
VROOO
SOUND OF THE ENGINE STARTING.
I HAVE TO GO POO.
THE ENGINE TURNING OFF.
FSSS
IT'S BECAUSE YOU TOOK A DUMP FOR HALF AN HOUR!
MAYBE HE'S CONSTIPATED.
JUST LIKE YOU, MIITZI!
YOU DON'T CALL ME BY MY NAME!
ALL RIGHT, MRS. NOHARA!
I'M ANNOYED ENOUGH AS IT IS, SO SHUT UP, THE BOTH OF YOU!!
ULTIMATELY, THEY GOT CAUGHT IN TRAFFIC.

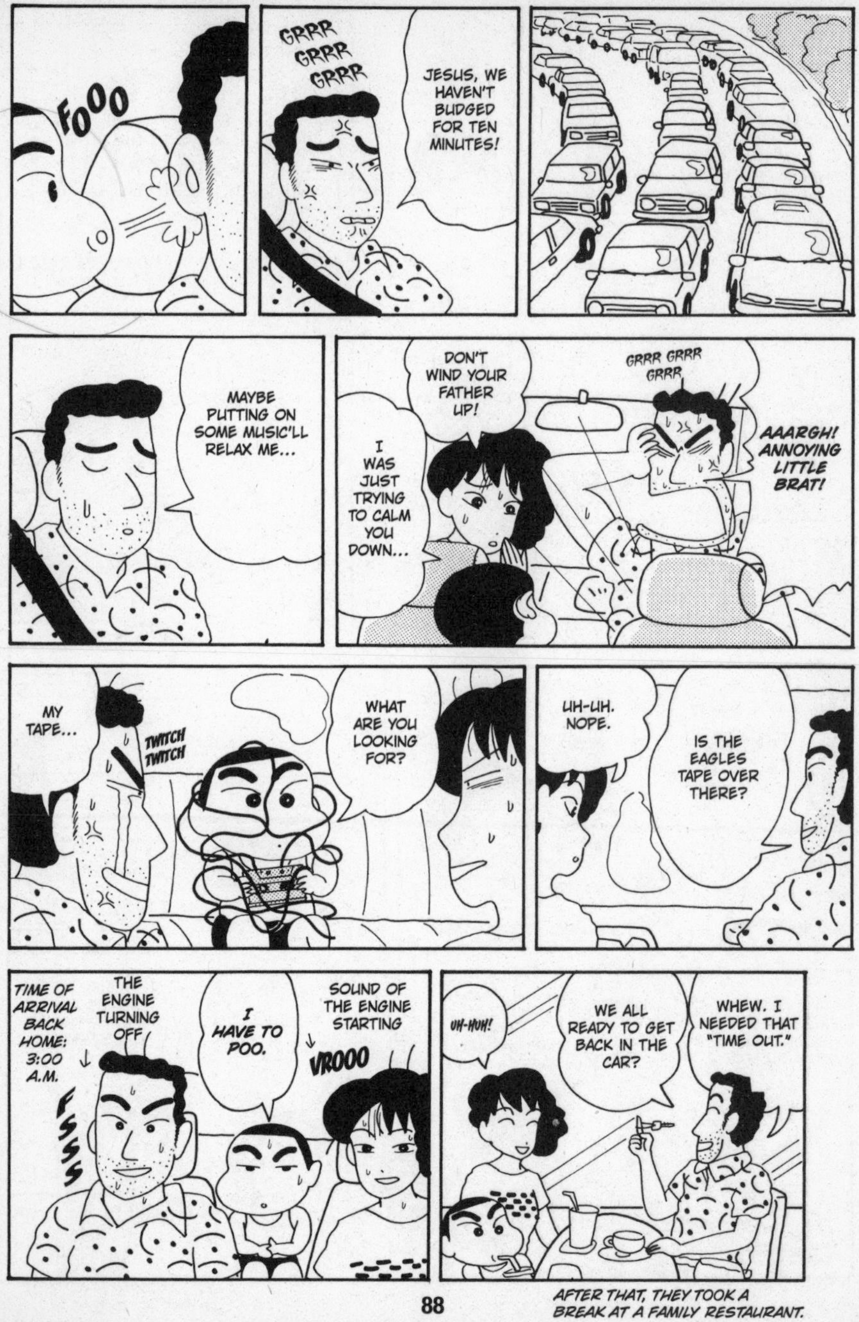
JESUS, WE HAVEN'T BUDGED FOR TEN MINUTES!
GRRR GRRR GRRR
FOOO
GRRR GRRR GRRR
AAARGH! ANNOYING LITTLE BRAT!
DON'T WIND YOUR FATHER UP!
I WAS JUST TRYING TO CALM YOU DOWN...
MAYBE PUTTING ON SOME MUSIC'LL RELAX ME...
IS THE EAGLES TAPE OVER THERE?
UH-UH. NOPE.
WHAT ARE YOU LOOKING FOR?
TWITCH TWITCH
MY TAPE...
WHEW. I NEEDED THAT "TIME OUT."
WE ALL READY TO GET BACK IN THE CAR?
UH-HUH!
SOUND OF THE ENGINE STARTING
VROOO
I HAVE TO POO.
THE ENGINE TURNING OFF
FSSS
TIME OF ARRIVAL BACK HOME: 3:00 A.M.

AFTER THAT, THEY TOOK A BREAK AT A FAMILY RESTAURANT.

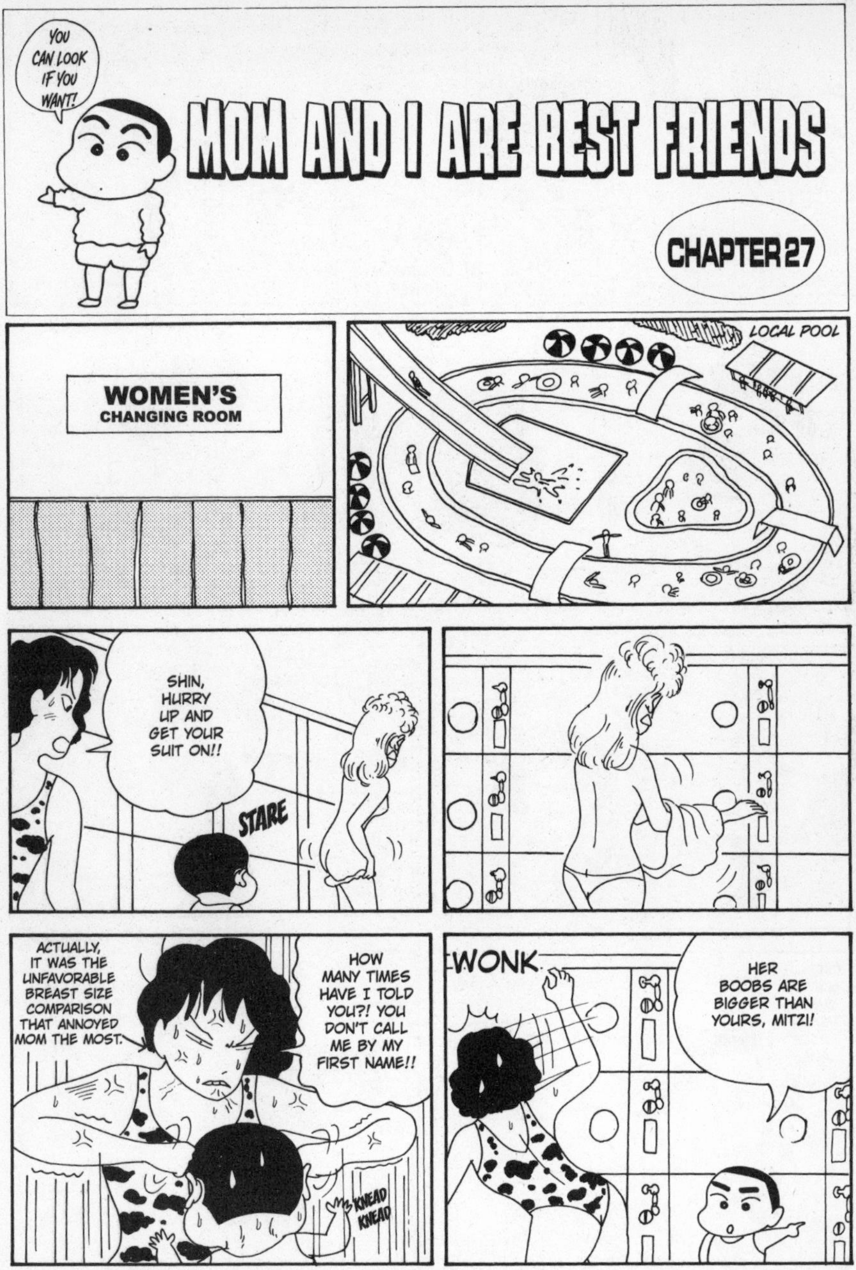
MOM AND I ARE BEST FRIENDS
CHAPTER 27
YOU CAN LOOK IF YOU WANT!
LOCAL POOL
WOMEN'S CHANGING ROOM
SHIN, HURRY UP AND GET YOUR SUIT ON!!
STARE
WONK
HER BOOBS ARE BIGGER THAN YOURS, MITZI!
HOW MANY TIMES HAVE I TOLD YOU?! YOU DON'T CALL ME BY MY FIRST NAME!!
ACTUALLY, IT WAS THE UNFAVORABLE BREAST SIZE COMPARISON THAT ANNOYED MOM THE MOST.
KNEAD KNEAD

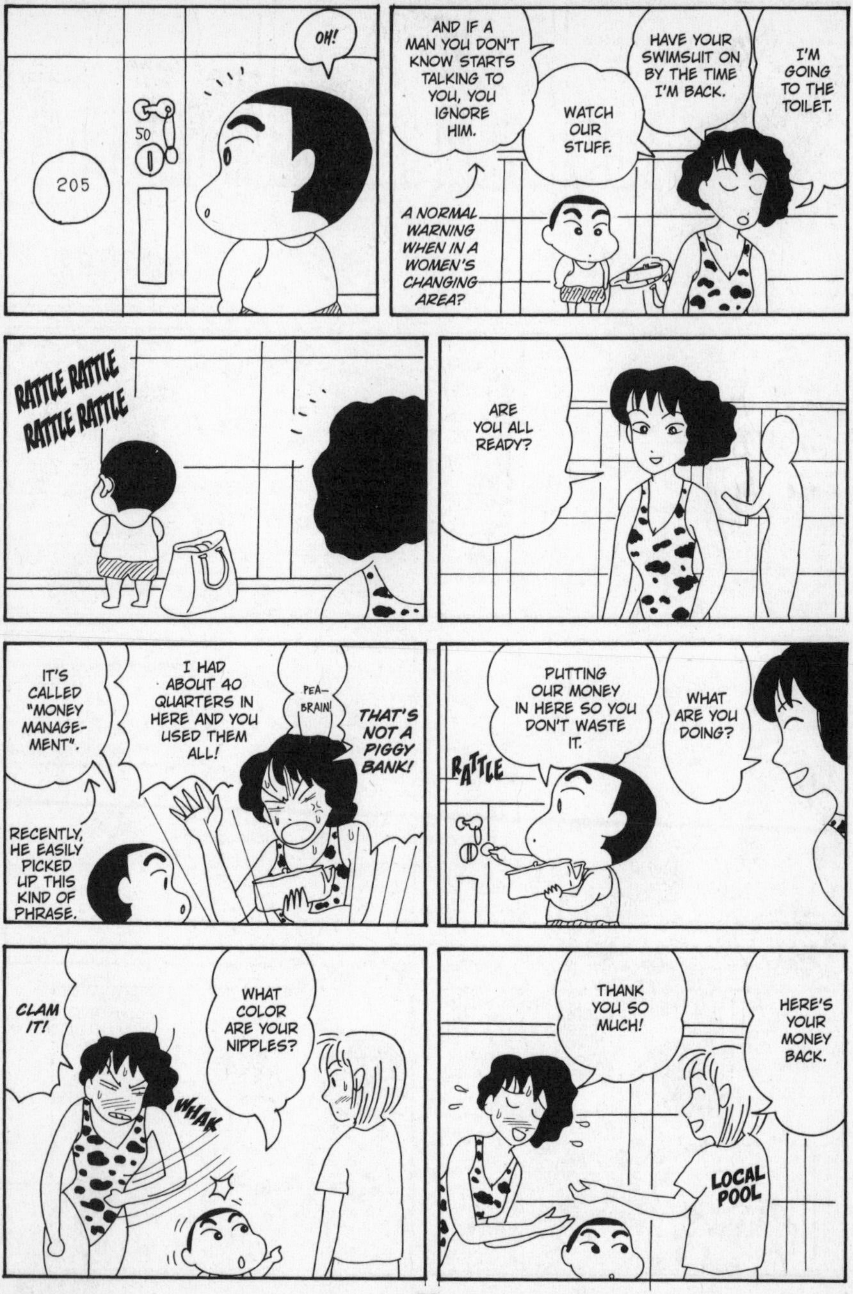
I'M GOING TO THE TOILET.
HAVE YOUR SWIMSUIT ON BY THE TIME I'M BACK.
WATCH OUR STUFF.
AND IF A MAN YOU DON'T KNOW STARTS TALKING TO YOU, YOU IGNORE HIM.
A NORMAL WARNING WHEN IN A WOMEN'S CHANGING AREA?
OH!
205
50
ARE YOU ALL READY?
RATTLE RATTLE RATTLE RATTLE
WHAT ARE YOU DOING?
PUTTING OUR MONEY IN HERE SO YOU DON'T WASTE IT.
RATTLE
THAT'S NOT A PIGGY BANK!
PEA-BRAIN!
I HAD ABOUT 40 QUARTERS IN HERE AND YOU USED THEM ALL!
IT'S CALLED "MONEY MANAGEMENT".
RECENTLY, HE EASILY PICKED UP THIS KIND OF PHRASE.
HERE'S YOUR MONEY BACK.
LOCAL POOL
THANK YOU SO MUCH!
WHAT COLOR ARE YOUR NIPPLES?
WHAK
CLAM IT!

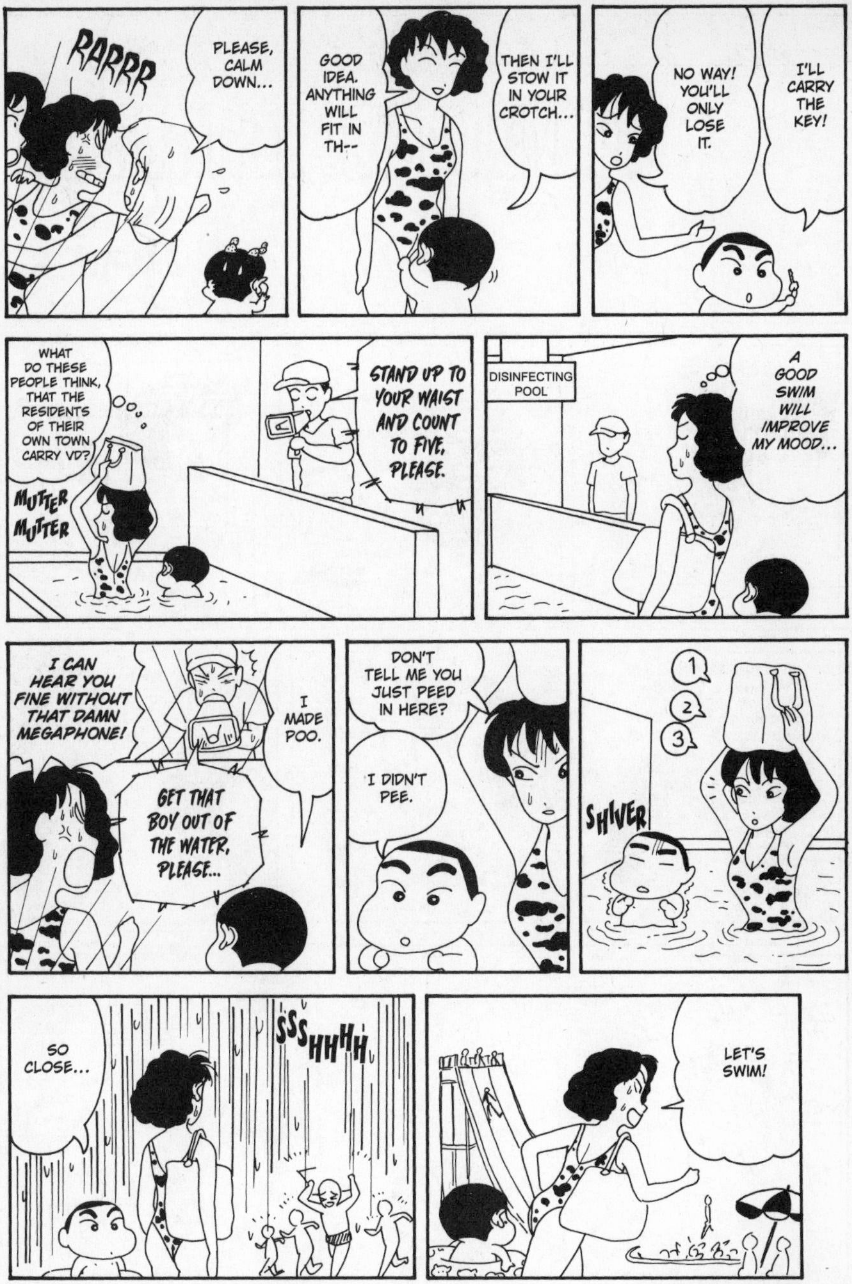

I'LL CARRY THE KEY!
NO WAY! YOU'LL ONLY LOSE IT.
THEN I'LL STOW IT IN YOUR CROTCH...
GOOD IDEA. ANYTHING WILL FIT IN TH--
PLEASE, CALM DOWN...
RARRR
A GOOD SWIM WILL IMPROVE MY MOOD...
DISINFECTING POOL
STAND UP TO YOUR WAIST AND COUNT TO FIVE, PLEASE.
WHAT DO THESE PEOPLE THINK, THAT THE RESIDENTS OF THEIR OWN TOWN CARRY VD?
MUTTER MUTTER
1
2
3
SHIVER
DON'T TELL ME YOU JUST PEED IN HERE?
I DIDN'T PEE.
I MADE POO.
GET THAT BOY OUT OF THE WATER, PLEASE...
I CAN HEAR YOU FINE WITHOUT THAT DAMN MEGAPHONE!
LET'S SWIM!
SSSHHHH
SO CLOSE...

AND AFTER THE POO WAS DISPOSED OF...

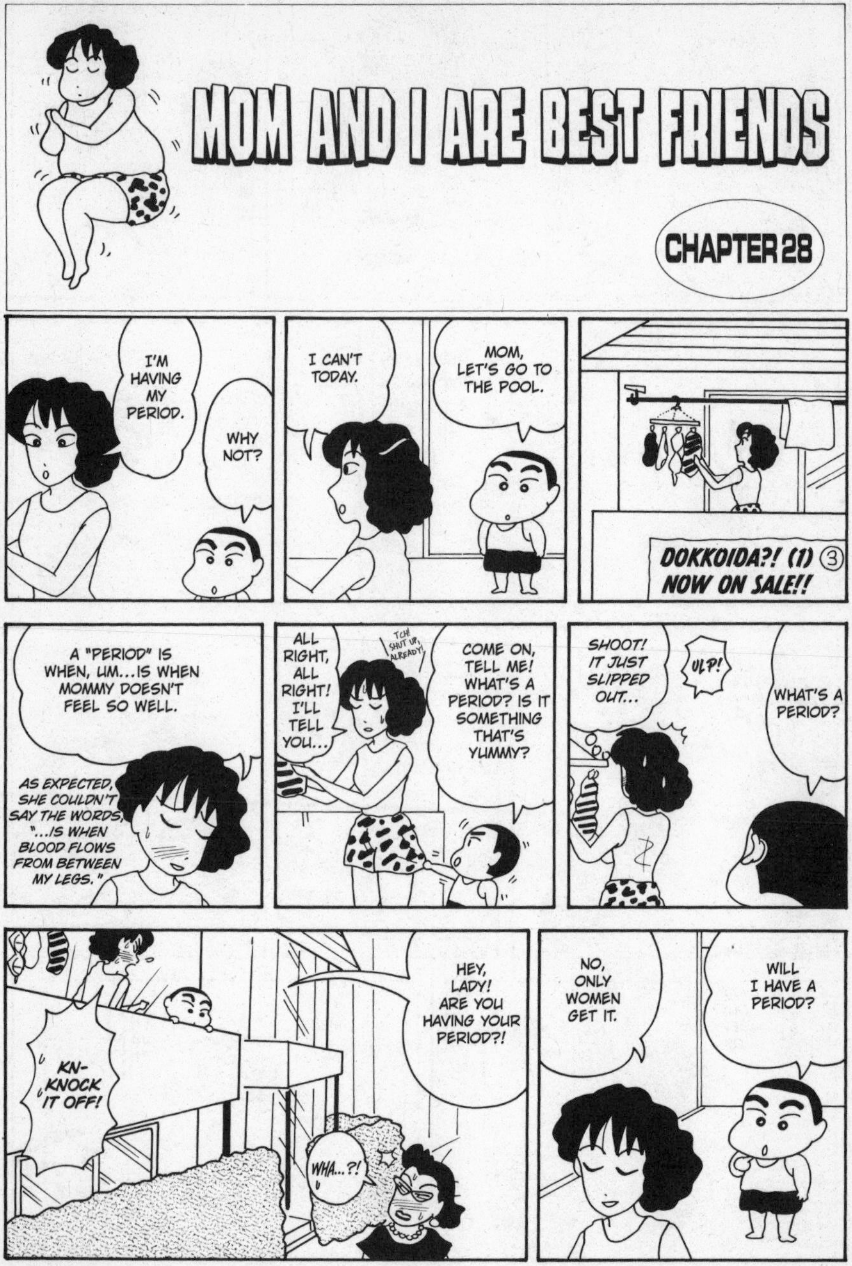
MOM AND I ARE BEST FRIENDS
CHAPTER 28
DOKKOIDA?! (1) ③ NOW ON SALE!!
MOM, LET'S GO TO THE POOL.
I CAN'T TODAY.
WHY NOT?
I'M HAVING MY PERIOD.
WHAT'S A PERIOD?
ULP!
SHOOT! IT JUST SLIPPED OUT...
COME ON, TELL ME! WHAT'S A PERIOD? IS IT SOMETHING THAT'S YUMMY?
TCH! SHUT UP, ALREADY!
ALL RIGHT, ALL RIGHT! I'LL TELL YOU...
A "PERIOD" IS WHEN, UM...IS WHEN MOMMY DOESN'T FEEL SO WELL.
AS EXPECTED, SHE COULDN'T SAY THE WORDS, "...IS WHEN BLOOD FLOWS FROM BETWEEN MY LEGS."
WILL I HAVE A PERIOD?
NO, ONLY WOMEN GET IT.
HEY, LADY! ARE YOU HAVING YOUR PERIOD?!
WHA...?!
KN-KNOCK IT OFF!

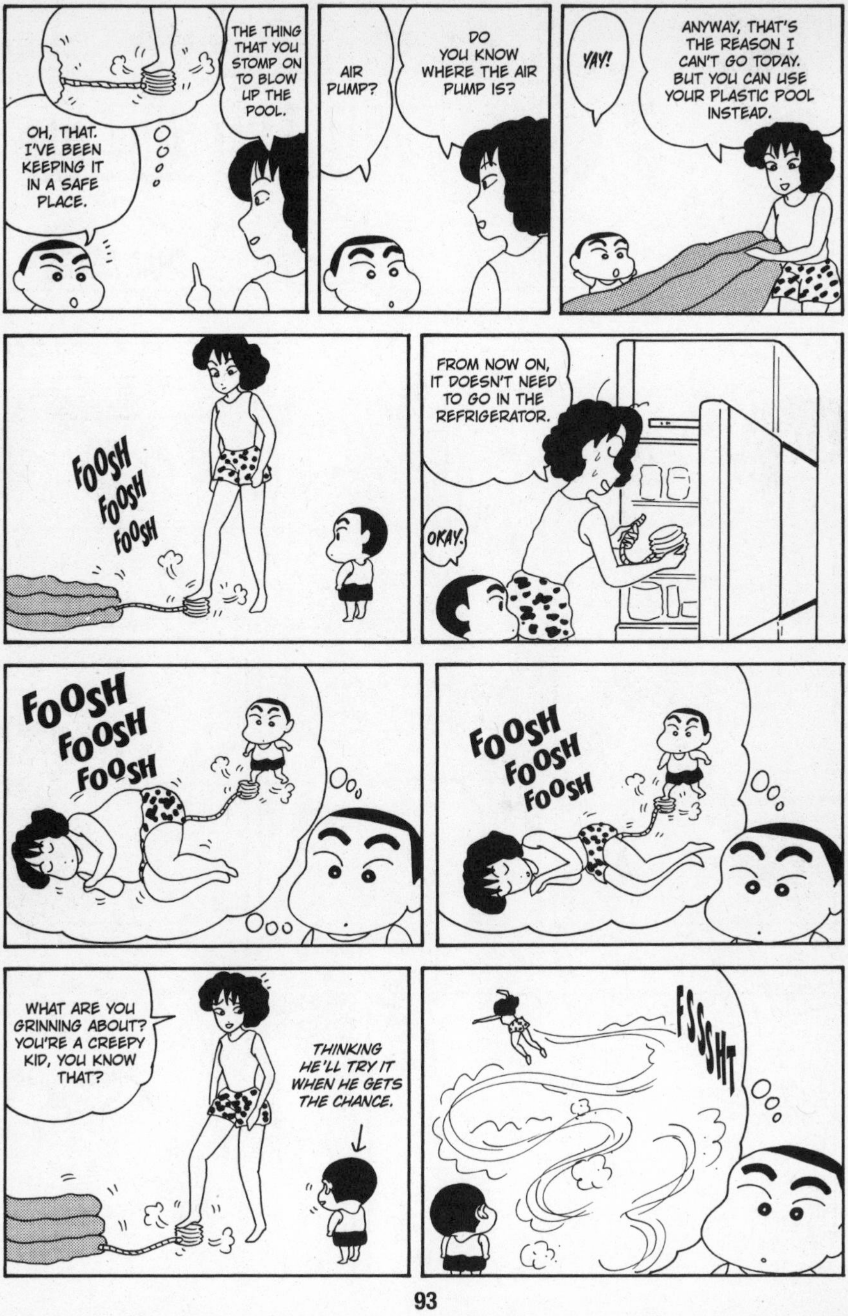
ANYWAY, THAT'S THE REASON I CAN'T GO TODAY. BUT YOU CAN USE YOUR PLASTIC POOL INSTEAD.
YAY!
DO YOU KNOW WHERE THE AIR PUMP IS?
AIR PUMP?
THE THING THAT YOU STOMP ON TO BLOW UP THE POOL.
OH, THAT. I'VE BEEN KEEPING IT IN A SAFE PLACE.
FROM NOW ON, IT DOESN'T NEED TO GO IN THE REFRIGERATOR.
OKAY.
FOOSH FOOSH FOOSH
FOOSH FOOSH FOOSH
FOOSH FOOSH FOOSH
FSSSHT
WHAT ARE YOU GRINNING ABOUT? YOU'RE A CREEPY KID, YOU KNOW THAT?
THINKING HE'LL TRY IT WHEN HE GETS THE CHANCE.

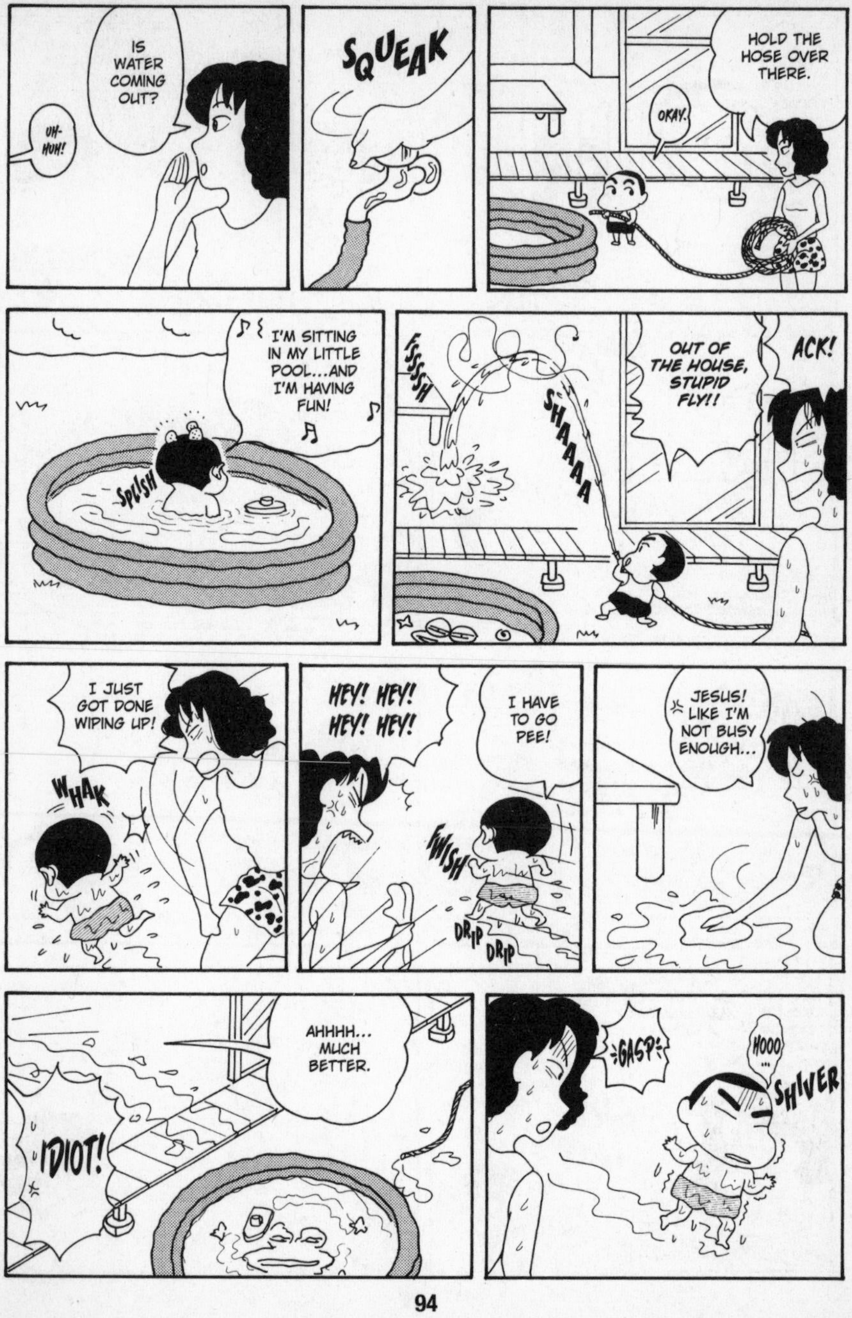
HOLD THE HOSE OVER THERE.
OKAY.
SQUEAK
IS WATER COMING OUT?
UH-HUH!
ACK!
OUT OF THE HOUSE, STUPID FLY!!
FSSSH
SHAAAAA
I'M SITTING IN MY LITTLE POOL...AND I'M HAVING FUN!
SPLISH
JESUS! LIKE I'M NOT BUSY ENOUGH...
I HAVE TO GO PEE!
HEY! HEY! HEY! HEY!
FWISH
DRIP
DRIP
I JUST GOT DONE WIPING UP!
WHAK
HOOO...
GASP
SHIVER
AHHHH... MUCH BETTER.
IDIOT!

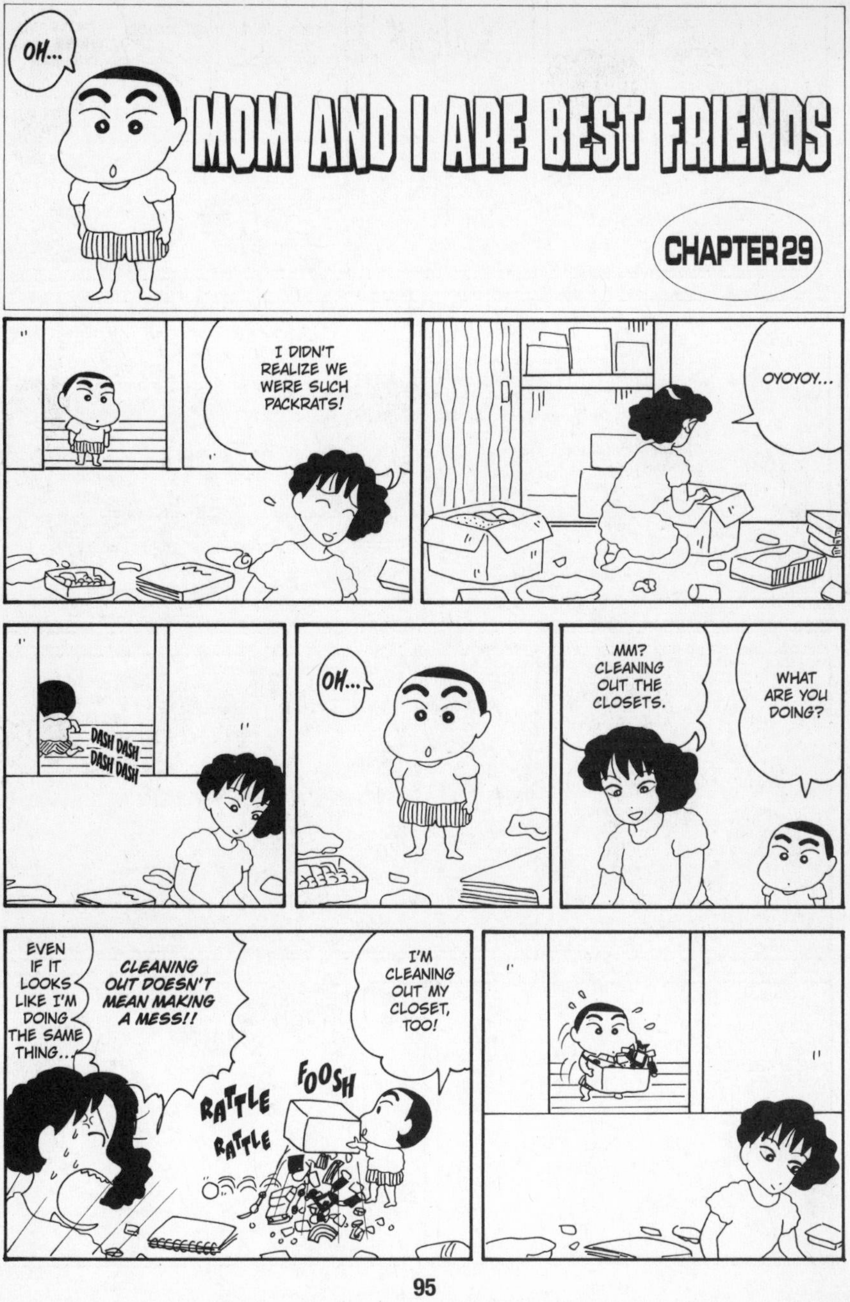
OH...
MOM AND I ARE BEST FRIENDS
CHAPTER 29
OYOYOY...
I DIDN'T REALIZE WE WERE SUCH PACKRATS!
WHAT ARE YOU DOING?
MM? CLEANING OUT THE CLOSETS.
OH...
DASH DASH
DASH DASH
I'M CLEANING OUT MY CLOSET, TOO!
FOOSH
RATTLE
RATTLE
CLEANING OUT DOESN'T MEAN MAKING A MESS!!
EVEN IF IT LOOKS LIKE I'M DOING THE SAME THING...

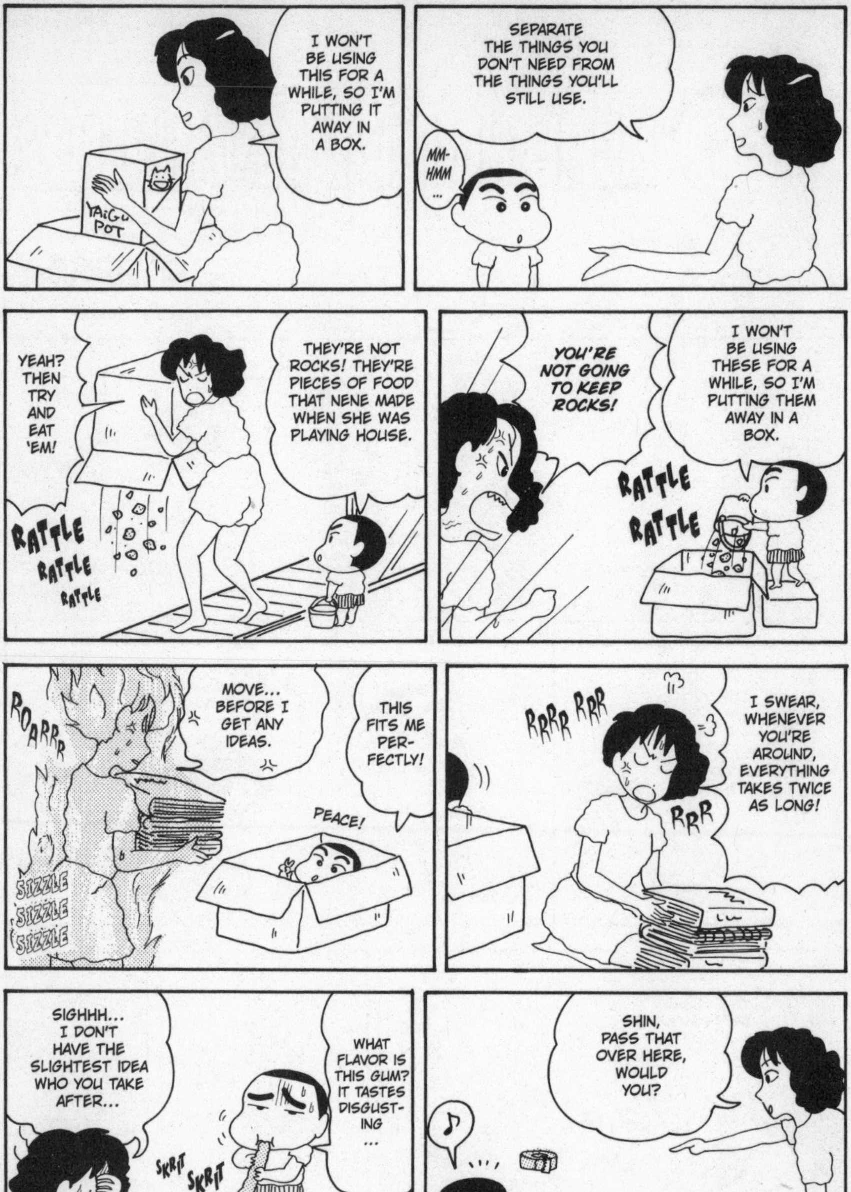
SEPARATE THE THINGS YOU DON'T NEED FROM THE THINGS YOU'LL STILL USE.
MM-HMM ...
I WON'T BE USING THIS FOR A WHILE, SO I'M PUTTING IT AWAY IN A BOX.
YAiGU POT
I WON'T BE USING THESE FOR A WHILE, SO I'M PUTTING THEM AWAY IN A BOX.
RATTLE RATTLE
YOU'RE NOT GOING TO KEEP ROCKS!
THEY'RE NOT ROCKS! THEY'RE PIECES OF FOOD THAT NENE MADE WHEN SHE WAS PLAYING HOUSE.
YEAH? THEN TRY AND EAT 'EM!
RATTLE RATTLE RATTLE
I SWEAR, WHENEVER YOU'RE AROUND, EVERYTHING TAKES TWICE AS LONG!
RRRR RRR
RRR
THIS FITS ME PERFECTLY!
PEACE!
MOVE... BEFORE I GET ANY IDEAS.
ROARRR
SIZZLE SIZZLE SIZZLE
SHIN, PASS THAT OVER HERE, WOULD YOU?
WHAT FLAVOR IS THIS GUM? IT TASTES DISGUSTING ...
SKRIT SKRIT
SIGHHH... I DON'T HAVE THE SLIGHTEST IDEA WHO YOU TAKE AFTER...

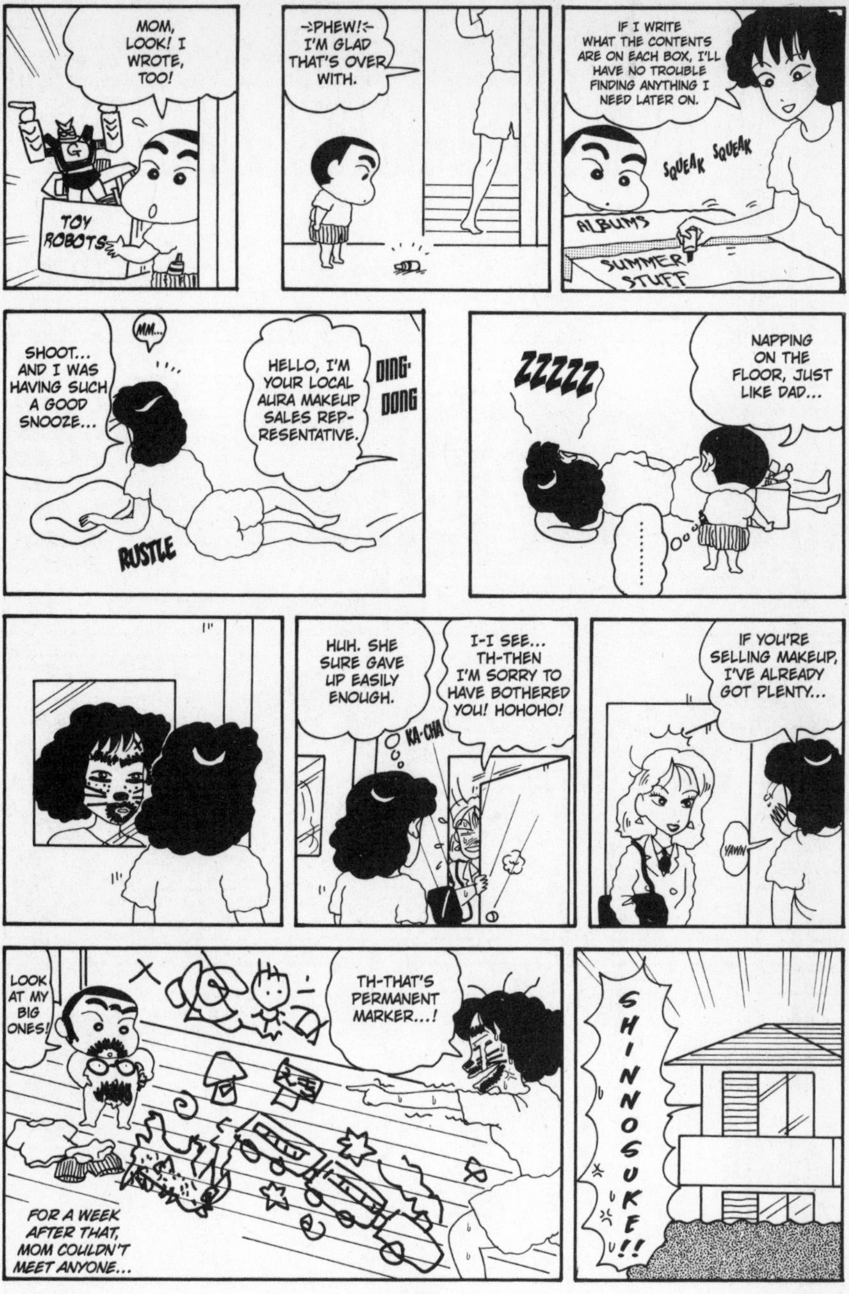
IF I WRITE WHAT THE CONTENTS ARE ON EACH BOX, I'LL HAVE NO TROUBLE FINDING ANYTHING I NEED LATER ON.
SQUEAK SQUEAK
ALBUMS
SUMMER STUFF
-PHEW!- I'M GLAD THAT'S OVER WITH.
MOM, LOOK! I WROTE, TOO!
TOY ROBOTS
NAPPING ON THE FLOOR, JUST LIKE DAD...
ZZZZZ
......
DING-DONG
HELLO, I'M YOUR LOCAL AURA MAKEUP SALES REPRESENTATIVE.
MM...
SHOOT... AND I WAS HAVING SUCH A GOOD SNOOZE...
RUSTLE
IF YOU'RE SELLING MAKEUP, I'VE ALREADY GOT PLENTY...
YAWN
I-I SEE... TH-THEN I'M SORRY TO HAVE BOTHERED YOU! HOHOHO!
KA-CHA
HUH. SHE SURE GAVE UP EASILY ENOUGH.
SHINNOSUKE!!
TH-THAT'S PERMANENT MARKER...!
LOOK AT MY BIG ONES!
FOR A WEEK AFTER THAT, MOM COULDN'T MEET ANYONE...

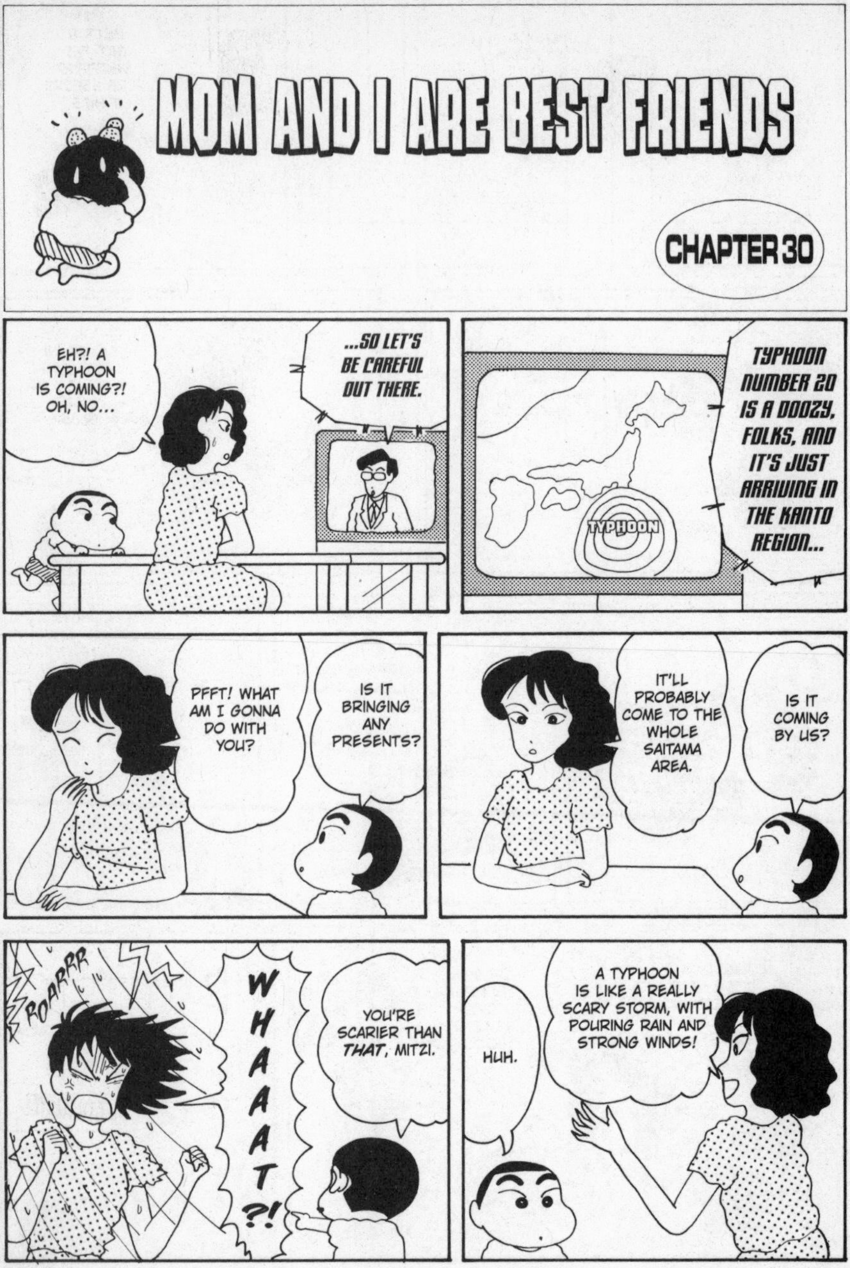
MOM AND I ARE BEST FRIENDS
CHAPTER 30
TYPHOON NUMBER 20 IS A DOOZY, FOLKS, AND IT'S JUST ARRIVING IN THE KANTO REGION...
TYPHOON
...SO LET'S BE CAREFUL OUT THERE.
EH?! A TYPHOON IS COMING?! OH, NO...
IS IT COMING BY US?
IT'LL PROBABLY COME TO THE WHOLE SAITAMA AREA.
IS IT BRINGING ANY PRESENTS?
PFFT! WHAT AM I GONNA DO WITH YOU?
A TYPHOON IS LIKE A REALLY SCARY STORM, WITH POURING RAIN AND STRONG WINDS!
HUH.
YOU'RE SCARIER THAN *THAT*, MITZI.
WHAAAAT?!
ROARRR

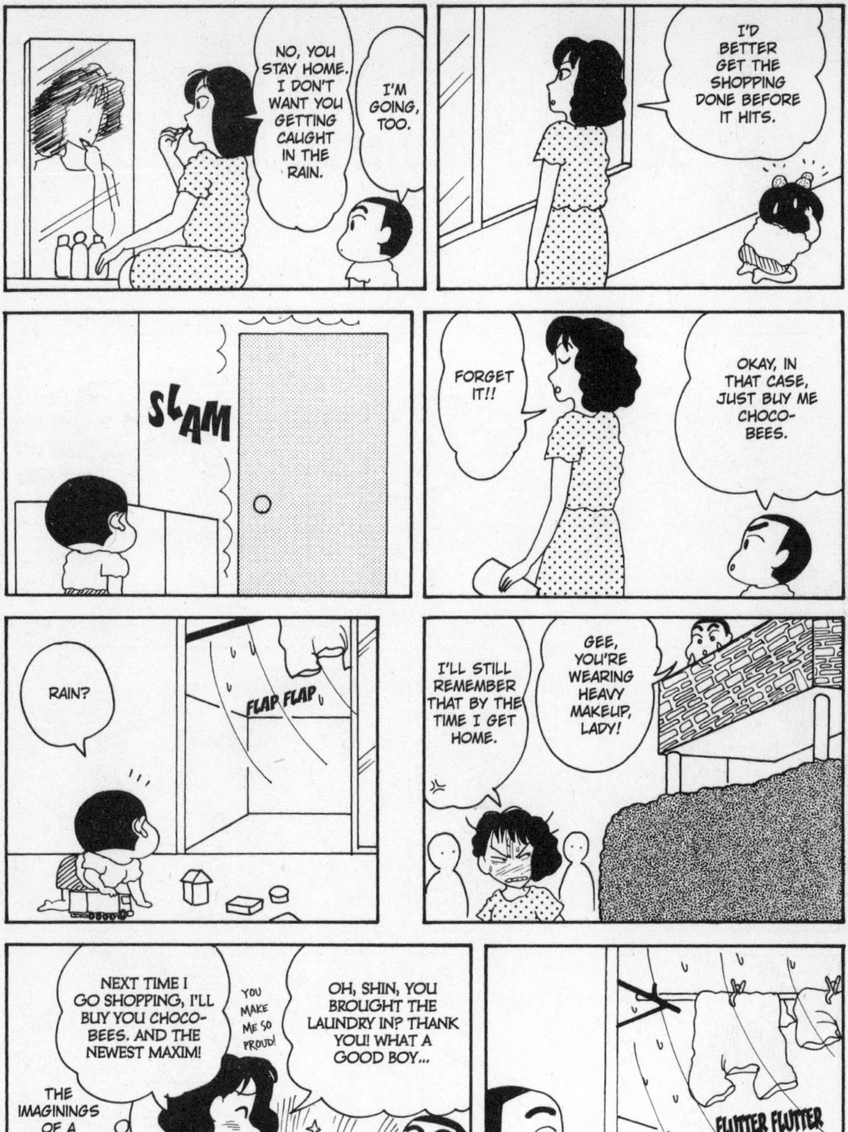
I'D BETTER GET THE SHOPPING DONE BEFORE IT HITS.
I'M GOING, TOO.
NO, YOU STAY HOME. I DON'T WANT YOU GETTING CAUGHT IN THE RAIN.
OKAY, IN THAT CASE, JUST BUY ME CHOCO-BEES.
FORGET IT!!
SLAM
GEE, YOU'RE WEARING HEAVY MAKEUP, LADY!
I'LL STILL REMEMBER THAT BY THE TIME I GET HOME.
FLAP FLAP
RAIN?
FLUTTER FLUTTER
OH, SHIN, YOU BROUGHT THE LAUNDRY IN? THANK YOU! WHAT A GOOD BOY...
YOU MAKE ME SO PROUD!
NEXT TIME I GO SHOPPING, I'LL BUY YOU CHOCO-BEES. AND THE NEWEST MAXIM!
THE IMAGININGS OF A FIVE-YEAR-OLD
GRIN...

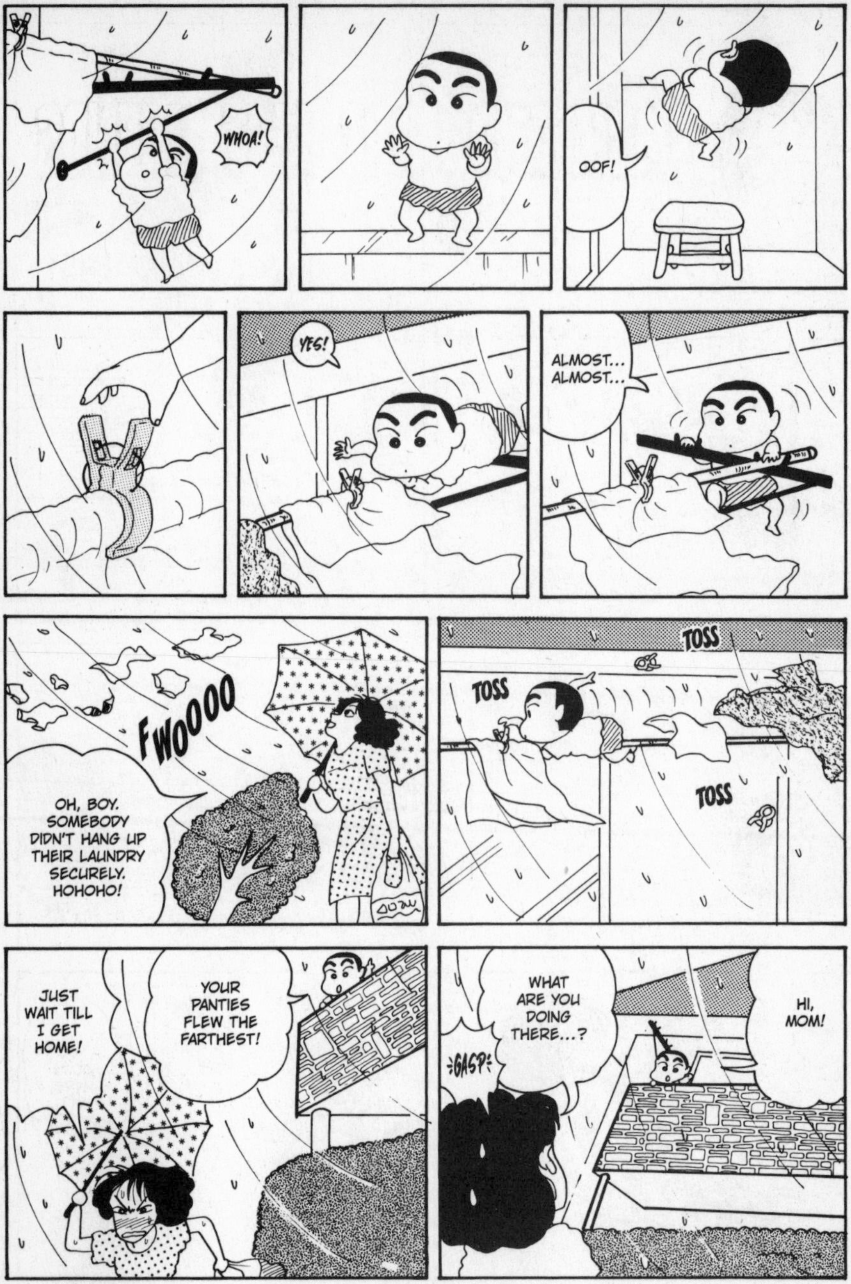
OOF!
WHOA!
ALMOST... ALMOST...
YES!
TOSS
TOSS
TOSS
FWOOOO
OH, BOY. SOMEBODY DIDN'T HANG UP THEIR LAUNDRY SECURELY. HOHOHO!
HI, MOM!
WHAT ARE YOU DOING THERE...?
GASP
YOUR PANTIES FLEW THE FARTHEST!
JUST WAIT TILL I GET HOME!

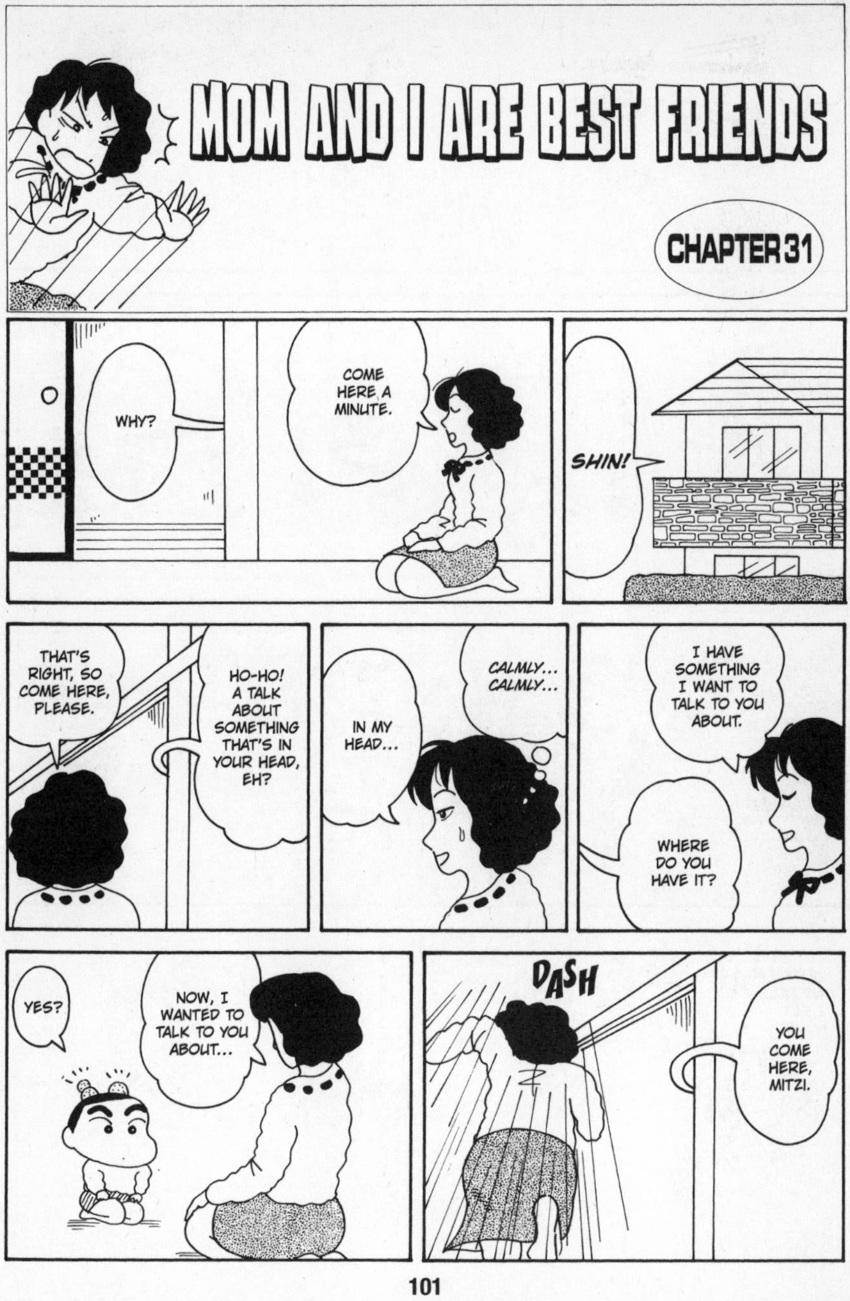
MOM AND I ARE BEST FRIENDS
CHAPTER 31
SHIN!
COME HERE A MINUTE.
WHY?
I HAVE SOMETHING I WANT TO TALK TO YOU ABOUT.
WHERE DO YOU HAVE IT?
CALMLY... CALMLY...
IN MY HEAD...
HO-HO! A TALK ABOUT SOMETHING THAT'S IN YOUR HEAD, EH?
THAT'S RIGHT, SO COME HERE, PLEASE.
DASH
YOU COME HERE, MITZI.
NOW, I WANTED TO TALK TO YOU ABOUT...
YES?

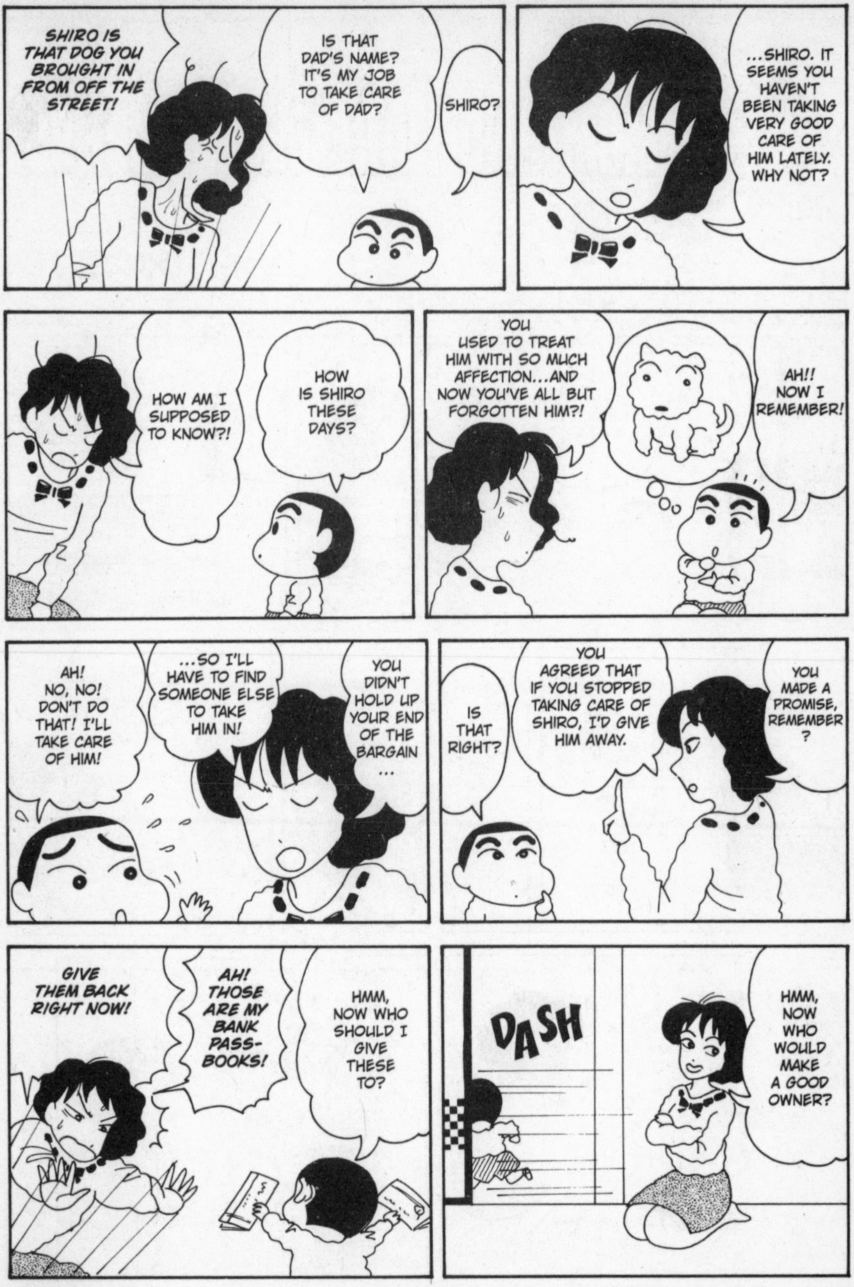
...SHIRO. IT SEEMS YOU HAVEN'T BEEN TAKING VERY GOOD CARE OF HIM LATELY. WHY NOT?
SHIRO?
IS THAT DAD'S NAME? IT'S MY JOB TO TAKE CARE OF DAD?
SHIRO IS THAT DOG YOU BROUGHT IN FROM OFF THE STREET!
AH!! NOW I REMEMBER!
YOU USED TO TREAT HIM WITH SO MUCH AFFECTION...AND NOW YOU'VE ALL BUT FORGOTTEN HIM?!
HOW IS SHIRO THESE DAYS?
HOW AM I SUPPOSED TO KNOW?!
YOU MADE A PROMISE, REMEMBER?
YOU AGREED THAT IF YOU STOPPED TAKING CARE OF SHIRO, I'D GIVE HIM AWAY.
IS THAT RIGHT?
YOU DIDN'T HOLD UP YOUR END OF THE BARGAIN...
...SO I'LL HAVE TO FIND SOMEONE ELSE TO TAKE HIM IN!
AH! NO, NO! DON'T DO THAT! I'LL TAKE CARE OF HIM!
HMM, NOW WHO WOULD MAKE A GOOD OWNER?
DASH
HMM, NOW WHO SHOULD I GIVE THESE TO?
AH! THOSE ARE MY BANK PASS-BOOKS!
GIVE THEM BACK RIGHT NOW!

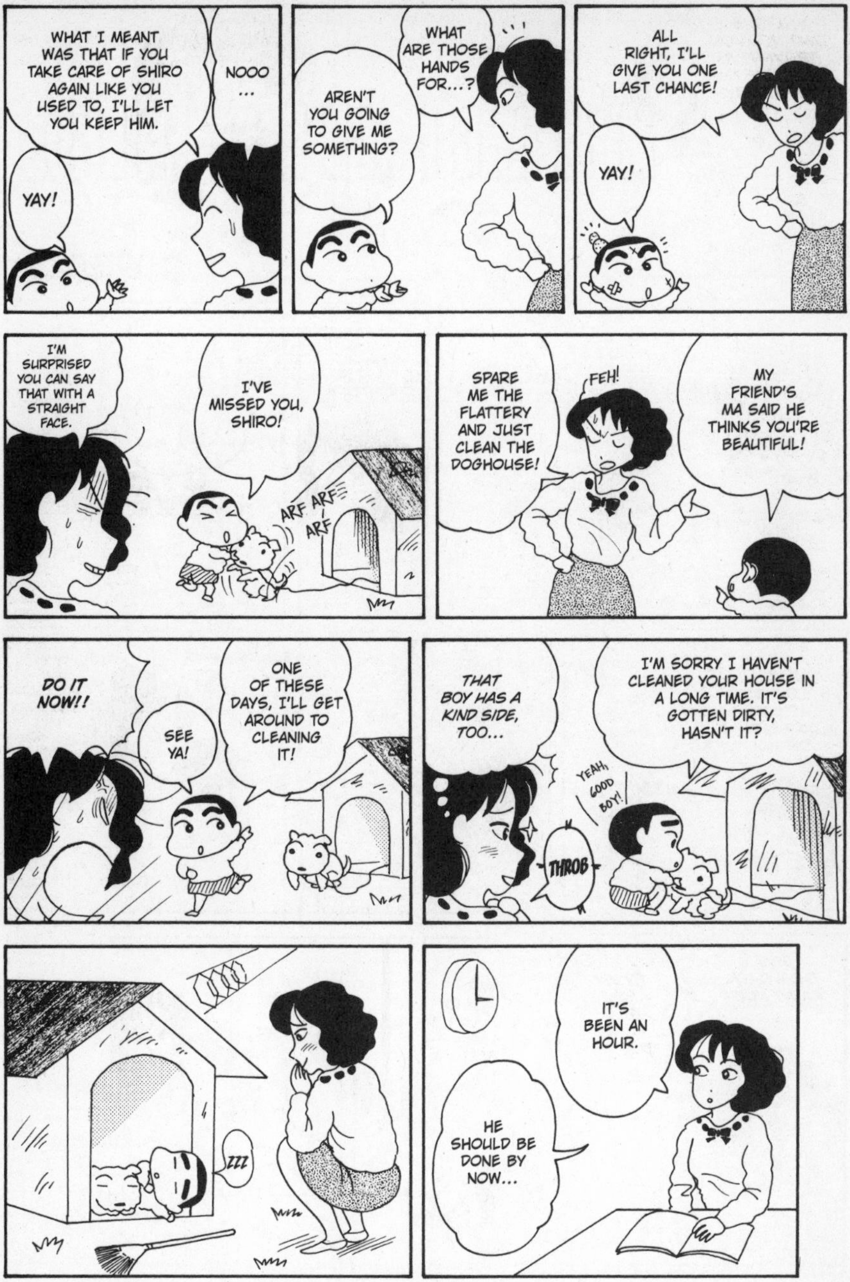
ALL RIGHT, I'LL GIVE YOU ONE LAST CHANCE!
YAY!
WHAT ARE THOSE HANDS FOR...?
AREN'T YOU GOING TO GIVE ME SOMETHING?
NOOO ...
WHAT I MEANT WAS THAT IF YOU TAKE CARE OF SHIRO AGAIN LIKE YOU USED TO, I'LL LET YOU KEEP HIM.
YAY!
MY FRIEND'S MA SAID HE THINKS YOU'RE BEAUTIFUL!
FEH!
SPARE ME THE FLATTERY AND JUST CLEAN THE DOGHOUSE!
I'VE MISSED YOU, SHIRO!
ARF ARF ARF
I'M SURPRISED YOU CAN SAY THAT WITH A STRAIGHT FACE.
I'M SORRY I HAVEN'T CLEANED YOUR HOUSE IN A LONG TIME. IT'S GOTTEN DIRTY, HASN'T IT?
YEAH, GOOD BOY!
THROB
THAT BOY HAS A KIND SIDE, TOO...
ONE OF THESE DAYS, I'LL GET AROUND TO CLEANING IT!
SEE YA!
DO IT NOW!!
IT'S BEEN AN HOUR.
HE SHOULD BE DONE BY NOW...
ZZZ

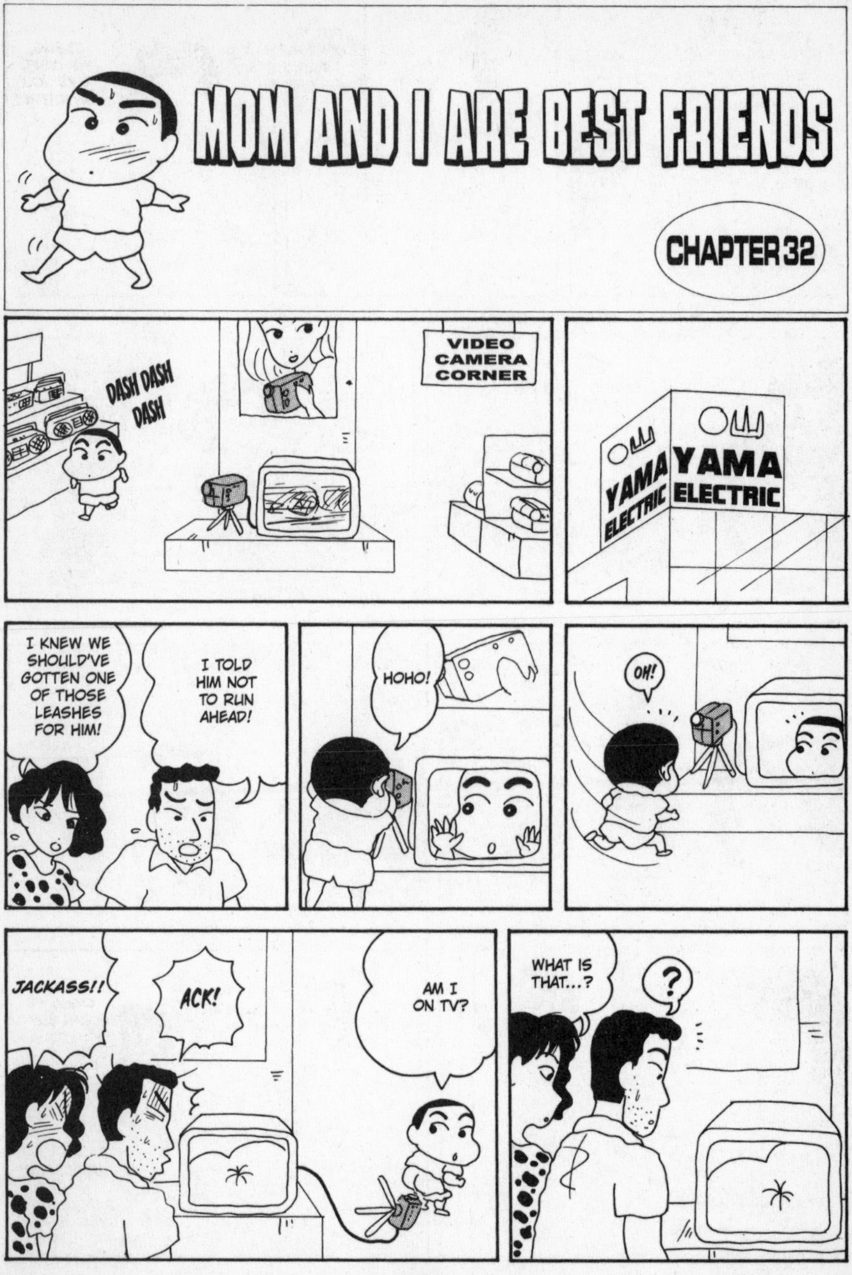
MOM AND I ARE BEST FRIENDS
CHAPTER 32
YAMA ELECTRIC
YAMA ELECTRIC
VIDEO CAMERA CORNER
DASH DASH DASH
OH!
HOHO!
I TOLD HIM NOT TO RUN AHEAD!
I KNEW WE SHOULD'VE GOTTEN ONE OF THOSE LEASHES FOR HIM!
?
WHAT IS THAT...?
AM I ON TV?
ACK!
JACKASS!!

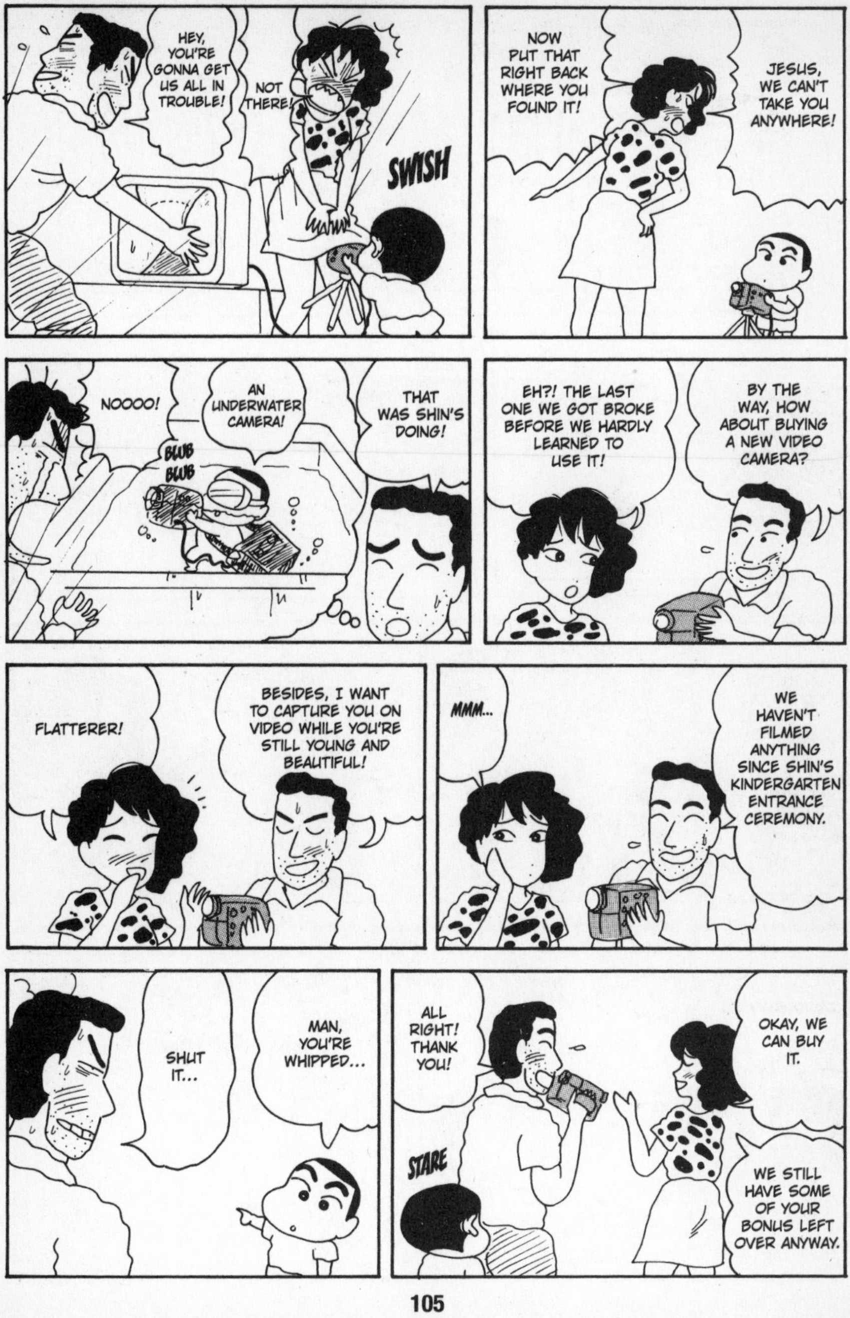
JESUS, WE CAN'T TAKE YOU ANYWHERE!
NOW PUT THAT RIGHT BACK WHERE YOU FOUND IT!
SWISH
NOT THERE!
HEY, YOU'RE GONNA GET US ALL IN TROUBLE!
BY THE WAY, HOW ABOUT BUYING A NEW VIDEO CAMERA?
EH?! THE LAST ONE WE GOT BROKE BEFORE WE HARDLY LEARNED TO USE IT!
THAT WAS SHIN'S DOING!
AN UNDERWATER CAMERA!
BLUB BLUB
NOOOO!
WE HAVEN'T FILMED ANYTHING SINCE SHIN'S KINDERGARTEN ENTRANCE CEREMONY.
MMM...
BESIDES, I WANT TO CAPTURE YOU ON VIDEO WHILE YOU'RE STILL YOUNG AND BEAUTIFUL!
FLATTERER!
OKAY, WE CAN BUY IT.
WE STILL HAVE SOME OF YOUR BONUS LEFT OVER ANYWAY.
ALL RIGHT! THANK YOU!
STARE
MAN, YOU'RE WHIPPED...
SHUT IT...

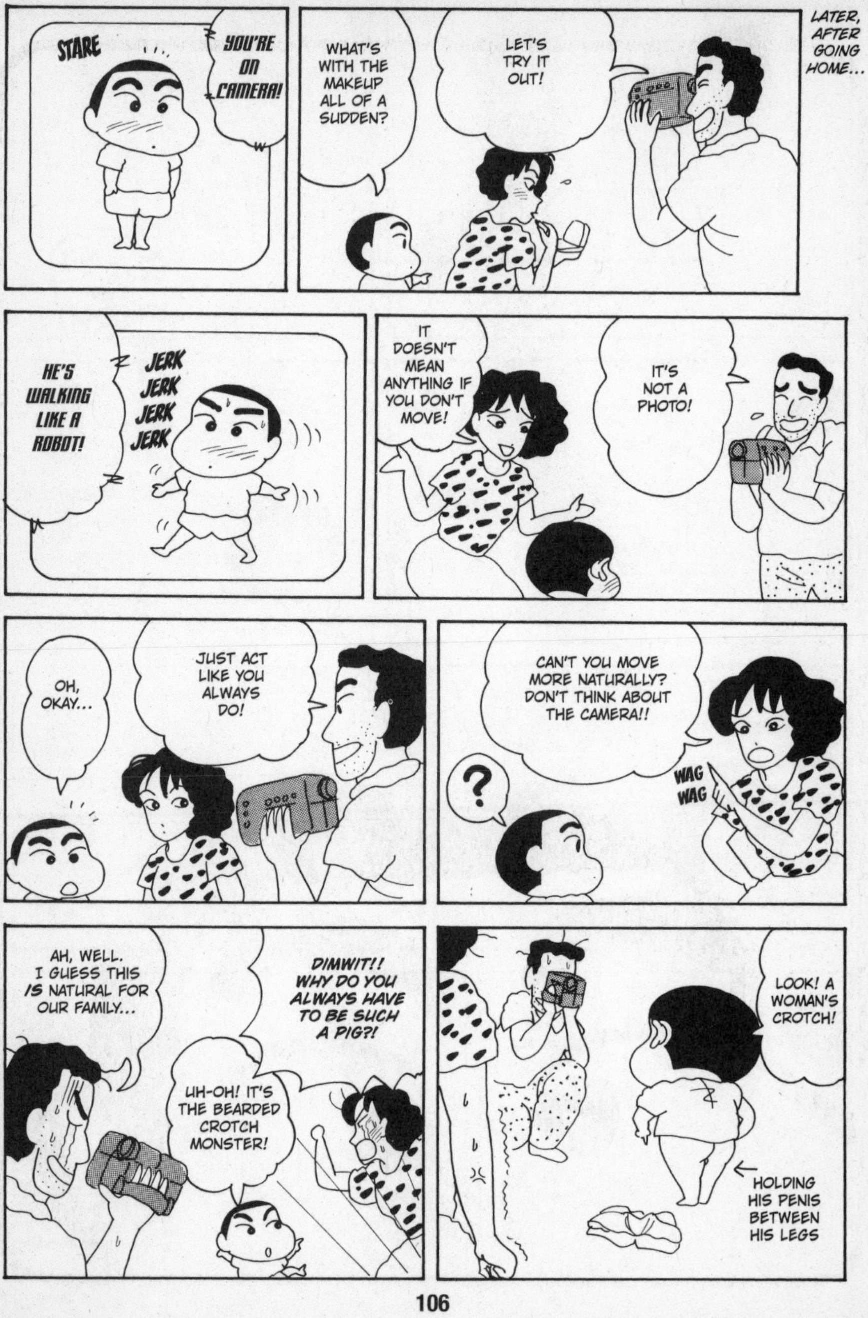
LATER, AFTER GOING HOME...
LET'S TRY IT OUT!
WHAT'S WITH THE MAKEUP ALL OF A SUDDEN?
YOU'RE ON CAMERA!
STARE
IT'S NOT A PHOTO!
IT DOESN'T MEAN ANYTHING IF YOU DON'T MOVE!
JERK JERK JERK JERK
HE'S WALKING LIKE A ROBOT!
CAN'T YOU MOVE MORE NATURALLY? DON'T THINK ABOUT THE CAMERA!!
WAG WAG
?
JUST ACT LIKE YOU ALWAYS DO!
OH, OKAY...
LOOK! A WOMAN'S CROTCH!
HOLDING HIS PENIS BETWEEN HIS LEGS
DIMWIT!! WHY DO YOU ALWAYS HAVE TO BE SUCH A PIG?!
UH-OH! IT'S THE BEARDED CROTCH MONSTER!
AH, WELL. I GUESS THIS IS NATURAL FOR OUR FAMILY...

KINDERGARTEN IS PARADISE

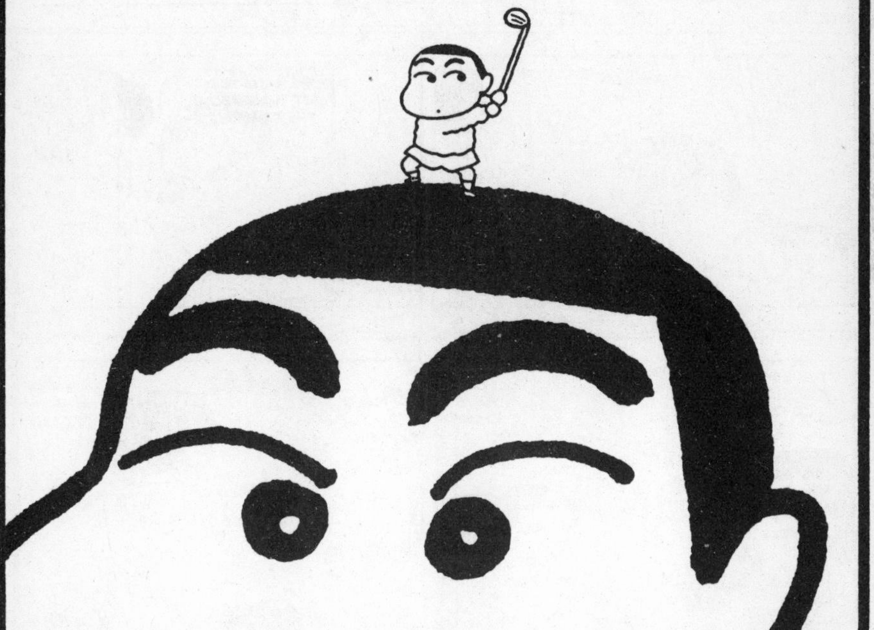

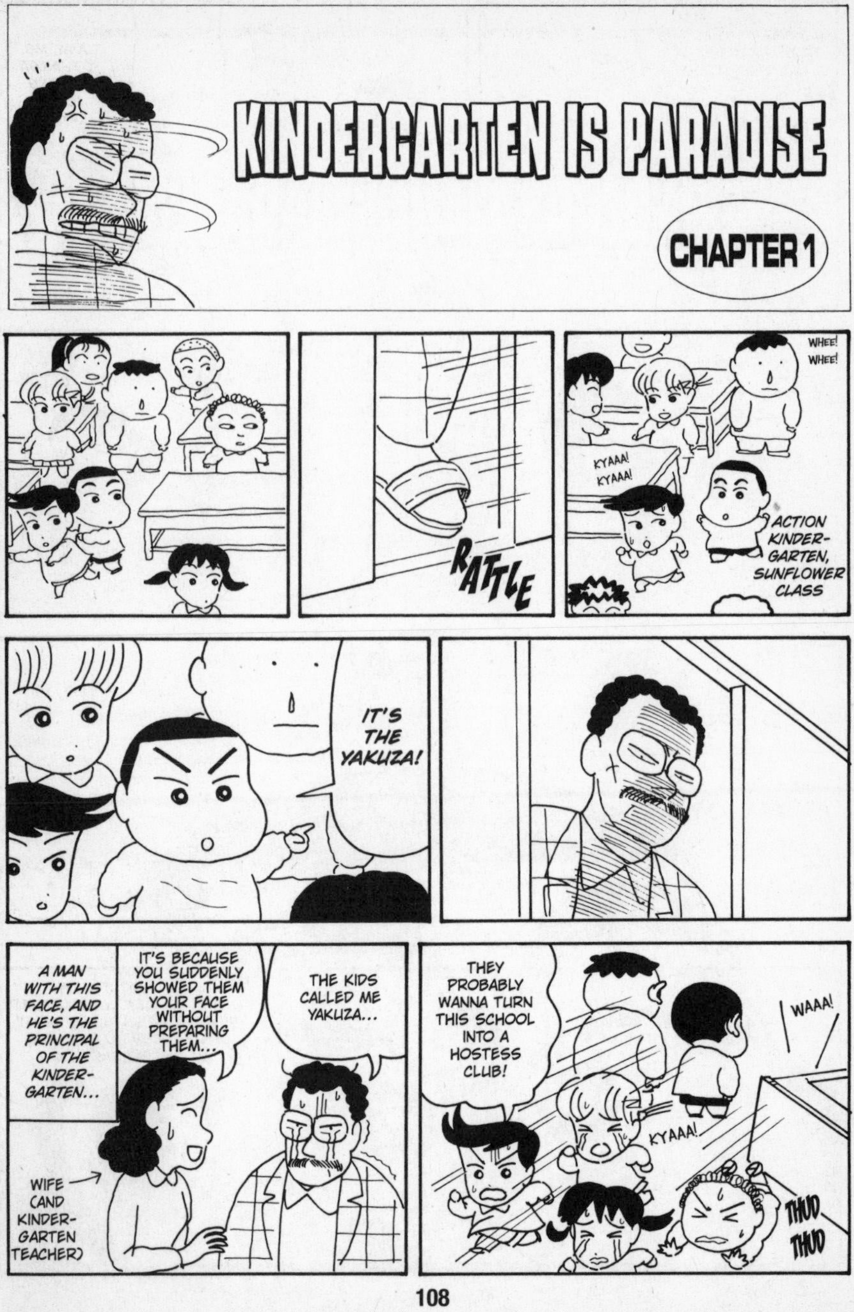
KINDERGARTEN IS PARADISE
CHAPTER 1
WHEE! WHEE!
KYAAA! KYAAA!
ACTION KINDER-GARTEN, SUNFLOWER CLASS
RATTLE
IT'S THE YAKUZA!
WAAA!
THEY PROBABLY WANNA TURN THIS SCHOOL INTO A HOSTESS CLUB!
KYAAA!
THUD THUD
THE KIDS CALLED ME YAKUZA...
IT'S BECAUSE YOU SUDDENLY SHOWED THEM YOUR FACE WITHOUT PREPARING THEM...
A MAN WITH THIS FACE, AND HE'S THE PRINCIPAL OF THE KINDER-GARTEN...
WIFE (AND KINDER-GARTEN TEACHER)

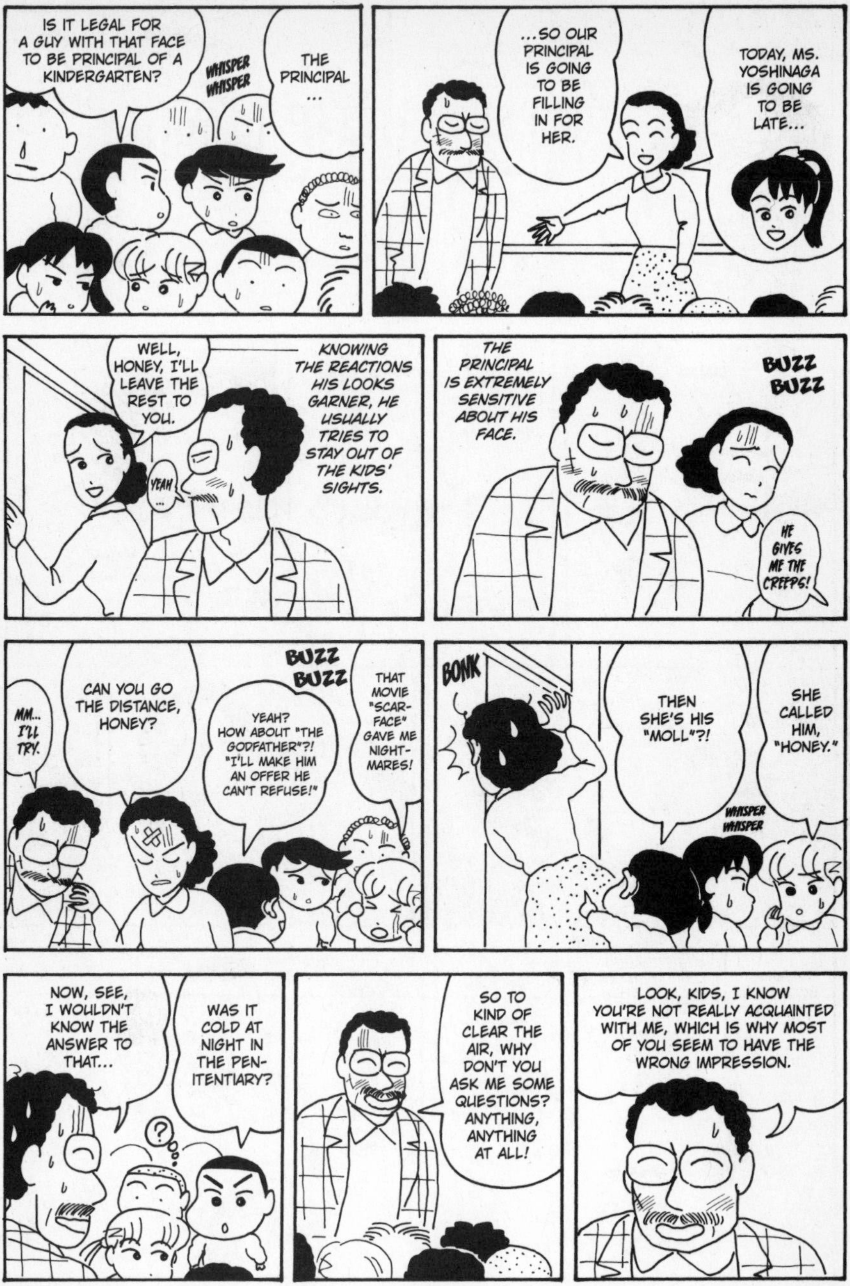
TODAY, MS. YOSHINAGA IS GOING TO BE LATE...
...SO OUR PRINCIPAL IS GOING TO BE FILLING IN FOR HER.
THE PRINCIPAL ...
WHISPER WHISPER
IS IT LEGAL FOR A GUY WITH THAT FACE TO BE PRINCIPAL OF A KINDERGARTEN?
BUZZ BUZZ
THE PRINCIPAL IS EXTREMELY SENSITIVE ABOUT HIS FACE.
HE GIVES ME THE CREEPS!
KNOWING THE REACTIONS HIS LOOKS GARNER, HE USUALLY TRIES TO STAY OUT OF THE KIDS' SIGHTS.
WELL, HONEY, I'LL LEAVE THE REST TO YOU.
YEAH ...
SHE CALLED HIM, "HONEY."
THEN SHE'S HIS "MOLL"?!
WHISPER WHISPER
BONK
THAT MOVIE "SCAR-FACE" GAVE ME NIGHT-MARES!
BUZZ BUZZ
YEAH? HOW ABOUT "THE GODFATHER"?! "I'LL MAKE HIM AN OFFER HE CAN'T REFUSE!"
CAN YOU GO THE DISTANCE, HONEY?
MM... I'LL TRY.
LOOK, KIDS, I KNOW YOU'RE NOT REALLY ACQUAINTED WITH ME, WHICH IS WHY MOST OF YOU SEEM TO HAVE THE WRONG IMPRESSION.
SO TO KIND OF CLEAR THE AIR, WHY DON'T YOU ASK ME SOME QUESTIONS? ANYTHING, ANYTHING AT ALL!
WAS IT COLD AT NIGHT IN THE PEN-ITENTIARY?
NOW, SEE, I WOULDN'T KNOW THE ANSWER TO THAT...
?

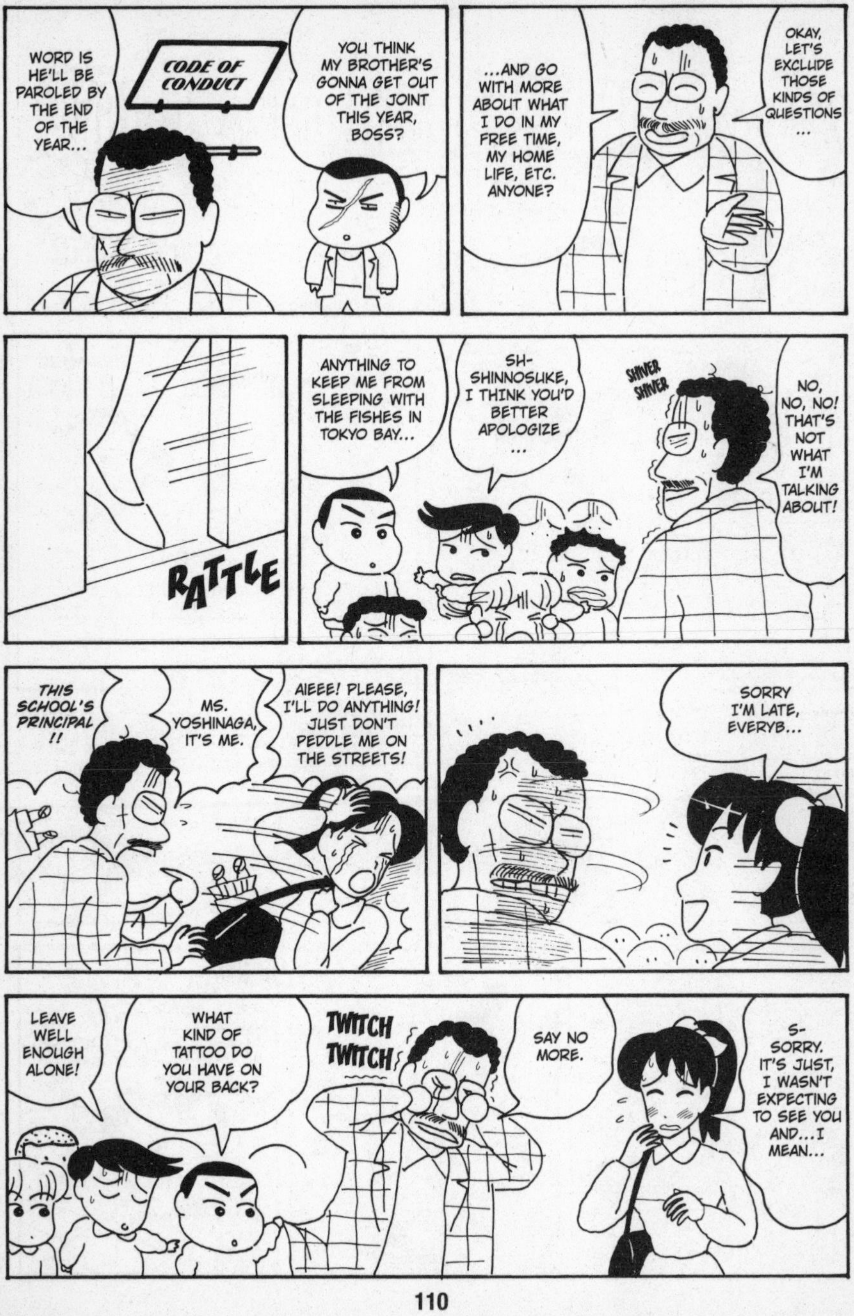
OKAY, LET'S EXCLUDE THOSE KINDS OF QUESTIONS ...
...AND GO WITH MORE ABOUT WHAT I DO IN MY FREE TIME, MY HOME LIFE, ETC. ANYONE?
YOU THINK MY BROTHER'S GONNA GET OUT OF THE JOINT THIS YEAR, BOSS?
CODE OF CONDUCT
WORD IS HE'LL BE PAROLED BY THE END OF THE YEAR...
NO, NO, NO! THAT'S NOT WHAT I'M TALKING ABOUT!
SHIVER SHIVER
SH-SHINNOSUKE, I THINK YOU'D BETTER APOLOGIZE ...
ANYTHING TO KEEP ME FROM SLEEPING WITH THE FISHES IN TOKYO BAY...
RATTLE
SORRY I'M LATE, EVERYB...
AIEEE! PLEASE, I'LL DO ANYTHING! JUST DON'T PEDDLE ME ON THE STREETS!
MS. YOSHINAGA, IT'S ME.
THIS SCHOOL'S PRINCIPAL !!
S-SORRY. IT'S JUST, I WASN'T EXPECTING TO SEE YOU AND...I MEAN...
SAY NO MORE.
TWITCH TWITCH
WHAT KIND OF TATTOO DO YOU HAVE ON YOUR BACK?
LEAVE WELL ENOUGH ALONE!

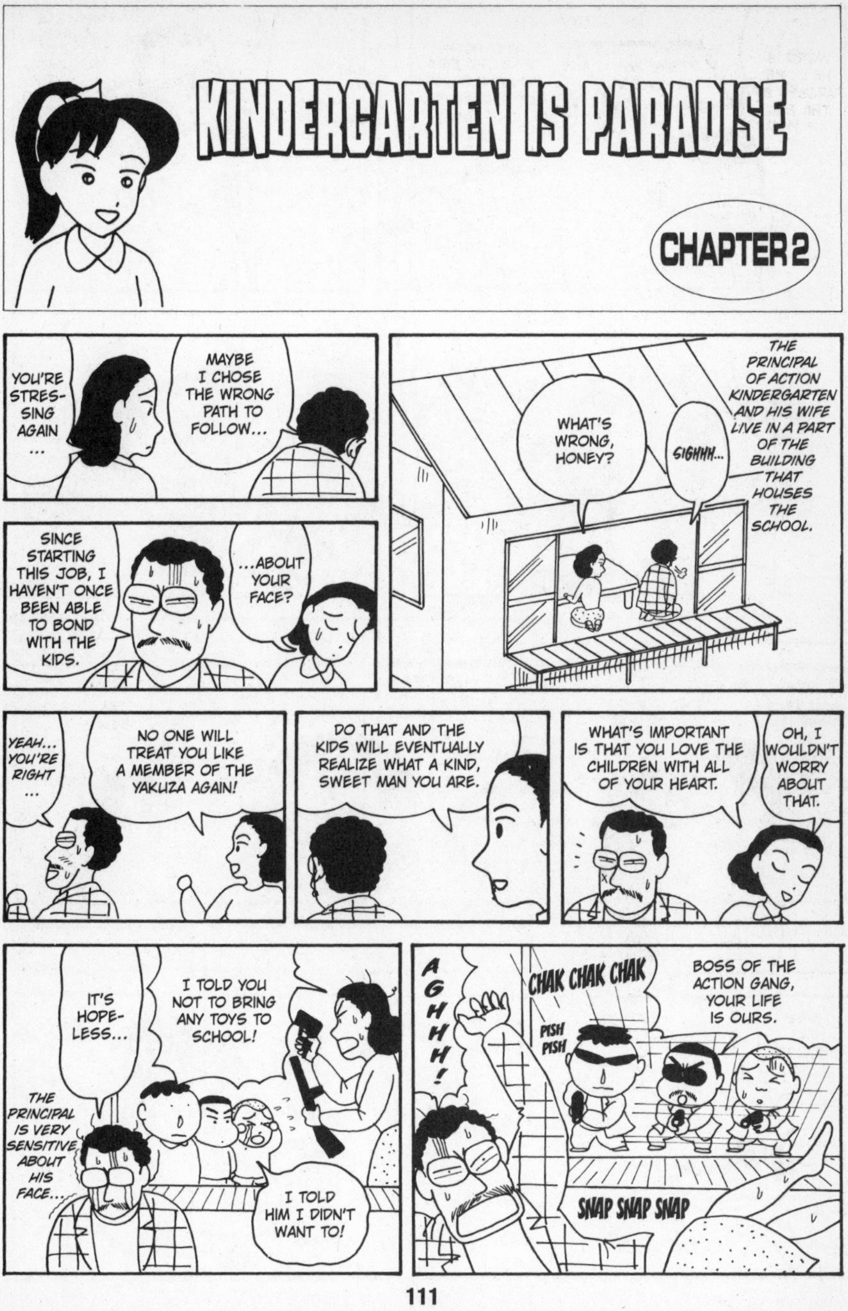
KINDERGARTEN IS PARADISE
CHAPTER 2
THE PRINCIPAL OF ACTION KINDERGARTEN AND HIS WIFE LIVE IN A PART OF THE BUILDING THAT HOUSES THE SCHOOL.
SIGHHH...
WHAT'S WRONG, HONEY?
MAYBE I CHOSE THE WRONG PATH TO FOLLOW...
YOU'RE STRES-SING AGAIN ...
SINCE STARTING THIS JOB, I HAVEN'T ONCE BEEN ABLE TO BOND WITH THE KIDS.
...ABOUT YOUR FACE?
OH, I WOULDN'T WORRY ABOUT THAT.
WHAT'S IMPORTANT IS THAT YOU LOVE THE CHILDREN WITH ALL OF YOUR HEART.
DO THAT AND THE KIDS WILL EVENTUALLY REALIZE WHAT A KIND, SWEET MAN YOU ARE.
NO ONE WILL TREAT YOU LIKE A MEMBER OF THE YAKUZA AGAIN!
YEAH... YOU'RE RIGHT ...
BOSS OF THE ACTION GANG, YOUR LIFE IS OURS.
CHAK CHAK CHAK
AGHHH!
PISH PISH
SNAP SNAP SNAP
I TOLD YOU NOT TO BRING ANY TOYS TO SCHOOL!
IT'S HOPE-LESS...
THE PRINCIPAL IS VERY SENSITIVE ABOUT HIS FACE...
I TOLD HIM I DIDN'T WANT TO!

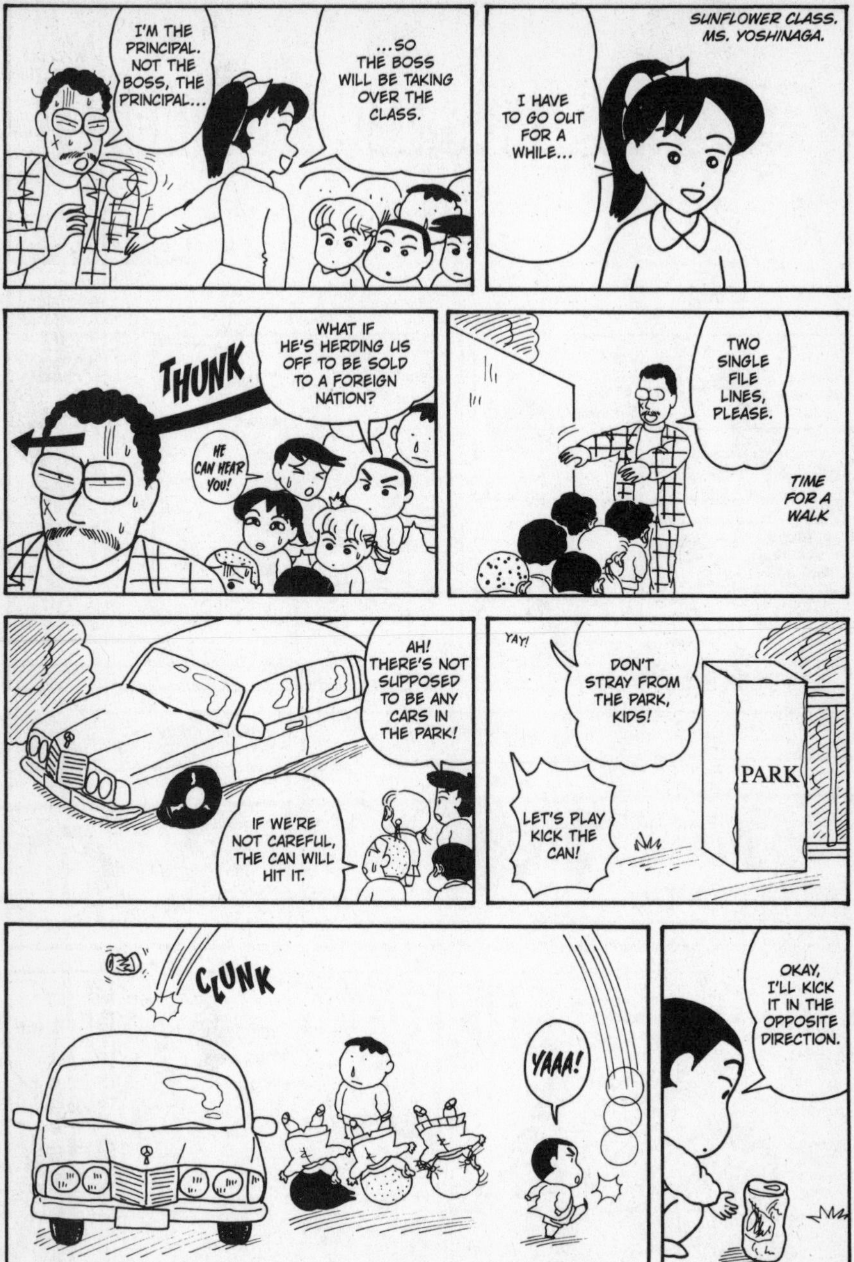
SUNFLOWER CLASS. MS. YOSHINAGA.
I HAVE TO GO OUT FOR A WHILE...
...SO THE BOSS WILL BE TAKING OVER THE CLASS.
I'M THE PRINCIPAL. NOT THE BOSS, THE PRINCIPAL...
TWO SINGLE FILE LINES, PLEASE.
TIME FOR A WALK
WHAT IF HE'S HERDING US OFF TO BE SOLD TO A FOREIGN NATION?
THUNK
HE CAN HEAR YOU!
YAY!
DON'T STRAY FROM THE PARK, KIDS!
PARK
LET'S PLAY KICK THE CAN!
AH! THERE'S NOT SUPPOSED TO BE ANY CARS IN THE PARK!
IF WE'RE NOT CAREFUL, THE CAN WILL HIT IT.
OKAY, I'LL KICK IT IN THE OPPOSITE DIRECTION.
YAAA!
CLUNK

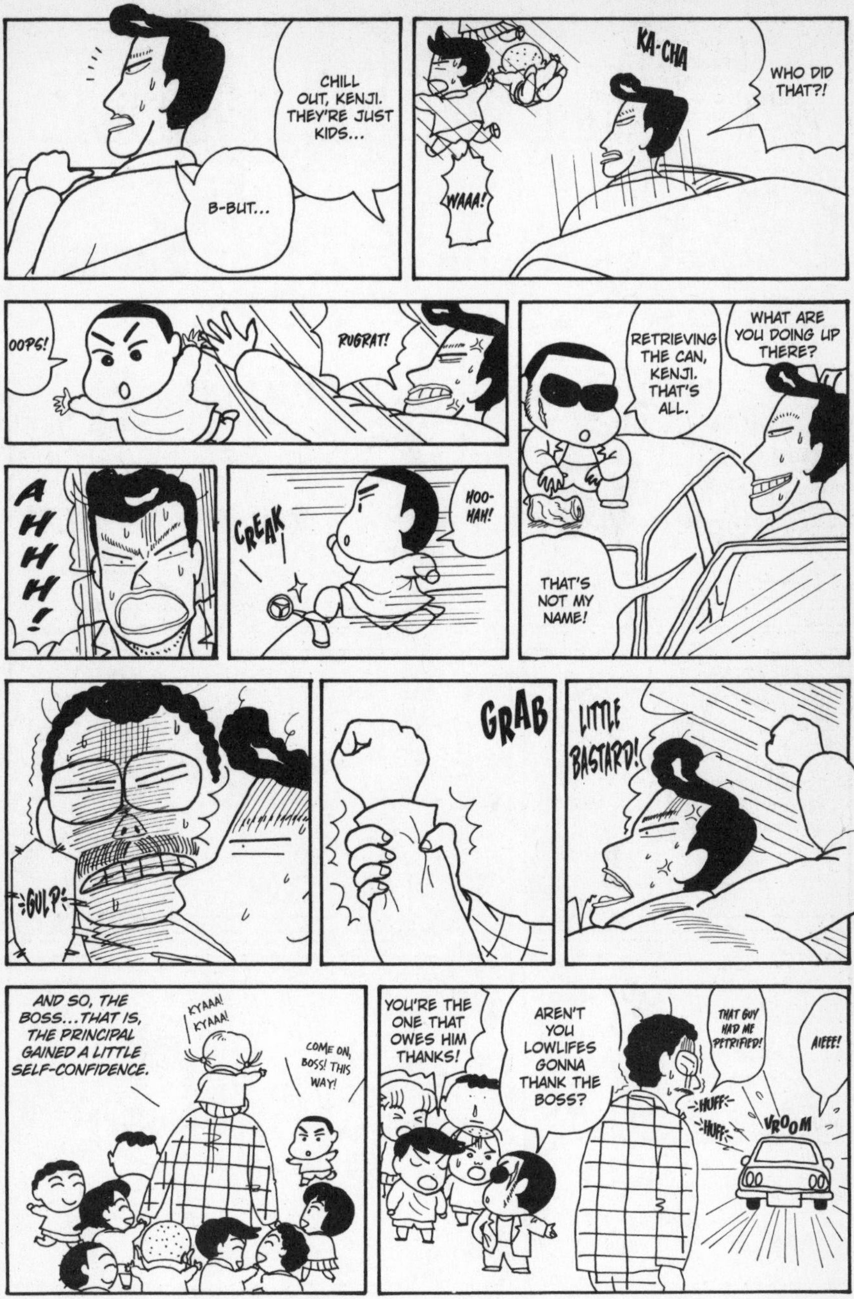
WHO DID THAT?!
KA-CHA
WAAA!
CHILL OUT, KENJI. THEY'RE JUST KIDS...
B-BUT...
WHAT ARE YOU DOING UP THERE?
RETRIEVING THE CAN, KENJI. THAT'S ALL.
THAT'S NOT MY NAME!
RUGRAT!
OOPS!
HOO-HAH!
CREAK
AHHHH!
LITTLE BASTARD!
GRAB
GULP
AIEEE!
THAT GUY HAD ME PETRIFIED!
HUFF
HUFF
VROOM
AREN'T YOU LOWLIFES GONNA THANK THE BOSS?
YOU'RE THE ONE THAT OWES HIM THANKS!
COME ON, BOSS! THIS WAY!
KYAAA! KYAAA!
AND SO, THE BOSS...THAT IS, THE PRINCIPAL GAINED A LITTLE SELF-CONFIDENCE.

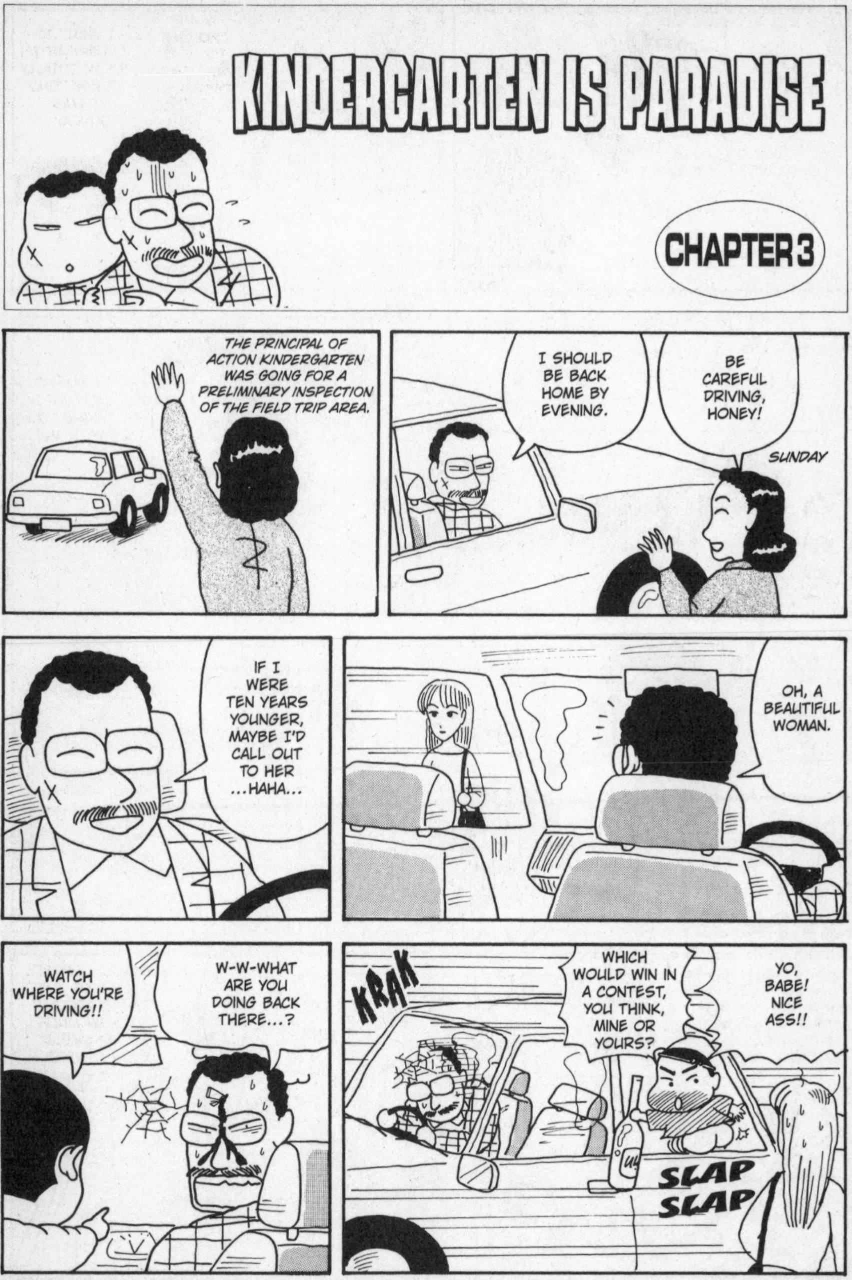
KINDERGARTEN IS PARADISE
CHAPTER 3
BE CAREFUL DRIVING, HONEY!
I SHOULD BE BACK HOME BY EVENING.
SUNDAY
THE PRINCIPAL OF ACTION KINDERGARTEN WAS GOING FOR A PRELIMINARY INSPECTION OF THE FIELD TRIP AREA.
OH, A BEAUTIFUL WOMAN.
IF I WERE TEN YEARS YOUNGER, MAYBE I'D CALL OUT TO HER ...HAHA...
YO, BABE! NICE ASS!!
WHICH WOULD WIN IN A CONTEST, YOU THINK, MINE OR YOURS?
KRAK
SLAP SLAP
W-W-WHAT ARE YOU DOING BACK THERE...?
WATCH WHERE YOU'RE DRIVING!!

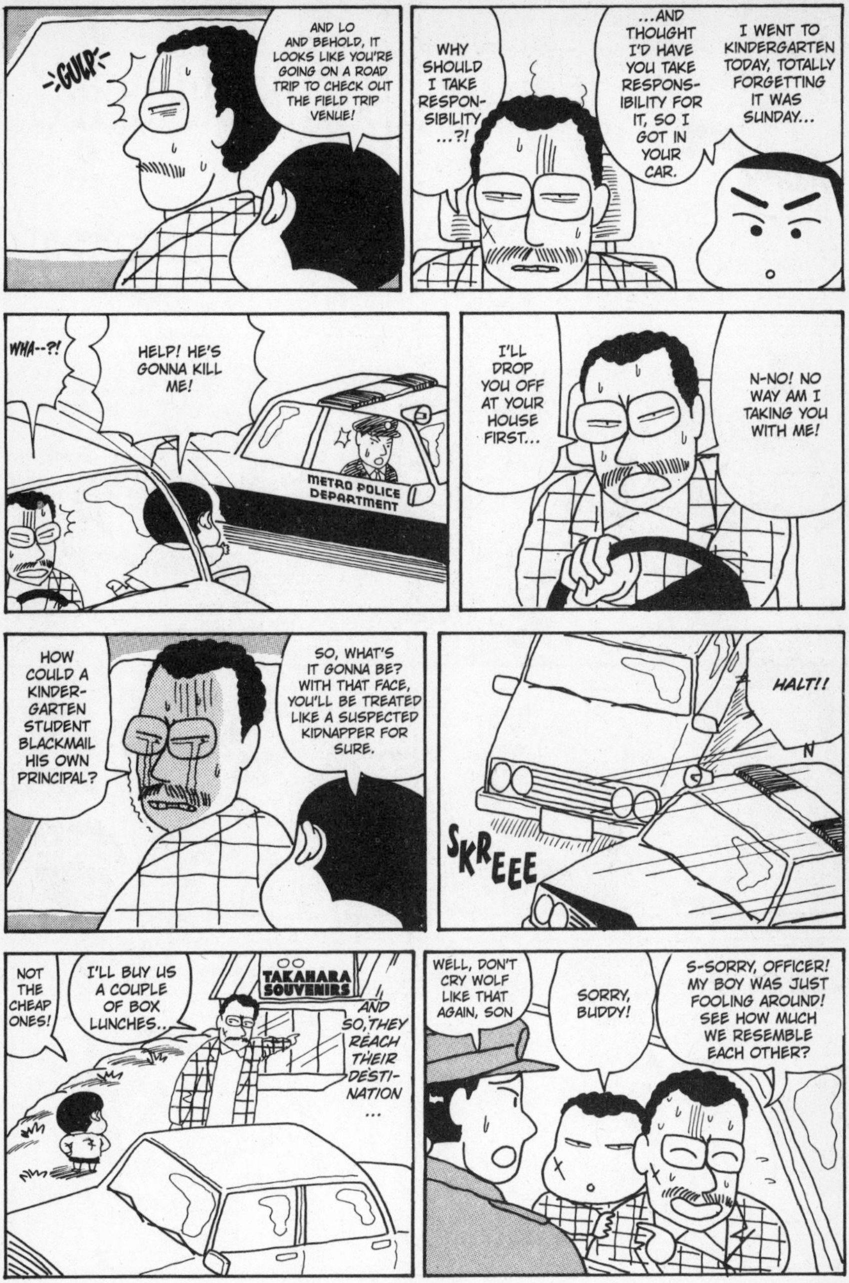
I WENT TO KINDERGARTEN TODAY, TOTALLY FORGETTING IT WAS SUNDAY...
...AND THOUGHT I'D HAVE YOU TAKE RESPONS-IBILITY FOR IT, SO I GOT IN YOUR CAR.
WHY SHOULD I TAKE RESPON-SIBILITY ...?!
AND LO AND BEHOLD, IT LOOKS LIKE YOU'RE GOING ON A ROAD TRIP TO CHECK OUT THE FIELD TRIP VENUE!
GULP
N-NO! NO WAY AM I TAKING YOU WITH ME!
I'LL DROP YOU OFF AT YOUR HOUSE FIRST...
HELP! HE'S GONNA KILL ME!
WHA--?!
METRO POLICE DEPARTMENT
HALT!!
N
SKREEE
SO, WHAT'S IT GONNA BE? WITH THAT FACE, YOU'LL BE TREATED LIKE A SUSPECTED KIDNAPPER FOR SURE.
HOW COULD A KINDER-GARTEN STUDENT BLACKMAIL HIS OWN PRINCIPAL?
S-SORRY, OFFICER! MY BOY WAS JUST FOOLING AROUND! SEE HOW MUCH WE RESEMBLE EACH OTHER?
SORRY, BUDDY!
WELL, DON'T CRY WOLF LIKE THAT AGAIN, SON
TAKAHARA SOUVENIRS
AND SO, THEY REACH THEIR DESTI-NATION ...
I'LL BUY US A COUPLE OF BOX LUNCHES...
NOT THE CHEAP ONES!

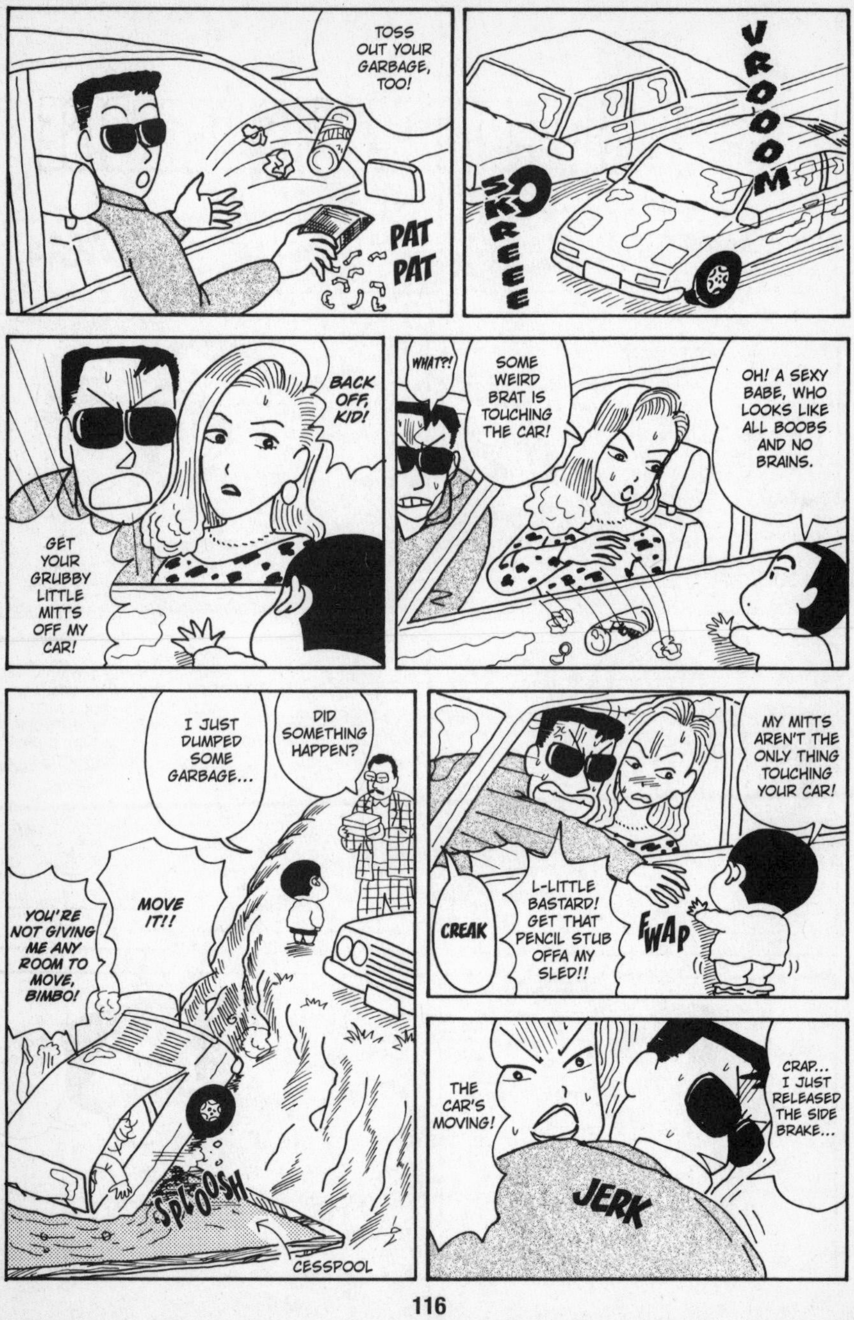

VROOOM
SKREEE
TOSS OUT YOUR GARBAGE, TOO!
PAT PAT
OH! A SEXY BABE, WHO LOOKS LIKE ALL BOOBS AND NO BRAINS.
SOME WEIRD BRAT IS TOUCHING THE CAR!
WHAT?!
BACK OFF, KID!
GET YOUR GRUBBY LITTLE MITTS OFF MY CAR!
MY MITTS AREN'T THE ONLY THING TOUCHING YOUR CAR!
L-LITTLE BASTARD! GET THAT PENCIL STUB OFFA MY SLED!!
FWAP
CREAK
CRAP... I JUST RELEASED THE SIDE BRAKE...
THE CAR'S MOVING!
JERK
DID SOMETHING HAPPEN?
I JUST DUMPED SOME GARBAGE...
MOVE IT!!
YOU'RE NOT GIVING ME ANY ROOM TO MOVE, BIMBO!
SPLOOSH
CESSPOOL

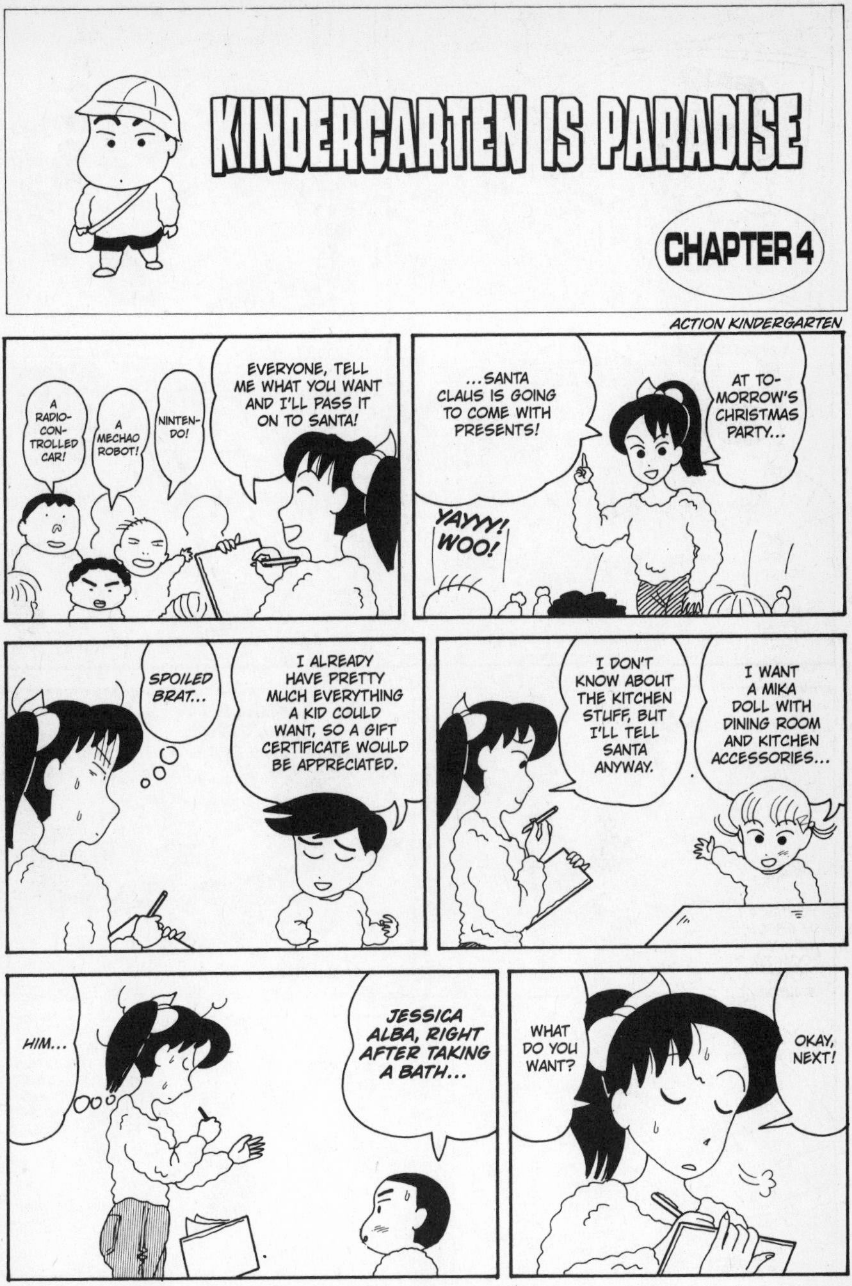
KINDERGARTEN IS PARADISE
CHAPTER 4
ACTION KINDERGARTEN
AT TO-MORROW'S CHRISTMAS PARTY...
...SANTA CLAUS IS GOING TO COME WITH PRESENTS!
YAYYY! WOO!
EVERYONE, TELL ME WHAT YOU WANT AND I'LL PASS IT ON TO SANTA!
NINTEN-DO!
A MECHAO ROBOT!
A RADIO-CONTROLLED CAR!
I WANT A MIKA DOLL WITH DINING ROOM AND KITCHEN ACCESSORIES...
I DON'T KNOW ABOUT THE KITCHEN STUFF, BUT I'LL TELL SANTA ANYWAY.
I ALREADY HAVE PRETTY MUCH EVERYTHING A KID COULD WANT, SO A GIFT CERTIFICATE WOULD BE APPRECIATED.
SPOILED BRAT...
OKAY, NEXT!
WHAT DO YOU WANT?
JESSICA ALBA, RIGHT AFTER TAKING A BATH...
HIM...

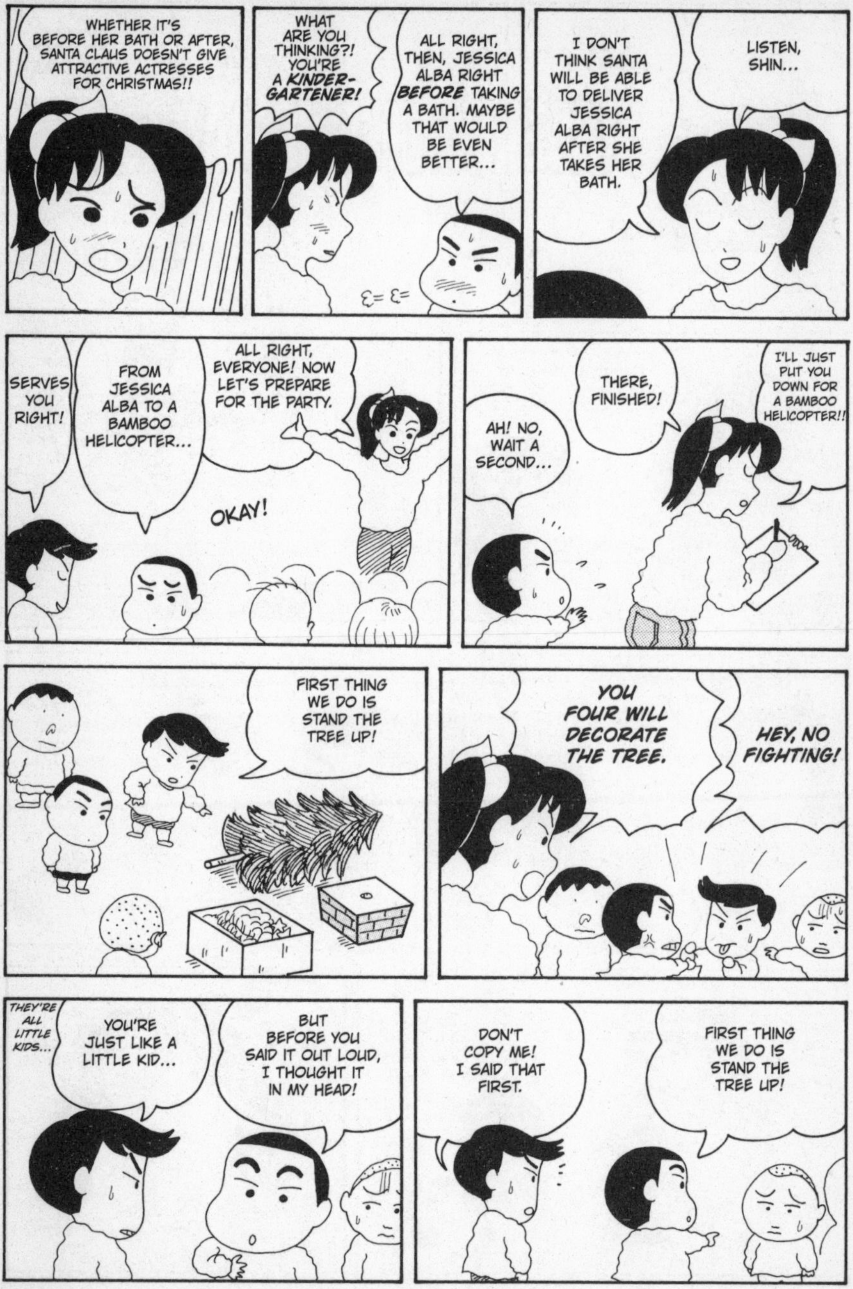
LISTEN, SHIN...
I DON'T THINK SANTA WILL BE ABLE TO DELIVER JESSICA ALBA RIGHT AFTER SHE TAKES HER BATH.
ALL RIGHT, THEN, JESSICA ALBA RIGHT BEFORE TAKING A BATH. MAYBE THAT WOULD BE EVEN BETTER...
WHAT ARE YOU THINKING?! YOU'RE A KINDER-GARTENER!
WHETHER IT'S BEFORE HER BATH OR AFTER, SANTA CLAUS DOESN'T GIVE ATTRACTIVE ACTRESSES FOR CHRISTMAS!!
I'LL JUST PUT YOU DOWN FOR A BAMBOO HELICOPTER!!
THERE, FINISHED!
AH! NO, WAIT A SECOND...
ALL RIGHT, EVERYONE! NOW LET'S PREPARE FOR THE PARTY.
OKAY!
FROM JESSICA ALBA TO A BAMBOO HELICOPTER...
SERVES YOU RIGHT!
HEY, NO FIGHTING!
YOU FOUR WILL DECORATE THE TREE.
FIRST THING WE DO IS STAND THE TREE UP!
FIRST THING WE DO IS STAND THE TREE UP!
DON'T COPY ME! I SAID THAT FIRST.
BUT BEFORE YOU SAID IT OUT LOUD, I THOUGHT IT IN MY HEAD!
YOU'RE JUST LIKE A LITTLE KID...
THEY'RE ALL LITTLE KIDS...

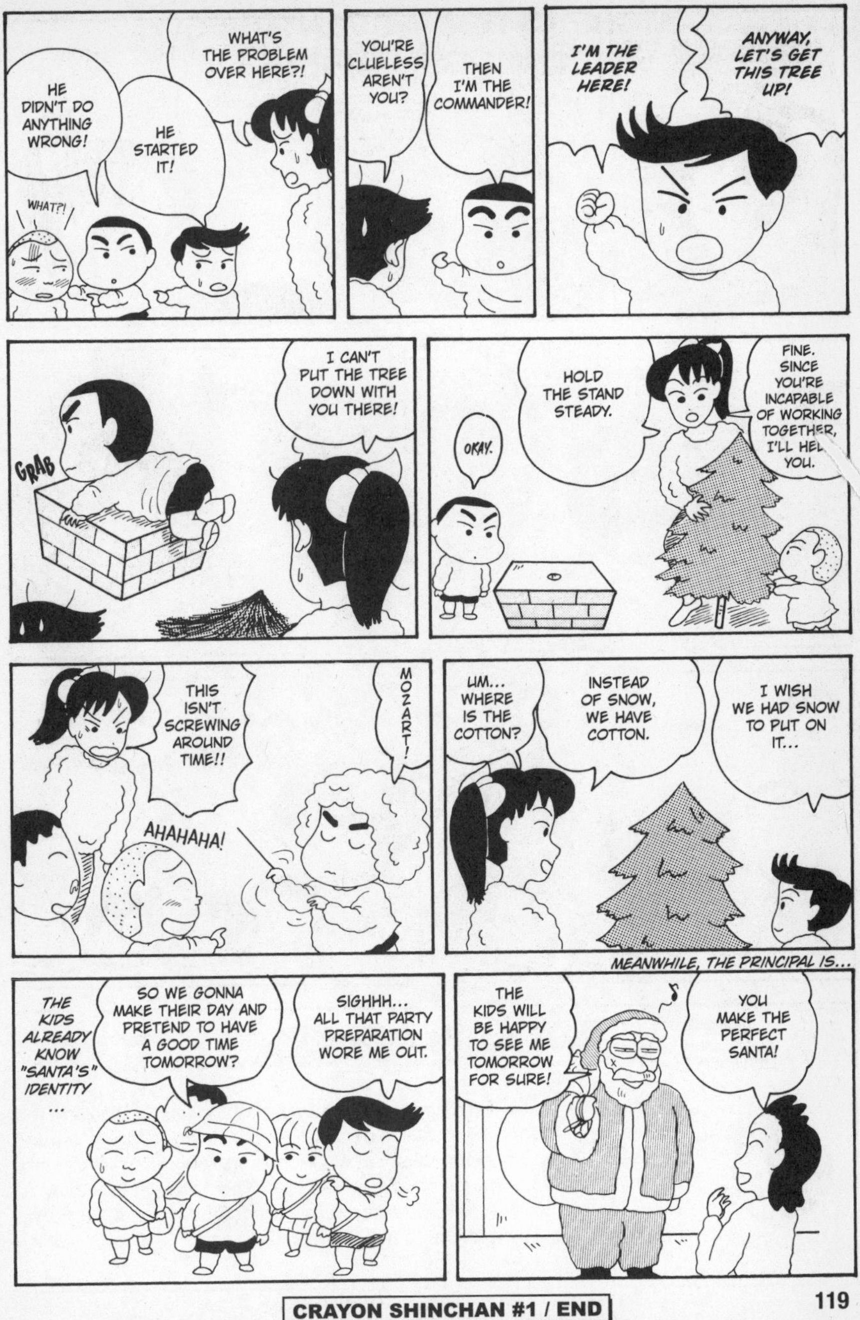
ANYWAY, LET'S GET THIS TREE UP!
I'M THE LEADER HERE!
THEN I'M THE COMMANDER!
YOU'RE CLUELESS AREN'T YOU?
WHAT'S THE PROBLEM OVER HERE?!
HE STARTED IT!
HE DIDN'T DO ANYTHING WRONG!
WHAT?!
FINE. SINCE YOU'RE INCAPABLE OF WORKING TOGETHER, I'LL HELP YOU.
HOLD THE STAND STEADY.
OKAY.
I CAN'T PUT THE TREE DOWN WITH YOU THERE!
GRAB
I WISH WE HAD SNOW TO PUT ON IT...
INSTEAD OF SNOW, WE HAVE COTTON.
UM... WHERE IS THE COTTON?
MOZART!
THIS ISN'T SCREWING AROUND TIME!!
AHAHAHA!
MEANWHILE, THE PRINCIPAL IS...
YOU MAKE THE PERFECT SANTA!
THE KIDS WILL BE HAPPY TO SEE ME TOMORROW FOR SURE!
SIGHHH... ALL THAT PARTY PREPARATION WORE ME OUT.
SO WE GONNA MAKE THEIR DAY AND PRETEND TO HAVE A GOOD TIME TOMORROW?
THE KIDS ALREADY KNOW "SANTA'S" IDENTITY...

CRAYON SHINCHAN #1 / END

MORE CRUDE ADVENTURES
COMING IN APRIL!

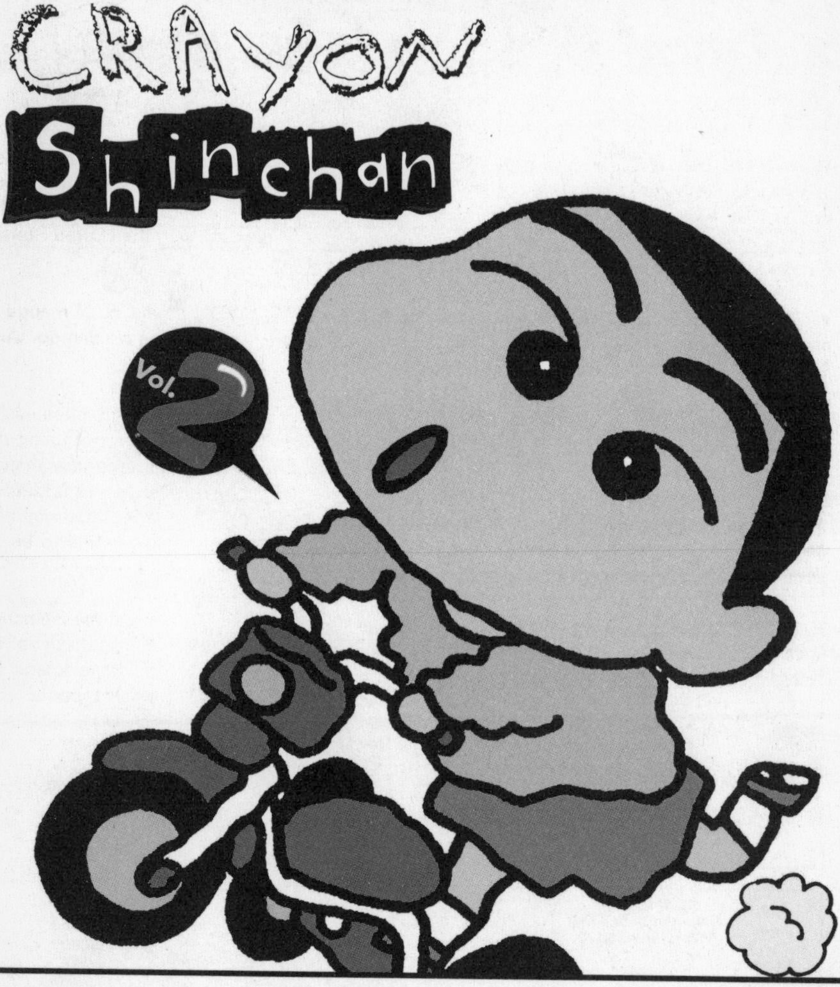
CRAYON
Shinchan
Vol. 2

By Yoshito Usui. Enjoy more adventures of Shinchan and Mitzi in the continuing "Mom and I Are Friends." These tales offer a unique perspective on domestic bliss – with cooking, shopping and potty training all getting the special Shinchan spin. Then he's off to school to wreak havoc on his fellow toddlers in "Kindergarten is a Fun, Fun Paradise." It's unwholesome family fun at it's finest.

CMX

Drop your pants and do a dance! Shinchan is here!

The original *Crayon Shinchan* manga by Yoshito Usui was first published by Futabasha back in 1990. In 1992, an anime version began airing on Japanese national TV, and Shinchan's notoriety quickly soared. In one form or another, Shinchan has been appearing around the world ever since. Currently, Shinchan is enjoying a wave of popularity in the United States, thanks to the recent appearance of the anime version in america.

We're happy to be bringing you the complete, translated, CRAYON SHINCHAN manga in all of its naughty glory, starting with the first volume and taking it as far as we can go. (And yes, we do mean that in more ways than one.)

If you are a fan of the TV series, you may be asking, "What's with this 'Crayon' business in the title?" Well, he's a little kid and he likes to draw with Crayons. (When not using his Mom's lipstick, of course.) This is how we believe the title appeared on the original manga and we're sticking to it. In fact, we're going to do our best to keep our version as faithful to the original manga as possible, give or take an occasional cultural reference that might be way too obscure for most American readers to get. (Hey, you didn't expect this to be an educational comic, did you?)

You will probably find some other minor differences between our manga and the Shinchan anime. (Obsessive nerd-types: start your engines!) But the important thing is that you will recognize the essential Shinchan in both: the same cluelessness, the same knack for enraging and embarrassing adults, and the same willingness to drop his pants at a moment's notice. Shinchan doesn't try to be bad – it's just his nature!

Meet the Noharas!

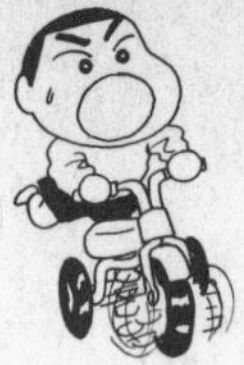

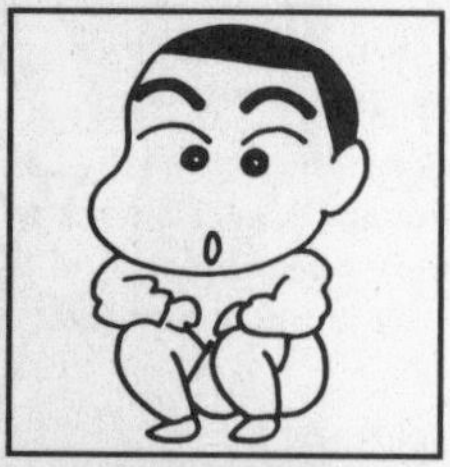

SHINNOSUKE NOHARA

(aka: Shin, Shin-chan, Shin chan, Shinchan)

5 years old. Likes pretty girls, drawing on himself, rolling around on the floor, and eating a tasty snack called Choco-bees. Frequently uses both words and his Mom's clothing in inappropriate ways. Also obsessed with bodily functions – his own and others'.

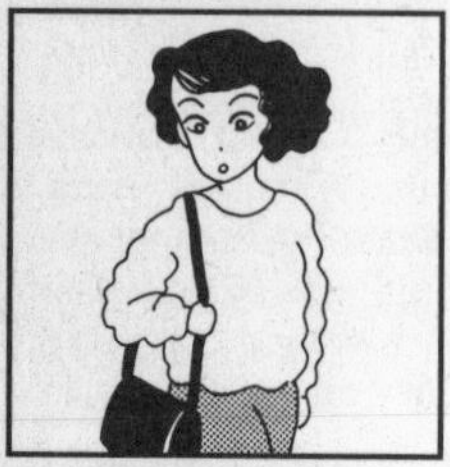

MITZI NOHARA

(aka: Misae)

Shin's easily frustrated mom. She's a stay-at-home housewife with the misfortune of being Shin's full time caretaker. Mitzi hasn't done much better in the husband department either, as Shin's Dad's behavior has to be closely monitored too. Frequently fantasizes about a better life.

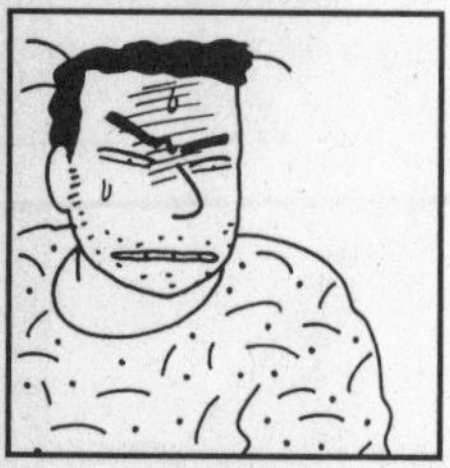

HIRO NOHARA

(aka: Hiroshi)

A browbeaten "salary man" who is the family's sole breadwinner. He's low on the totem pole at work and doesn't get much respect at home either. Like son, like father: Hiro has the eye for the pretty girls too, and Mitzi's none too tolerant of it. He talks a lot in his sleep, which doesn't help things much.

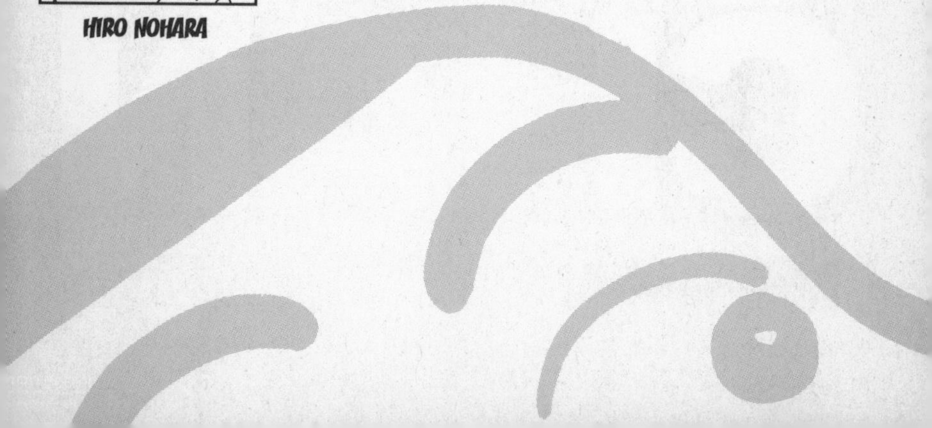

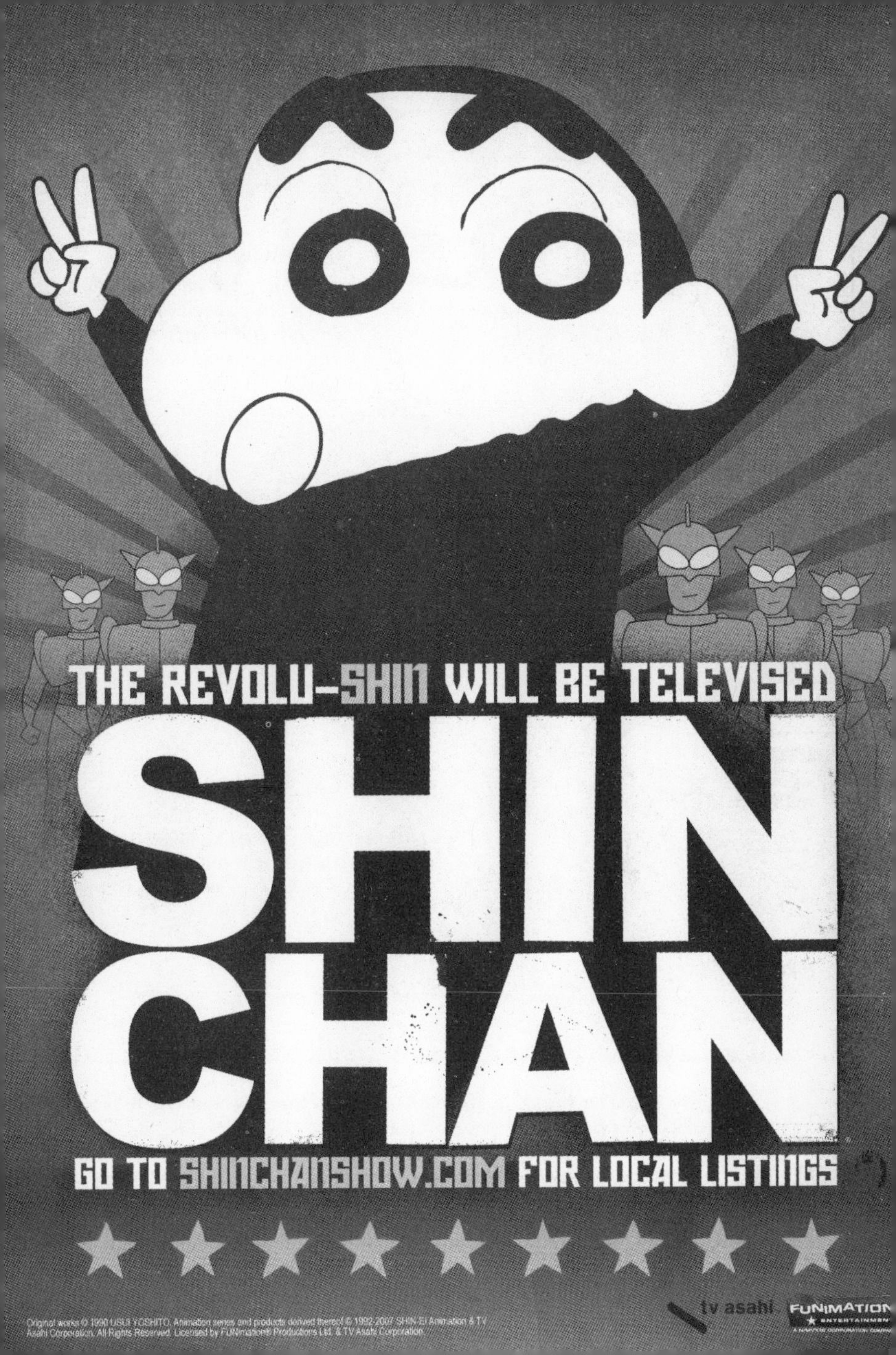
THE REVOLU-SHIN WILL BE TELEVISED
SHIN CHAN
GO TO SHINCHANSHOW.COM FOR LOCAL LISTINGS
tv asahi
FUNIMATION ENTERTAINMENT
Original works © 1990 USUI YOSHITO. Animation series and products derived thereof © 1992-2007 SHIN-EI Animation & TV Asahi Corporation. All Rights Reserved. Licensed by FUNimation® Productions Ltd. & TV Asahi Corporation.

PRESENTS

Volume 3

By Kanako Inuki. A common mask that the Japanese use to protect children from germs hides a bizarre secret for one young girl. As for Kurumi, she meets an old fortuneteller who turns out to be one of the girls who didn't give Kurumi a present when she was a child. She's been searching for Kurumi all these years, and now has a very special gift for her. Then find out what it is about an incredibly long scarf that creeps out even Kurumi!

IS SUZUO READY TO BECOME A SUPER-HERO? FIND OUT NOW!

Volume 1

By Yu Yagami. Original story by Taro Achi. Suzuo's in search of a job when he runs into a girl who offers him work testing out a "transformation belt." Allegedly the product of a toy company, this belt will turn him into a character named Dokkoida. In reality, she's working for the Galaxy Federation Police, an organization that needs to test out power suits to beef up their forces. Then a giant robot attacks, and Suzuo must put on his belt and spring into action!

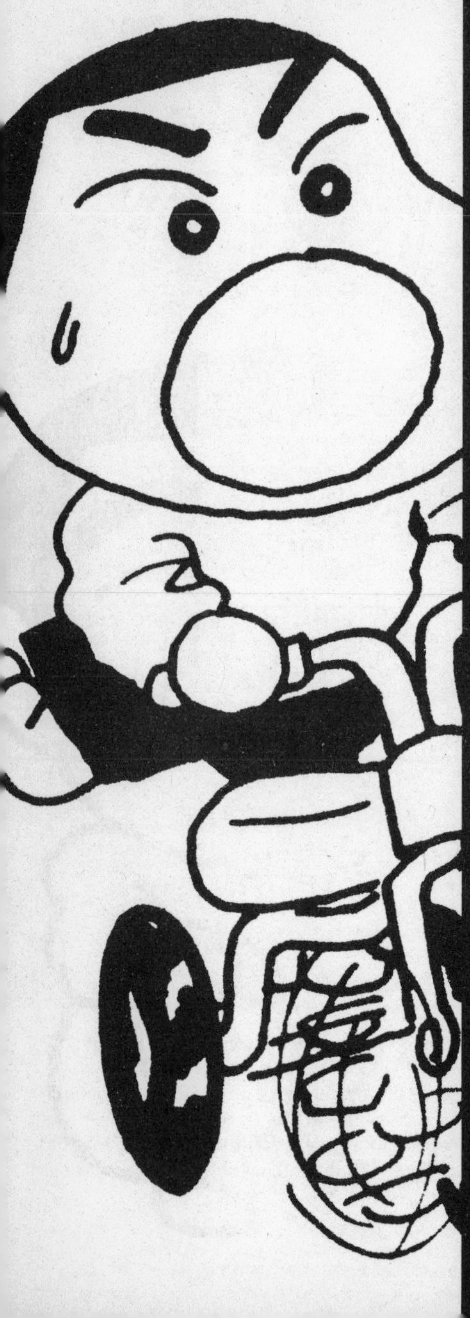

KNOW WHAT'S INSIDE

With the wide variety of manga available, CMX understands it can be confusing to determine age-appropriate material. We rate our books in four categories: EVERYONE, TEEN, TEEN + and MATURE. For the TEEN, TEEN + and MATURE categories, we include additional, specific descriptions to assist consumers in determining if the book is age appropriate. (Our MATURE books are shipped shrink-wrapped with a Parental Advisory sticker affixed to the wrapper.)

E

EVERYONE

Titles with this rating are appropriate for all age readers. They contain no offensive material. They may contain mild violence and/or some comic mischief.

T

TEEN

Titles with this rating are appropriate for a teen audience and older. They may contain some violent content, language, and/or suggestive themes.

T+

TEEN PLUS

Titles with this rating are appropriate for an audience of 16 and older. They may contain partial nudity, mild profanity and more intense violence.

M

MATURE

Titles with this rating are appropriate only for mature readers. They may contain graphic violence, nudity, sex and content suitable only for older readers.

CMX

Sheldon Drzka – Translation and Adaptation
Wilson Ramos – Lettering
Larry Berry – Design
Jim Chadwick – Editor

ISBN: 978-1-4012-1715-0

RIGHT TO LEFT?!

Traditional Japanese manga starts at the upper right-hand corner, and moves right-to-left as it goes down the page. Follow this guide for an easy understanding.

For more information and sneak previews, visit cmxmanga.com. Call 1-888-COMIC BOOK for the nearest comics shop or head to your local book store.

FLIP IT!

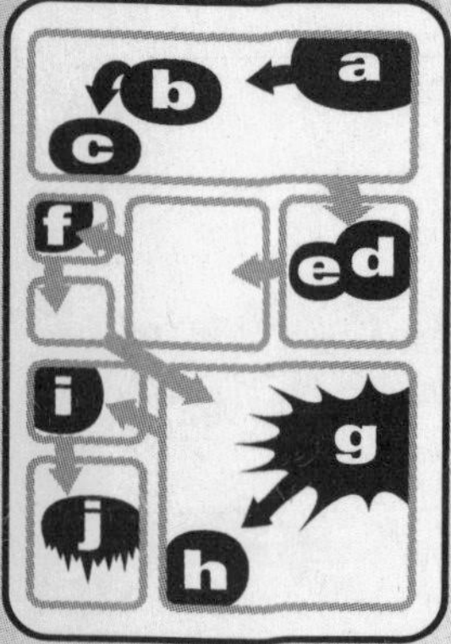
a
b
c
d
e
f
g
h
i
j

All the pages in this book were created—and are printed here—in Japanese RIGHT-to-LEFT format. No artwork has been reversed or altered, so you can read the stories the way the creators meant for them to be read.

cmx™

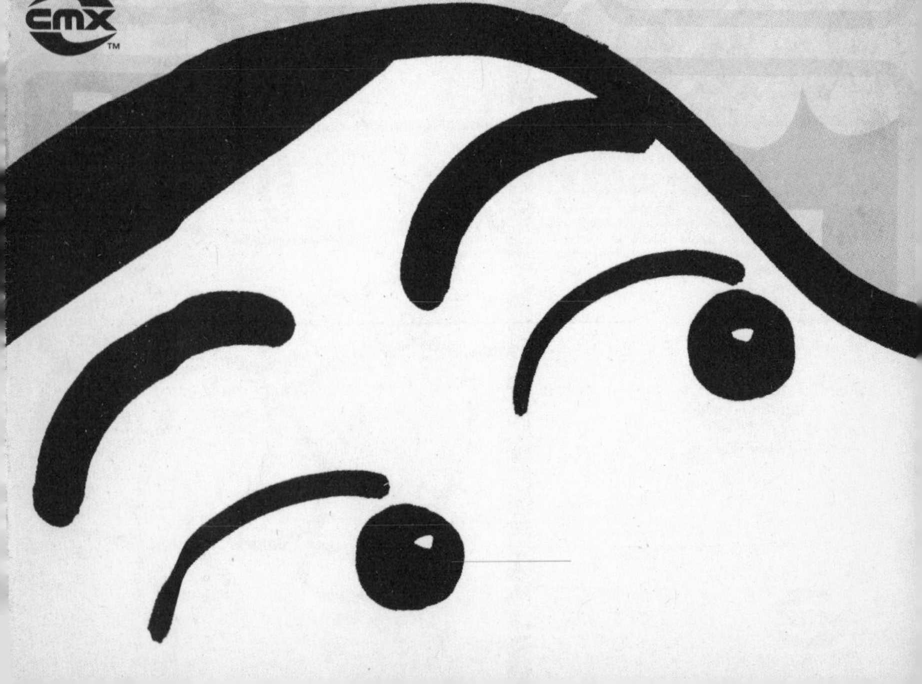